In loving memory of my dear sweetheart, and wife, Lois Bollinger who has passed on to go home to be with Jesus. I miss you so.

The Elven Chronicles: The Exiled

Lois and M. John Bollinger

The Eleven Chronicles
The Exiled
by Lois and M. John Bollinger

Printed in the United States of America.

ISBN 9781498497961

Unless otherwise indicated, Scripture quotations taken from the King James Version (KJV)–*public domain.*

www.xulonpress.com

We would like to dedicate our book in loving memory to Nada and James Hunter, Cleo and John Bollinger, and Martha Bollinger who have gone ahead to be with our Lord and Savior Jesus Christ.

This book is lovingly dedicated to our daughters Mindy, Martha, and Mary.

Table of Contents

Acknowledgements

We would like to thank David Limbaugh, and Jack Langer. Their help made this book possible.

Chapter 1

The Great Battle

Liam Midir stood staring through the leaves at the valley below his feet. The night breeze caressed his face as he listened to crickets singing in the night. With the perfume of flowers wafting through the trees, he filled his lungs with the sweet smelling air. His mind went back to the Elven Realm, to nights not so long ago when he stood laughing with his friends in the Royal Gardens, his ears filled with the ancient melodies of his people. His life had been a peaceful one back then.

Liam's father Brig was High King of the Realm. Two-hundred years earlier he had faced a coup by the corrupt Dark Elves, and many elves perished on both sides in the ensuing Battle for the Realm. After Brig emerged victorious, the surviving Dark Elves escaped through the Rift to Earth.

Then one night a scout came running into the Royal Court, his face pale with the news he carried from Earth. Having found a small fortress used by the Dark Elves, he had stood underneath a window listening to their conversation. What he heard chilled him to the bone.

The Dark Elves had discovered that the One meant to send his Son to die for the sins of all. The arrogant Dark Elves were deeply insulted that the One would waste His love on humans, a race they considered no better than cattle. If they could not have all the One's love and attention, no one else would either. In their rage the Dark

Elves not only turned away from the One; they set out to destroy every last human on earth. They planned to start with the small island of Eire and work their way across the planet like locusts, killing any human who came in their path. Liam immediately sent a messenger to deliver the news to his father.

Concerned for his human brethren, Brig appointed his son, Crown Prince Liam, as King of the Light Elves on Earth. He sent Liam through the Rift with over twenty thousand troops. They were joined by an entire branch of the Eagle clan, led by the great eagle Mighty Fiacra, a close friend of Liam's. Brig smiled as he saw hope and courage shining from the eyes of eagle and elf alike. They had only one order: protect the humans from the Dark Elves at all costs. Liam vowed in his heart not to fail them or his father.

The Light Elves had their hands full trying to keep the humans safe from the depredations of the Dark Elves, whose attacks could be subtle and cunning. Sometimes they would appear as friendly elves, then use their serpent's tongue to turn brother against brother until the entire village was in an uproar and someone got killed. On a larger scale, they would turn chieftain against chieftain until entire clans went to war.

Other times, their assaults were direct and brutal. They would catch travelers unaware in the forest and torture them. They would slip into houses in the middle of the night and quietly kill any children they found, often hanging around the village until morning so they might enjoy the families' wails of grief.

Liam sent a messenger to the Dark Elves demanding they stop harming humans, but in reply he received the warning "Don't interfere again" carved into his messenger's dead body. Finally Liam declared all-out war on the Dark Elves.

So now the war had come down to one valley on an island destined to be named Ireland. Its human inhabitants were warlike but primitive. They would have no defense against the subtle brutality of the Dark Elves.

Liam's troops waited for his signal to move from the concealment of the trees. Fiacra and the other eagles had warned him two hours earlier of the Dark Elves' approach. The moonlight shone on the eagles' broad wings as it peeked momentarily through the thick clouds. They hovered high in the night sky, closely watching the enemy draw near the Light Elves. Liam had mounted his best archers on Fiacra and his children to help protect his troops from the air. He had twenty thousand soldiers on the ground and 500 airborne archers.

Fiacra fluttered his wings to signal that the enemy was near. Liam watched from the trees as the enemy army came over the mountaintop and slithered down the mountainside like a ghostly serpent. There were thousands of them, all intent on wiping out the only thing that could prevent them from annihilating the human race.

The Dark Elves were almost invisible even to Liam's elven eyes, their faint outlines barely discernible in the pale moonlight. They had sunk so deep into the darkness of this world that any nearby shadow would swallow them up and conceal them until their victims were in their grasp.

Liam looked up at the thick clouds and frowned – it would be difficult to fight in this light. He summoned his massive strength and willed a wind to blow the clouds away from the battlefield. As the clouds moved, the moon lit up the ground in a silvery glow, fully exposing the Dark Elves to their enemies. Cursing, the Dark Elves contorted their faces in anger as the light glanced off their swords.

Smiling grimly, Liam gave the order to attack. As Liam's troops charged, the great eagles moved into position above them. The archers were led by Captain Gildas, the swordsmen by Captain Kendhal. Liam himself commanded the Elite Guard.

The group of soldiers known as the Fianna moved swiftly through the mass of enemy soldiers, their arrow-point formation sweeping all before them. They reached the center of the battlefield quickly, dividing the enemy into two groups. The rest of the Light Elf army attacked ferociously, beating their enemies back as they converged from both sides. The Dark Elves were trapped between three groups of Liam's soldiers on the ground and the eagle clan and Liam's archers from the air.

The field was a swirl of color, the emerald green and gold uniforms of the Light Elves clashing with the red and black of the Dark Elves. The eagles flew over the battlefield dropping logs and boulders on the Dark Elves. Their riders rained arrows on their adversaries while the eagles swooped down to rescue imperiled Light Elves. The

Dark Elves fought back viciously, capturing some eagles and hacking them to pieces alongside their elven comrades.

The dance of death continued far into the night as the two armies fought over the future of humanity.

Liam ducked and swiftly moved under his opponent's sword stroke, delivering one of his own to the midsection. His enemy crumpled to the ground and was quickly replaced by two more swordsmen who lunged at him at once. Liam dropped to the ground, sweeping out his leg and toppling the two soldiers to the ground. He put his sword through the first one's chest, while he blocked the second's blow with his dagger. He and his remaining opponent jumped to their feet and squared off again.

The snarling Dark Elf pulled back his sword and sent the blade flying at the elf king's neck. Deftly stepping aside, Liam swung his leg up and kicked his opponent soundly in the head, sending him stumbling forward. Trying to recover, the Dark Elf shook his head and moved towards Liam again, his eyes full of hatred. As he drew back his arm to deliver a blow, Liam saw his opening and took off his head.

Suddenly Liam felt a blade pressing against his neck. He spun away instantly and swept his sword up in an arch, its blade slamming into the sword that had been at his throat. The shock of the blow sent the weapon flying from the hands that wielded it. The adversary quickly turned and grabbed a pike. With the grace of a bullfighter, Liam stepped lightly away from the charge and brought his sword down through the back of his opponent's neck.

Scanning the battlefield, Liam saw that the Light Elves were winning but at a horrendous cost. The ground was littered with bodies from both groups.

Then a flash of red caught his eye. A Dark Elf, most of his face obscured by the hood on his red cloak, stood over one of Liam's soldiers. Liam recognized Evan, a fighter from his own household. He had helped Evan take his first steps as a baby and later trained him to use a sword.

Liam fought through the sea of bodies to reach Evan, who had the shattered end of a pike protruding from his chest. Evan held up his hands to plead with the Dark Elf, his long, sand-colored hair becoming matted with his own blood and his gray eyes burning bright with pain. The attacker raised his sword and swung, taking off both of Evan's hands. The young elf uttered a heart-wrenching scream. As Liam watched in horror, the Dark Elf grabbed the pike and ground it further into Evan's chest, eliciting another bloodcurdling scream of agony that sent an icy dagger of horror through Liam's heart.

The Dark Elf laughed and jerked the pike from Evan's chest, sending a spray of blood through the air. Then he raised it and slammed the end of it through Evan's heart. He licked the blood from his fingers and smiled before turning and walking away. Evan's fair face relaxed into the peaceful look of eternal sleep.

With cold rage burning in his heart, Liam fought to reach the Dark Elf, but Evan's killer disappeared into the swarming mass of fighting bodies.

Liam's heart twisted in grief as he looked at Evan's ruined body. Suddenly, two Dark Elves lunged forward, slicing at him with their swords. The serrated blades flashed in the moonlight as Liam struggled to put aside his grief and rejoin the battle.

Evan's slayer looked back at Liam through the raging battlefield. Braen relished the thought of killing the young Elf in full view of the Light Elves' leader. His sense of triumph, however, did not override his sense of self-preservation – he discarded his red cloak, the symbol of a Dark Elf leader, since he expected Liam would seek to reap vengeance on him before the battle was over.

As Braen walked past some wounded Dark Elves, he saw one lunging desperately for a water-skin just out of his reach. Braen snatched up the skin, drank deeply, and poured out the rest next to the soldier. The stricken elf moaned and collapsed back onto the ground.

Chuckling, Braen walked away and found a nice hiding place under an overturned cart. The battle wasn't going his way, so he concentrated on surviving. There would be plenty of time later to pay back Liam for all his interference. In the meantime, Braen would relax under the cart and then surrender. He knew the Light Elves would show compassion and mercy, and they would eventually release him or he'd escape. Then he'd repay the favor by making Liam beg nicely before he finally ended his pathetic existence. He laughed again and waited out the battle.

Meanwhile, at Liam's signal, his lieutenant Eryn lifted a golden horn to his lips and blew one note. The Light Elves regrouped on the ground while Fiacra and his children gathered together in the sky. Eryn blew another note and all of Liam's troops made one last determined charge.

The Light Elves glowed with an inner light as they swept over the Dark Elves like a flood. The eagles swooped down, scattering the enemy. Most of the Dark Elves fought to the bitter end, preferring to die rather than suffer the indignity of mercy at the hands of their enemies. They took many Light Elves and eagles down with them, striking out for hate's sake with their last breath.

Many heroic Light Elves lost their lives that day. Many elven families would wait in vain for their loved ones to come home. When Fiacra discovered he had lost half his children, the great eagle's heart almost failed him, and Liam had to give him a calming herb. His surviving children kept watch over him as he grieved. Liam spent the rest of the night doing the grisly business of caring for the wounded and dying.

As the sun rose the surviving Dark Elves were taken to the foot of Krewabrig, an icy summit whose name meant Bloody Mountain. It was quite fitting, Liam thought grimly, considering their propensity to violence.

The group stopped near the village of Cluse, where the Dark Elves would immediately stand trial for their crimes against humanity. King Liam sat in the judgment seat, which was a wooden bench provided by the human villagers that lived at the foot of the mountain. Some of Fiacra's children cruised overhead, keeping a keen eye on the prisoners.

Liam was tall – a good 6'7" – and powerfully built. He was still dressed in his battlefield uniform – a dark green tunic and pants, with a gold and silver belt, a golden sword hanging at his side. Around his broad shoulders was draped a dark green cloak with an emerald clasp. His dark brown, waist-length hair was still pulled back from his face in battle braids, his silver circlet adorning his brow. His face had an ethereal beauty, with high cheekbones, compelling dark gray eyes, and a soft generous mouth beneath a proud strong nose set in a square jaw. Power emanated from him like the rush of an immense river about to overflow its banks, causing the Dark Elves to shrink back from his seat.

Sitting silently, Liam cast a penetrating gaze on the prisoners as witnesses testified to the endless crimes of the Dark Elves. He sighed deeply as the list went on and on until the listeners were numbed by the incomprehensible cruelty of it all.

Finally he heard the last witness. The crowd – comprising humans as well as the surviving Light Elves, who numbered no more than seven hundred soldiers – grew restless. The Dark Elves shifted anxiously within their ring of guards. Only fifty had survived, those who had fallen on their knees before their captors and begged for their lives. They stood and awaited the judgment of Liam Midir.

Liam motioned to General Arth and the prisoners were brought before him. He stood, his eyes hard, his face cold, as he began to pronounce his judgment.

"How many times have you appeared as a kindly stranger, only to sow discord and death? How many rooftops have you sat upon, snickering as you listened to the wails of families who found infants smothered in the night? How many elven families have you ambushed and murdered, including my wife, my daughter, her husband, and my unborn grandchild?"

The Dark Elves shifted uncomfortably. They couldn't deny the charges, but neither would they repent. Liam continued, this time addressing the crowd.

"They committed acts of pure malice for anything living and thriving. Their crimes went on and on until we had no recourse but to gather ourselves and destroy these evil monsters. Most were unrepentant to the bitter end, but those before you begged for their lives. They will be exiled to the snow and barred from the realms of mankind forever, until the very memory of elves in this world is the merest whisper of a dream."

Liam motioned to Tiernan, his Chief Counselor, who turned and drew his sword. The elven guards herded the Dark Elves together to walk the road to the top of the mountain and their snowy exile. The humans hurriedly moved out of the way as the evil beings were led through the village.

Kara looked up from her dolly to see the procession approaching. Elves! She loved elves. They were always so kind and gentle to her, often passing her a piece of fruit or a sweet as they walked through the small village on their way to who knows where. She knew the grownups held them in awe. She thought they were pretty and loved to look at them.

So she followed the solemn parade, oblivious to the raven-haired prisoner who watched her out of the corner of his jade-colored eye. He made his way to the edge of the group as they were nearing the end of the village.

Kara's attention was drawn to Kendhal, Captain of Liam's Swordsmen, who favored her with a dazzling smile as he brushed his gentle hand through her golden curls. "You can't be more than five years old, little one. What a beautiful child you are."

She giggled as her proud father Condan picked her up.

"Her name is Kara," said her mother Isha.

"She is our only child, my lord," added Condan. "She is the apple of our eye." He gave his little daughter an affectionate hug and allowed the elf to reach out and take her in his arms.

Typical of Light Elves, Kendhal loved children. Kara's sweet face lit up in laughter when the elf kissed her gently on the forehead. "You are very blessed to have such a treasure," he said smilingly as he gave her back to her proud parents.

"Thank you my lord. She is our whole life," her father replied. Kara squirmed in her father's arms.

"Papa, dolly's laying in the dirt," she said indignantly. Her father set her down to retrieve her dolly and continued speaking with the elven lord.

Then Kara heard her name whispered on the wind. As she picked up her dolly her eyes were drawn to a beautiful elf with long black hair and the greenest eyes she'd ever seen. Braen smiled at her, and she giggled and smiled back. But she soon tired from the walk and sat down in the grass. At that moment, Braen slipped his hand under his cloak and brought out a *carhakt* – a deadly, worm-sized snake that was covered with brightly colored bands. He whispered softly to it and covertly dropped it in the thick grass near Kara.

The serpent made straight for the little girl, who sat rocking her doll and singing. She started to get up and it stopped, watching her. As she stood she caught sight of the rainbow colored snake. Laughing, she bent down and picked it up.

Time seemed to slow down as Liam, running from the back of the procession, saw the tragedy unfold. Kara's mother gasped in horror as she caught sight of her daughter with the snake. Her father moved toward her, his eyes wide with fear. Several of Liam's elves turned at the mother's horrified cry and moved toward the girl. Waiting until just before they reached her, Braen nodded to the snake and it sank its needle-sharp fangs into her tiny hand. As she collapsed the snake quickly disappeared into the surrounding shrubbery.

Her mother's scream rang in Liam's ears. His cry of rage rang out over those of his warriors.

He raced to the girl and cradled her in his arms. He reached deep within himself, praying to the One to help him save this child. He gathered all his strength, trying desperately to use his healing powers to counter the deadly poison. But it was no use. Within seconds it was over. Kara lay dead in his embrace as he choked back tears. Tiernan gently took the child from his arms and gave her to her grieving parents. Elves crowded around the parents to comfort them, while those guarding the prisoners looked from one Dark Elf to another trying to determine which was responsible for this last senseless act of violence.

The elves helped the anguished parents bury the tiny child. Liam gave Isha a cordial to relax her and then with a quiet prayer sent her to sleep. Condan was so shaken by the loss of his child that he could not speak; he sat silently staring into the flames of the fire, not touching his own cordial prepared by Liam. The Elf King dispatched his aides to find neighbors to stay with the grieving parents. Normally he would have stayed with them himself, but he had fifty dangerous prisoners to remove from the village before they caused any more trouble. He offered Condan a few quiet words and a gentle hand on his shoulder before stepping out the door.

The guards had herded the prisoners to a small patch of ground just outside of town. Liam looked at the group of Dark Elves, barely able to contain his anger. He knew one of them had dropped the snake, but he couldn't prove anything. He gripped his sword hilt in helpless rage and motioned for the rest of his angry warriors to move the prisoners up the long road to the mountaintop.

Braen laughed to himself as he walked amid the other Dark Elves. He could still strike out at Liam even as a prisoner. This war wasn't over yet; his day would come. He smiled as the group trudged slowly to the peak of the mountain. When they neared the icy top, the guards stopped the group and stood them before Liam.

Liam made a formidable figure, his cape and hair blowing in the fierce wind. The snow swirled around his tall form, his face stern and unrelenting as he glared at the prisoners before him. They were as beautiful as any living creatures that had ever walked the earth, but Liam knew their hearts. Inside they were as hideous as the monsters they had tried to create to plague mankind. The time had come to rid the earth of these creatures of the night.

Cold and solemn, Liam pronounced their doom.

"Your disdain of all living things is despicable. You have killed and maimed for the pleasure it brings your twisted hearts. You have sown discord and death wherever you go. You are a plague that the earth cries out to be rid of. You are forever condemned to the snow, where little else lives but where you can survive. And may the earth never again groan with the torment of your footsteps."

The guards stepped forward, their swords drawn. The Dark Elves turned and walked toward the cold mountaintop. The freezing wind pulled at their cloaks and hair, whipping them unmercifully, as if the very earth could not rid itself of them quickly enough.

Braen stopped and looked back through the raging snowstorm. He laughed again at Liam's weakness. If the roles had been reversed, he would have killed Liam slowly while informing him that it was he – Braen – who had killed Liam's loved ones. But for now, Braen contemplated the prospect of someday reaping vengeance on the elf responsible for his exile. He imagined Liam's final torment upon learning that he had let the elf live who had slaughtered his own family members.

Braen's position as leader of the Dark Elves was a well-kept secret – at his own insistence of course. Why tempt fate? And little did they know he had prepared a secret contingency plan in case the Dark Elves lost the battle.

He had ordered his faithful underling Natha to hide during the battle and keep ready to activate the plan: he was to poison mankind's mind against the Light Elves, ensuring they were blamed for everything the Dark Elves had done. He was to incite the humans to such hatred for the Light Elves that they would hunt them to extinction. Smiling at his own cunning, Braen turned and walked through the driving snowstorm.

Brennus shot him a contemptuous look. He had watched helplessly during the battle as Braen had butchered Evan, Brennus' older brother. Unable to break through the wall of fighting troops to rescue his brother, he had seen Braen cut off Evan's hands and torture and kill him. Anger rose in his fair heart as he watched Braen simply walk away. Even telling Liam had not eased the pain.

Tears sprang to his young eyes and his brother's screams of agony rang through his mind. Suddenly, he pulled an arrow from his quiver and fitted it to his bow in one swift motion. Before anyone could stop him he let it fly at Braen's head. The gale pushed the arrow slightly off-target, merely slicing a gash in Braen's cheek.

Braen turned in rage as Brennus fitted another arrow in his bow. But as he raised it to fire, Liam stepped in his path. Brennus froze in place. His eyes filled with compassion, Liam gently took the bow and arrow from his grasp. The young archer fell to his knees and sobbed. Liam knelt down and held Brennus, speaking quietly to him before helping him back to his feet. Tiernan came over, put his arm around Brennus' shoulders, and led him to the back of the group of Light Elves, where his friends crowded around him, offering words of comfort.

Liam turned toward Braen, reaching for his healer's kit. Braen stared defiantly at Liam and then spat in the snow toward the elf king. Turning on his heel, he walked away, the blood already congealing on his face.

Liam watched the Dark Elves disappear into the driving snow. He looked back at his own battle weary warriors. Their faces showed grim satisfaction as the Dark Elves disappeared from sight. Many had lost family members to these evil creatures. It had been a long, exhausting battle, but the One had given them the strength they needed to send the Dark Elves into a well-deserved exile. Never again would they depredate on mankind. Never again would dark words be whispered in sleeping ears, only to result in war and the deaths of the innocent. Their malice and hatred of humankind was like a poison, filling the earth with terror.

Sighing, Liam turned and looked at General Arth. He nodded at Liam and motioned for the troops to gather around their king. Liam looked at them, pride and devotion shining from each fair face.

"You know what we are about to do, my people. It will require all our strength, and it is entirely possible that we will not survive. None are compelled to stay who wish to leave through the Rift. You may go back to the Realm freely with my blessing and my gratitude." He paused. Not one elf stirred.

"We are wasting precious time, my lord," whispered Brennus with a respectful bow of his head. His fellows all nodded in agreement. Liam looked at his troops one more time, his heart swelling with joy and gratitude.

With a fervent prayer to the One for guidance, Liam reached deep within himself, bringing to bear all the awesome power the One had given him as king. He directed this power to create a barrier around the top of the mountain – a barrier that Braen's power could never undo.

Around him his elves sang a song of praise for the One. As his massive strength drained from him, he felt himself drawn into the song, felt the overwhelming power of the One begin to give him a new strength and determination. As he sang, he felt himself being swept away by the One's awesome strength and love until his heart soared with joy and purpose.

A golden mist formed in the air, impervious to the mountainside gales. The barrier wound itself around the mountaintop like an impenetrable wall. As it settled into place with an echoing rumble, Braen looked back. He saw Liam and his elves through the barrier, singing their praise for the One. Braen flinched as the sweet notes reached his ears. He did not worship the One. He worshiped something else; something that loved the darkness as much as he did.

As the song faded, Liam felt the One speak to him, telling him the strength of the Light Elves had faded too. They would never again wield the awesome power they had as the guardians of mankind. Now they would have a different strength, the strength of the heart and the soul. Instead of protectors, they were now assigned to be comforters and healers.

As the song ended Liam quietly acknowledged the commands of the One, thanking Him for giving the Light Elves a new purpose, now that they had voluntarily given up most of their power to protect mankind from the likes of Braen. As the last note ended, the elves looked at each other. There was a light of determination in their eyes, a new hope and joy. Many laughed for joy, rejoicing that they would still be able to keep company with their beloved mankind. Liam's heart rang as he and his elves started back down the mountain, singing another song of praise for the One.

The last remnant of the Dark Elves had been exiled to the snow, no longer to prey upon humankind, the ones the Light Elves had sworn to protect. They were forever removed from the realms of mankind; the sentence was final.

Or was it?

As the moon rose, Natha waited for his chance. It wasn't long in coming. After retiring to his bed, Kara's father heard the soothing song of a bird. With a sigh he drifted off to sleep. Natha smiled and slithered the rest of the way into the room.

Lulling this human to sleep was easy. Using his grief as a catalyst for Braen's plan would be even easier. As the bereaved father lay sleeping, the Dark Elf whispered in his ear. Evil, subtle lies mixed with just enough truth to sound plausible. Despicably, he blamed Liam for failing to save Kara. Condan moaned in his sleep, a tear running down his face.

"Good," thought Natha, "he's listening."

This would be one visit of many. Within a month the man would be ready to lead the humans to war against the Light Elves. He was an admired Chieftain and eloquent speaker who could convince his people of the Light Elves' mendacity. With any luck he would soon be leading hunting parties against the Light Elves. Once they were annihilated, Natha could find a way to break the barrier around the mountaintop and free his compatriots. Natha smiled to himself, imagining the rewards he would receive from Braen. The father moaned again, whispering his daughter's name.

"Oh shut up." whispered Natha. He ran his fingernail down the man's right cheek, making a long gash that would heal into an ugly scar.

"Liam did that to you for questioning his healing ability," he whispered. He snickered as he slithered back through the window and was swallowed up into the night.

Later that night Liam awoke with a start, his father's impatient voice ringing in his head.

"Liam, wake up!"

"Yes Athair. What is wrong? Is Mather alright?" he asked anxiously. He often worried about his parents, even though they lived in the safety of the Realm.

"Yes, of course your mother is alright," responded his father Brig. "I called you because there is an electromagnetic storm passing close to the earth. The Rift is closing rapidly and I don't know when it will open again. I'll have to see how much damage the storm will do. I don't know when you can get back through to the Realm."

"We will be alright Athair," replied Liam, smiling at the concern in his father's voice. "The Dark Elves are exiled and humanity is safe. Don't worry."

"I do worry son. I have a bad feeling about this. In a few moments you will be trapped in the world of Men. If something happens, no one in the Realm will be able to help you."

"What could happen?" Liam responded, smiling.

"Funny," said his father grimly. "That's what you asked just before your hunting accident, when you stepped into a bear trap and almost bled to death."

"We are in the hands of the One, Athair. He will watch over us," said Liam.

"That is my fervent prayer son," said his father solemnly. "Just . . . be careful."

Liam was puzzled. "Be careful of what?"

"I don't know," his father sighed. "I just have a bad feeling and you have been in my heart lately. Somehow I feel as if you were about to step into another bear trap. Just be careful."

The worry was plain in his voice as they both felt the Rift beginning to close.

Liam could feel his father's love and concern wrap around him like a warm blanket. "I will be careful Athair," he told him. "I promise."

The Rift was almost closed.

"I love you son." Brig paused. "And Liam, I know you love humanity, but sometimes that love is not returned. Please be care . . ." His father's voice was cut off as the Rift sealed tight.

"I love you too, Athair," Liam whispered. He lay his head back down on his pillow and fell asleep praying to the One.

It was a cold, gray morning when Liam's troops came riding into the village of Cluse a month later. Liam had come to check on Condan and his grieving wife, and to make sure the humans had sufficient supplies for the harsh winter he knew was coming. Liam's elves began to unload their gifts and supplies, including bundles of smoked meats, sweet elven cakes, healing herbs, rare fruits, warm blankets, and heavy furs. Liam dismounted his horse and turned to greet the villagers who had crowded around his group.

Condan was at the back of the crowd talking to several men in Celtic. Celtic was the elven native language and had been taught to the humans generations before. Liam noticed he had a long, ugly scar running down his right cheek. What had happened since he saw him last?

Before he could speak, Condan shoved his way to the front of the crowd and growled, "Come to try to buy off your guilt, Elf King?"

There were shocked looks from some of Liam's warriors. Never had they heard a human repay their king's kindness and generosity with such words. Liam looked at Condan as he recalled Kara's death. He would not respond in kind. The poor man was suffering enough.

"I only thought to bring supplies for your people," said Liam quietly.

"You'd do better giving us better weather, Elf King," snapped Condan. "Or don't you care if we worthless humans freeze to death?"

"You know we cannot control the seasons, Condan," responded Liam gently. "That is in the hands of the One."

"Humph!" answered Condan. Turning to the rest of the villagers he retorted, "He seems to think he can control everything else!" The villagers turned pale, refusing to meet the eyes of the elves. There was a long, uncomfortable pause.

Finally Liam's quiet voice broke the silence. "You are better than this."

"But not good enough for you to save my daughter, Elf!" shouted Condan defiantly.

The words stabbed at Liam's heart and he winced at the pain.

General Arth frowned and stepped forward to speak in defense of his king. Liam's upheld hand stilled him.

"It is well, Arth," Liam said. "He is still suffering. Do not add to his torment." He smiled kindly at Condan. "We will be in the area until tomorrow morning, my dear friend. If there is anything you need."

"If I need anything I won't lower myself by asking it of an elf!" He spat angrily on the ground near Liam's boot. The hurt in Liam's eyes gave him pause, but only for a moment. This elf let my daughter die, he reminded himself. His face hardened again and he turned and stalked back home. The other villagers shifted uneasily as he passed. Then they quietly picked up the Light Elves' gifts and, without a word of thanks, went quickly back into their houses and shut the doors, leaving the Light Elves standing in the street in stunned, hurt silence.

Arth put his hand on Liam's shoulder. "Come, my king, we should leave this place." He gazed over the village, sensing a malice that made him fear for his king's safety. After taking one last look, Liam sighed sorrowfully, quietly turned, and walked back to his horse.

As they rode out of the village every elf felt an itch between their shoulder blades, as if an enemy had an arrow trained there. Fearing for his troops, Liam quickly moved off the road. The elves melted into the forest out of sight.

As the months went by the humans grew more aggressive. In a mere six months they went from being the elves' faithful allies to riding in packs looking for trouble. Soon it became unsafe for any elf to be caught alone by the groups of human thugs that roamed their beautiful woodlands.

The great eagles began hovering over the woodlands, ready to sound the alarm if humans approached the elves' encampments. Liam set up an illusion around the eagles, yet the humans often would spot the birds anyway and unleash a volley of arrows. Several of Lord Fiacra's children died in these patrols, yet they kept their faithful watch over their friends. Times grew increasingly perilous for Liam's people; simply walking their beloved forest became dangerous.

One sunny morning Ranal was heading to the small lake in the heart of the forest, where a picnic was being held to celebrate the warm weather's return. Feeling uneasy upon hearing about the excursion, the golden-haired elf lord had set off for the lake to check on the mothers and children there. As he walked, a feeling of dread overtook him and he quickened his pace. His blood ran cold at the sound of hoofbeats on a nearby path. He raced ahead of the riders and onto the grassy picnic area. He bolted into the midst of the elves and shouted one word.

"Run!"

Chapter 2

Hunted

The entire group of mothers and children dropped what they were doing and instantly disappeared into the forest.

Ranal knew he needed to buy time to let them put some distance between themselves and their human pursuers. When the riders arrived at the encampment, he was lounging on a boulder basking in the sun, his golden head laid back against his interlaced fingers, his long thick hair flowing like waterfalls down his shoulders, his handsome face turned toward the warm sun. As the riders stopped in front of him, he lazily cracked one bright blue eye open.

"Excuse me good sir, but you seem to be blocking my sunshine," he murmured lazily.

Sitting motionless on his horse, the lead rider surveyed the campsite. There had obviously been more elves here.

"Where is the rest of your party, elf?" he demanded harshly.

Ranal yawned and slowly stretched before sitting up. Smiling, he gazed at the group of riders. The malice in their eyes was unmistakable. The handsome elf lord yawned again, a twinkle of mischief in his eye. "Party my lords? Is there a party hereabouts and no one told me?"

He stood up on the rock, hands on his hips and a grin on his face. "Ah, I am always the last invited to a party and the first asked to leave, it seems," he murmured sadly. He shrugged. "I ask you, what am I to do, my lords?"

The rider grew impatient. "You can start by telling us where the rest of the elves are! We told you elves before, all the lakes are ours, and you'd get a good thrashing if we caught you near one again."

Ranal's sapphire blue eyes widened in mock fear. He bowed deeply, his hand over his heart. "My lords, I assure you I would never do anything to incur the displeasure of such formidable opponents," he intoned with a twinkle in his eye.

The exasperated rider got off his horse and stalked over to Ranal's rock. "Get down here," he demanded.

Ranal jumped lightly from his rock and landed gracefully right in front of the man's nose. The man stepped back in bewilderment and blinked up at the tall elf lord. Ranal towered over him, purring like a cat with a mouse as he looked the human up and down. Frowning, he reached out and felt the man's shirt.

"My goodness, what crude material. I wouldn't put this on my horse if he were freezing," he quipped.

The rider scowled and slapped Ranal's hand away. Ranal held his own hand as if sorely offended. "Oh dear, now I've insulted you. Please accept my apology in the spirit it is given," he said in a silken voice.

Having enough of the mockery, the rider drew his sword and pointed it at Ranal's throat. Ranal stepped back in exaggerated fear. "Oh my. You are a big fellow aren't you?" he said sarcastically.

"Big enough to take you down, elf," smirked the human. The others laughed.

Ranal folded his arms across his broad chest. "You know, bigger isn't always better," he said softly, his handsome face lit up in a dazzling smile.

Suddenly, moving in a blur of motion, he grabbed the human and lifted him over his head. He threw him effortlessly at the other riders, knocking them all off their horses.

"Indeed, sometimes bigger isn't better at all," he chuckled. He ordered their horses to run to the lake. As the horses stampeded away, he disappeared into the forest before the humans were on their feet.

The entire group of elves was halfway back to Liam's encampment before the humans had caught their own horses.

Months passed as Natha worked to corrupt Condan's heart and soul. Each night brought new bitterness to his heart until even his wife Isha began contemplating leaving him. The village of Cluse was now a place of fear. Anyone who criticized the rising aggression against the elves was quickly dealt with by Condan's growing band of thugs.

One day Isha decided she could stand it no longer – she would leave him that night. Days before, she had started writing a scroll describing the events leading up to the Great Battle, the trial of the Dark Elves, her daughter's death, and her husband's transformation from a kind and gentle father into a murderous bully.

She described how one night she had walked to her bedroom door and stood in horror as she saw a Dark Elf leaning over her husband, whispering into his ear. She remained hidden, fearing the evil power of the Dark Elves. She wanted to bring this up to her husband, but by then she was terrified of him. She tried to tell the men in the village, but they were as evil as Condan. How she had longed for King Liam's help, but the elves had long since gone into hiding.

A faint noise outside caught Isha's attention. She quickly rolled up the small scroll and hid it in her tunic. Seconds later the door swung open and Condan swaggered into the room, smelling of wine. Without bothering to greet her, he sat down at the table and waited for Isha to serve his supper.

She felt a brief moment of sadness as she set the food before him. In better days her little family would have been gathered around the table laughing and talking. But those days were gone forever.

She looked at the small, empty chair that Condan had lovingly prepared for his little daughter. He had told her she was a princess and that was her throne. They had spent so many happy hours gathered round that little chair.

Choking back tears, Isha looked into the hard face of her husband. Living with him had become more than she could bear. She was leaving him and going back to her parents. Not that it would matter to Condan, who barely even looked at her anymore.

Isha sat down at the table when there was a loud knock at the door.

"Enter," Condan shouted gruffly.

One of his thugs came through the door. "Sir, we caught one of the farmers trying to help an elf captive escape. We killed the elf but we thought you might like to take care of the sympathizer yourself."

Isha shuddered. The glint in the thug's eye told her he couldn't wait for the "show" Condan would put on for the townspeople. He had made public torture a regular ritual in this once quiet village. All were expected to attend.

"Who is it?" Condan barked.

"Erin O'Connell."

Condan grinned. He had been after this one for a long time. He meant to take his time and enjoy himself tonight. O'Connell would pay dearly for the trouble he'd caused.

He got up from the table and headed for the door. When he stopped to reach for the handle, he turned his intense eyes on his frightened wife.

"You will be there won't you, my heart? I expect my wife to be there when I triumph over one of my enemies." His menacing eyes warned her not to say no.

"Of course I'll be there Condan," she lied. "Where else would I be?"

The conversation was interrupted by a noise in the street followed by shouting. Condan quickly stepped outside to see what was causing the commotion. His right hand man Dougal came running. "Condan, O'Connell's escaped," he declared. "We're gathering a hunting party to go after him."

"Make sure every available man in the village goes. I want them all to see what happens to troublemakers like O'Connell."

Dougal nodded. Condan raced to his horse and was gone with the others in a cloud of dust.

Isha breathed a sigh of relief and slipped out the door into the street. She casually picked up a basket and headed for the barn. If people saw her, they would think she was going to the barn for more food.

She walked into the barn, slipped into a stall, and quickly saddled her little mare Nightwind, the fastest horse in the valley. If Isha could make it into the forest undetected, Nightwind could carry her swiftly to the safety of her parents' keep.

Isha cautiously led Nightwind into the pens. Using the cattle for cover, she made her way to the edge of the pens and then out the back gate. She moved silently from shadow to shadow until she made it to the safety of the forest. Once there she mounted Nightwind and rode as if the devil himself were after her.

Eventually she came to the valley where the Great Battle had occurred. It had been renamed The Black Valley because it seemed that the battle had soaked the entire valley in elven blood. She rode gingerly across the valley until she came to a small cave hidden by an outcropping of boulders. Looking around cautiously, she quickly led Nightwind inside the cave. She had found the small cave one day while she and Kara were picking berries. She had already placed a water jar there to hide the scroll, and had hidden a pot with some tar to seal the jar.

Isha took the scroll from her tunic and looked at it one last time. She felt someone had to know the events of the past year even if they discovered the scroll too late. But she was reluctant to hide it in an easily discovered place.

Working quickly, she started a fire and heated the tar. She put the scroll into the jar and sealed it with the tar. Then she set it gently in the hole she had dug in a corner of the cave. After covering it with dirt and mounting Nightwind, she moved to the entrance of the cave and peeked out. No one was about.

She nudged Nightwind with her heels and the pair shot from the cave like an arrow. She didn't stop until she was safely within her parents' impenetrable gates, never to return to Cluse.

When Condan returned to his empty home, he shrugged indifferently. There were plenty of old women in the village who could be made to do his cooking and cleaning. Her skulking and cringing in corners had begun to wear on his nerves, and he had been planning to do away with her anyway.

Condan concentrated on his burgeoning campaign against the Light Elves, constantly warning nearby villages of their depredations. The messages were read to the villagers and then posted for all to see. Natha made midnight visits to their leaders, whispering his corruption further into the human population.

Finally, Condan convened a large gathering in Cluse. Leaders and scholars arrived from many other villages to decide one thing: how to eliminate the Light Elves.

Condan stood on a platform and looked over the excited crowd. Smiling, he stepped forward and raised his hand for quiet.

"My friends, we all know why we are here. We have been lied to and used. It's time to shake off the yoke of the oppressor! These elves have enslaved us long enough. If violence is the only thing they understand then I say violence it shall be! Who will stand with me against these evil beings?"

As the crowd cheered, a look of sadness passed over the red-haired Light Elf watching from the trees. Egan slowly turned and started back toward his waiting king. Suddenly, a woman's scream rang out. Egan had his horse run toward the sound, originating in a small glen a few miles from the village.

There, a thug was backing a young girl up against a tree, his knife inches from her face. "Now you'll see what we do to elf sympathizers," he said darkly. Suddenly there was an elven sword at his throat.

"Now good sir, I ask you," Egan whispered in his ear. "Is this any way to treat such a fair creature?" His silken voice purred but his green eyes held a spark of anger.

He favored the young girl with his brightest smile. She smiled back uncertainly. Her face had a few bruises where the brute had slapped her.

With one swift movement, the elf lord knocked the man unconscious and swept the girl up onto his horse. "I apologize for my abruptness Lady, but you must get out of this area immediately. I am afraid some of your people might be a tad overwrought if they thought you were sympathetic to elves."

"But I *am* sympathetic to elves," the girl said. "I have no other place to go." She looked at her hands as a tear rolled down her cheek. Egan reached out and gently wiped it away. "There now my Lady, don't cry," he said reassuringly. "I promise I will find a safe place for you."

He settled her on his horse, preparing to take her back to the elven encampment. Her face was still solemn. Egan tipped her chin up with his fingertip to look into her eyes.

"My Lady, this frowning must stop," he told her with mock sternness. "Otherwise I will be forced to tickle you senseless. Please don't force me to resort to such extreme measures." A laugh threatened to erupt from his smiling lips and his eyes twinkled with merriment.

The girl looked at him in shock. Then, as his kind smile melted her defenses, she smiled back. "That is much better my Lady. Now let us make haste to get back to camp. I hear the cook is preparing the most succulent deer," he whispered to her, as if revealing a state secret. The girl's giggle could be heard ringing through the small vale as the pair rode off toward Liam's encampment.

Liam stood in the small glade gathering his power. The warm summer sun shone down on the glade, its light reflecting from the water onto the leaves overhead. A feeling of peace pervaded the place. Liam had come here often to pray and ask for God's guidance for his people. This time he had a different purpose.

It had been months now, and there was no sign of the Rift opening by itself. Liam decided to try to open it using what strength he had left. His people needed a way of escape before they were wiped out entirely.

He tried to stifle a nagging doubt. The Rift had never stayed closed this long – what if it never reopened? What if they couldn't get back?

He shook his head and cleared his mind. Years ago, he had followed the Redeemer Jesus all through his ministry, learning all he could from his God. Jesus had assured him He would always be there when needed, that He would never leave or forsake those that loved Him.

Liam's heart warmed at the memory, and his face broke out in a gentle smile. No, He would not leave them here alone. He would be with them and help them.

He knelt in the grass beside a little stream and bowed his head.

"Mighty Father, I know You can do all things and that You can deliver us out of this trial. If it is Your will please deliver us from those that seek our lives. And forgive those that would hurt us. I feel they don't really know what they are doing. Make a way of escape for us soon, Mighty God. Please make the Rift open so that we may return home to those that love us. I ask in the Name of the Redeemer, Jesus the Christ. Amen."

Liam arose and started to unleash his power, willing the Rift to open. He felt it shudder. Exerting every bit of strength he had, Liam ordered it to open. It trembled again and then was still, an immovable wall between his people and their safety.

Liam closed his eyes and sighed. He would try again later. He knew his father had seen his attempt from the other side, where he must be working just as hard to open the Rift. Perhaps together, with the One's help, they would find a way.

Later that day the entire camp was in an uproar. Liam's Chief Counselor Tiernan had been captured by humans. Liam heard the news from his oldest son Teagan, who had been found lying exhausted a mile down the trail to Liam's camp. Captain Gildas, Lord of the Archers, had found the elfling and quickly brought him back to camp.

Liam listened as a tearful Teagan related that he'd been out hunting with Tiernan when they were set upon by a gang of humans. Teagan explained how Tiernan sent him to safety while he kept the thugs busy. Liam's heart burned with anger at the thought of his good friend suffering at the brutal hands of their aggressors.

Liam sent several search parties to look for Tiernan. General Arth rode out of the camp, his face grim with determination. Fiacra and his clan rose high in the air, searching for the elven lord. One of the eagle's daughters finally spotted Tiernan's horse beside a trail leading into a dense part of the forest. It had been gutted.

Deep in the forest Tiernan awoke to the sound of another hard slap. With a slight shock he realized *he* was the one being struck. Strange how it didn't hurt anymore, he mused.

Tiernan stood with his back against a large boulder that sat between two trees. His captors watched as the elf struggled to keep his feet. This proved difficult, as his arms were stretched behind him with ropes tied to the strong trees. His back was cut and bruised by the rough rock he was forced to lean against. The ropes pulled him back against the rough surface so forcefully that he was sure both his shoulders were dislocated. The elf's swollen, blood-smeared face was cut and bruised, framed by his dark hair that hung like dirty ropes.

It seemed like ages ago when he and young Teagan had been chased by Condan's thugs. Actually it was only a day since their ill-fated hunting expedition. The humans appeared unexpectedly and were savage in their pursuit, gutting Tiernan's horse as the elves tried to escape. Tiernan knew the humans could not catch him on foot, but the small prince had started to tire. Tiernan sent him off to safety while drawing the humans toward himself. He remembered the stricken look in Teagan's frightened eyes as he ordered him to run.

He opened a swollen eye and looked at his tormentors. "Excuse me my lords. A question if you please."

The human bully stopped and shot his fellows a surprised glance. They shrugged. He turned back to his victim. Tiernan waited patiently as his tormentor, panting with the exertion of abusing the elf, looked at him again and finally nodded.

"Can we possibly finish up anytime soon?" he smirked with his swollen lips. "I have a pressing engagement with the most enchanting she-elf and she doesn't like to be kept waiting." His answer was the back of a fist across his face.

"I suppose she will accept the excuse that I was detained by acquaintances," he smiled painfully.

His eyes dark with anger, the bully punched the elf across the face with all his strength.

Tiernan didn't make a sound. When the lights stopped flashing before his eyes and his head stopped spinning, he began to laugh.

The sound startled the humans, who looked silently at the battered elf. Had he gone mad?

Tiernan watched his persecutors for a moment then spoke again. "One more question, my lord."

The human frowned. "What is it, elf?" he demanded roughly.

Tiernan lifted his head with a roguish look in his eyes. "Have you perchance been sick lately, my lord?"

"No. Why?"

Tiernan's eyes glittered with defiance. "Because you hit like a little girl," he purred. He was rewarded with a blow that sent him back into unconsciousness.

The bully pulled out a knife. "I'll shut your mouth for good," he spat, stepping forward and moved the dagger toward Tiernan's throat.

Suddenly a shower of arrows rained down on the humans, and all was still in the small encampment.

General Arth stepped out of the underbrush. His face turned grim as he caught a glimpse of Tiernan's bloodied features. Silently, the elves cut the ropes and gently wrapped Tiernan in soft blankets. He was handed up to General Arth, who settled the beaten elf in front of him in the saddle. The elves then raced for their camp, where King Liam's healing skills would be put to the test.

As they rode off, the wind blew mournfully over the dead campsite.

Liam breathed a sigh of relief as he stepped out into the night air. He had worked on Tiernan half the night, carefully healing the worst of his wounds and gently salving his battered body with a sweet smelling healing ointment. Now he stood outside the tent looking at the beautiful, far-away stars.

The thought brought the Rift to his mind. If he could not get it open soon, he'd have to find another way of escape. He looked around the camp. Ranal was sitting nearby in front of a fire watching a she-elf sing her baby to sleep. The sight of the mother and child spurred him to action. He was their king, their protector. He could not let them down.

Liam took a deep breath. He would try again – he had to. His people's survival was at stake.

He knelt on the ground and bowed his head humbly as he prayed. "Dear Father, please help me to open the Rift. My people are in grave danger and I have found no means of escape. Please hear my prayer and rescue us. I ask in the Name of the Blessed Redeemer, Jesus."

He stood and began to gather his strength. He concentrated on the Rift, summoning all his power to will it to open. But it was in vain. He felt a chill as the realization of his failure swept over him like a cold rain.

"My Lord, stop," cautioned Ranal beside him. "You will only harm yourself. The Rift simply will not open right now."

Liam grew dizzy as he continued his futile efforts. Finally he passed out from the exertion, only faintly aware of Ranal's concerned voice. Ranal caught his king just before he fell to the ground.

Liam awoke with the morning sun peeking through the doorway of his tent and shining in his eyes. Sensing someone else in the tent, he turned his head and locked eyes with Ranal. He grimaced and put his arm over his eyes.

"Please don't say it."

"I told you so," retorted Ranal, laughing at Liam's irritation. "What did you expect, old friend? I told you it would not work."

"I had to try. I owe my people that much."

"I know," said Ranal kindly. "I love them too."

Liam sat up, fighting a headache. "We must find an answer. I cannot let my people be slaughtered like sheep."

"There is a way, Liam. We just have to find it." He paused. "What did your father tell you to do when you couldn't find a solution to a problem?"

"Ask the One," admitted Liam.

"Well?" Ranal smiled.

"Call Egan," said Liam. "There is power in the faith of many hearts. We will pray again."

Ranal stepped outside and hailed his friend. They walked inside Liam's tent expectantly.

Liam paused to gather his thoughts. "My friends, we must find a way of escape before our mothers and children are slaughtered. Gather everyone together for prayer."

His friends nodded and quickly left the tent. In an hour all who could be spared from guard duty were assembled in front of Liam's tent along with all the surviving families and orphans. Fiacra and his clan floated high in the sky, keeping a sharp eye out for intruders.

Liam and his followers knelt and bowed their heads. Liam's quiet, gentle voice carried over the camp.

"Mighty Father, we ask for your help. We are trapped far away from our home and kin. Please make a way of escape for us. We are surrounded by our former friends who now want our blood. Please show us what to do. And forgive those who seek our destruction. They do not realize what they are doing. We ask in the Name of the Blessed Redeemer Jesus. Amen."

As Liam finished his prayer, he heard a bird squawk overhead. He looked up and saw a sea gull floating in the breeze. It hovered over him for a moment, then slid away on the wind toward the sea. Liam frowned, perplexed. What was it doing so far from the sea?

The answer came from a small, still voice in his heart: "*Leading the way.*"

Liam's eyes lit up. They were to go over the sea – but where? He immediately decided to find a destination.

Liam made a covert visit to the coast and called a porpoise from the sea. The animal told him of rumors of a large island far to the south. He even volunteered to guide them there. Liam sent Fiacra back with the porpoise to check on the island's location. After Fiacra corroborated the porpoise's story, Liam ordered twenty huge ships prepared for the journey.

His ship builders began work in a small bay that Liam had covered in an illusion. To the human eye it appeared as a small, fogged-in body of water, not fit for a decent harbor. To the elves, it was a peaceful haven where they could build their ships and prepare their escape. The ships, designed to carry both elves and eagles, included many compartments for the numerous plants and animals they would take with them. They had no intention of leaving their animal allies to the mercy of the brutal humans.

Six hard months after the attack on Tiernan, a final tragedy struck the Light Elves.

Of the many war orphans in Liam's camp, two of the smallest were Kallan and Kayne. By human standards they would have been only six and eight years old. They were the last two surviving members of a noble family, one that had played a major role in stopping the attempted coup by the Dark Elves in the Realm.

They had lost their parents during the first hunts. Liam's cook had always made an extra effort to look after them. On this day, however, he was busy tending to a large influx of elven refugees from the lands to the north.

Kallan and Kayne had gone back down the trail from the camp after lunch. Having spotted some large berry bushes, the brothers wanted to surprise the cook with the sweet fruit. The small elves hadn't had tarts since before the hunts started, and their mouths watered thinking of the treats.

They were just coming back with the berries when Condan's riders surprised them on the trail. To keep from giving away the location of their camp, the young elves ran in several different directions. But the relentless riders chased them for hours, cutting off the tiring elven children at every turn. Finally, Kallan and Kayne were driven around a bend in the path and ran right into a group of Condan's thugs. The exhausted young elves struggled but could not break free.

"Well now," said Condan, "What have we here?" He grabbed Kallan by his hair, jerking his head back to get a better look at his ears. "Why, it's two elf brats." He turned to the younger brother. "Where are you from, Whelp?"

"We serve in the house of Liam, the great king, my lord," said Kallan meekly.

An evil thought came to Condan's mind: perhaps it was time to pay back Liam for letting his daughter die.

"You two will do just fine," he muttered as he shoved Kallan toward his men. He went to his horse and pulled a coil of rope from his saddlebag.

The elves looked at each other, their hearts beating wildly.

Hours later Liam came rushing into the clearing. He and several others had been searching frantically all afternoon for the brothers. Liam felt a sense of dread when he found hoof prints following the youngsters.

A sob escaped his lips as he took in the scene before him. Kayne and Kallan stood tied to two trees, their small bodies riddled with arrows.

Liam ran to the youngsters. Kayne was dead, an arrow protruding from his slender throat. Feeling a weak pulse on Kallan's neck, Liam quickly cut him down and gently laid him on the ground. He had been shot several times, the arrows imbedded deeply into his little frame. He moaned weakly as Liam vainly tried to stop the bleeding.

Liam stopped and laid his hand on the child's forehead, willing the pain away.

"It doesn't hurt anymore," Kallan whispered as he smiled up at Liam. "Thank you, my king."

Liam choked back tears and managed a smile. "I am glad, little one."

"Can I sleep now, my lord? I am so tired." Kallan looked up at Liam with trusting eyes.

"Yes," Liam answered softly as a tear rolled down his cheek. "You can sleep now."

His cherub face relaxed, and Kallan closed his eyes in death. Liam bent his head and wept over the small body. That's how General Arth and the rest of the search party found him.

Liam walked into camp carrying Kallan. He was followed by General Arth, who held Kayne's body. Liam's face was stone, and no one dared speak. He walked to the fire where Tiernan and the rest of his Counselors sat reading patrol reports. They rose at the sight of the dead children.

"Prepare the ships to set sail," Liam whispered, his eyes black with anger.

Fiacra and his children were dispatched to every known elven settlement, telling them of Liam's plans to leave in one year and urging them to make their way to Liam's encampment.

Ranal looked over the valley one more time. He knew every inch of this land, which was why Liam had sent him to ensure all the elves had safely left for the ships. Indeed, they were all gone now – Ranal had sent the last two young elves back to Liam on his own horse. As he turned to go, an arrow suddenly flew up from the valley floor and struck his left thigh. Wincing, he pulled it out. Before he had time to bind the wound, a shower of arrows chased him away.

There were shouts below and the sound of horses' hooves pounding toward him. Gasping in pain, Ranal turned and ran as fast as his wound allowed him, dodging around trees and rocks. He had been captured once and had no intention of repeating the horrendous experience. His pursuers seemed to surround him, blocking his exit at every turn. He was chased for hours before the loss of blood began to slow his flight.

As he rounded some trees, his left foot caught on a tree root and he fell with sickening force onto the ground. A white-hot pain shot through his wounded leg and exploded into his brain.

He struggled to his feet and ran through the trees toward a house standing in a clearing. Praying to the One that it was empty, he ran in the door and carefully shut it behind him. He peeked back out through a crack in the door.

He was startled by a human voice behind him. "What happened to your leg, my lord?"

Ranal whirled around, his heart pounding. He saw a woman no more than twenty years old with golden hair down to her waist and beautiful blue eyes filled with concern and fear.

She stepped beside him and looked through the crack in the door. Seeing the riders approaching, she grabbed Ranal's arm and herded him toward her bed. "Quick, get under the covers. I'll send them away, but you must stay under the covers."

Trembling with shock and exhaustion, Ranal fell onto the bed and the woman swiftly covered him from head to foot. Just then someone pounded on her door. She squared her shoulders, looked at the door, and yelled harshly, "What is it?"

The pounding continued. She stepped to the door and flung it open wide enough to push her head and shoulders through. "I said, what do you want?" she demanded gruffly.

From the bed, Ranal could smell the sweat of the hot, dirty human riders. He closed his eyes and shuddered, growing dizzy from the pain in his leg.

He heard the woman's voice again, cracking like a whip. "I asked you what you want. I haven't got all day to be bothered with a bunch of drunkards riding the countryside. Now what is it?"

Finally a man's voice answered, "We are looking for an elf, lady. And we think he ran this way."

"You *think* he ran this way?" she retorted with a derisive snort. "And why pray tell would I be entertaining an elf when I have a paying customer waiting on me right now?"

After an embarrassed silence, Ranal heard the humans move off. But one remained, who Ranal heard whisper, "I'll be back in a week, lady, with gold." Then he too left.

Ranal heard the door shut and the security bar placed across it. The woman stepped to the bed and pulled the covers off his head. He looked up at her, gratitude shining from his eyes. "Many, many thanks great lady. I will leave now so as not to be here when your customer arrives."

He tried to rise. Weak from blood loss and shock, he was easily pushed back down. "Don't be an idiot," admonished the woman. "I have no customer. I'm a farmer, not a veiled woman. And besides, you aren't in any condition to go running off into the woods. They would catch you before you got past my cow pasture." Her voice softened slightly. "And I've seen what they do to elves."

Her face was grim as she looked at his wounded leg. "You just lie back and let me patch you up. Maybe you can move tomorrow, but for now, lie still." Ranal lay back against the goose down pillow and smiled weakly.

"Your wish is my command, my lady."

"The name is Eve," she said smiling, fire flashing in her bright, blue eyes.

It would be several days before Ranal could safely move to Liam's encampment. By that time he had fallen hopelessly in love with his human guardian.

The skirmishes and battles went on for another horrific year, taking its deadly toll on the Light Elves. Friends and loved ones never returned from patrols, and entire elven households were decimated. Finally the huge ships were stocked and ready for the elves' flight from their persecutors.

Liam sat in camp, weary from the day's ride. It had been a grueling trip, with the Light Elves being pursued by their human hunters.

How ironic, he thought. *We are running from the very people we have sworn to protect.*

He looked around the camp. His four young sons lay exhausted, sleeping on their blankets. He hated to disturb them, but they had to reach the ships ahead of their pursuers.

He rose to his feet and nodded to his counselors Tiernan, Ranal, and Egan, who began gathering the group to leave. Tiernan gently sat Liam's oldest son Teagan in front of him in the saddle. Liam, Ranal, and Egan did the same with Owain, Barram, and Rigalis, without even disturbing their slumber. Ranal's wife Eve carried in front of her a small elven girl orphaned by humans. Then they all rode away, followed by the surviving Light Elves.

There were only three hundred Light Elf warriors and their families left from an initial group of thousands. Liam watched the remnant of his people ride wearily toward the bay and the waiting ships. Looking to the One, he silently prayed they would make it safely to the ships before it was too late.

For the next three days, Liam's elves fought a delaying action with the humans, giving bits of ground to gain time for their families to safely reach the ships. General Arth held the main forces at bay along Cnoc Mor Seamlas since the terrain was favorable for defense. The boulder-strewn, tree-covered ridge and slopes gave cover to the elves. Their superior eyesight, hearing, and marksmanship with the bow served them well.

Finally, General Arth led his troops in a circuitous route around their enemies and laid several false trails for the humans to follow away from the bay where Liam's ships were anchored. Then the small elven army swiftly made for the bay and their waiting families. As soon as they were safely aboard, the ships moved onto the open sea. Liam had covered the ships in a thick mist, so anyone standing on the shore saw only a mass of fog stretching from the bay to the sea outlet.

The porpoise and his mate were waiting for Liam's ships outside the harbor. The animals turned and led the ships to the south. Instead of flying above the fleet, Fiacra and his clan – only fifty of whom had survived the hunts – stayed on the ships so they would not give away their location.

With a prayer to the One for guidance, Liam ordered the ships to follow. If they could reach the haven before the humans were able to catch them, perhaps he could throw an illusion around the island, shielding it against intruders. He still had enough strength left for that.

They sailed for many days until one sunny morning Fiacra called down from the top of the main mast. "An island my lord, a large one," he called excitedly.

Liam climbed to the top of the mast and looked for himself. He saw an enormous island surrounded almost entirely with steep cliffs, only accessible by a small strip of beach on the west side. It was flanked on the right by a two-hundred-foot waterfall that fell from the cliffs beside the beach, plunging into the ocean to cast a rainbow across the golden sand. As he looked the island over he could see tall green mountains and miles of lush jungle. It was a perfect haven for elves. He stared at it a moment as he sent a prayer of thanks to the One. Finally he spoke. "I name you Brisal, for Land of the Blessed you shall be."

Liam swiftly climbed down to the deck and signaled the other ships to make for the island. In front of the ships the porpoises leapt into the air with delight at the sight of the huge island. "Many thanks my friends," Liam called down to them. Liam's delighted sons shouted and sang songs to the animals as they danced before the great elven ships. The animals sang back in their own language, telling of the birds and trees and wildlife on the island. Liam listened carefully, then sent Fiacra and his sons to scout out the island and report back on the best location for a settlement.

From the ships, the elves packed into smaller boats and landed on the narrow beach. In no time they disembarked with all their worldly possessions, the great eagles carrying the largest bundles and animals. When the last bundle had been brought ashore, Liam ordered the ships and boats to be taken out to deep water and scuttled. It pained Liam to do it, but their presence near the island would have given them away.

He watched as the last boat was pulled onto the shore after carrying the last elves from the burning ships. It was quickly concealed in nearby trees. The elves stood watching the burning ships solemnly, knowing there was no turning back now. They were here to stay.

Liam felt a sense of relief as he prepared to throw an illusion over the entire island.

He shut his eyes and began to sing. As his melodious voice rang through the air, a golden mist formed around the island and solidified into an illusion. Instead of a lush paradise, the island now appeared to outside eyes as a forbidding place with inhospitable stony mountains, quicksand, and treacherous pits.

The elves stood together on the beach with their king and raised their voice in a song of praise and thanks to the One for His safe guidance to this refuge. Their voices blended together in a harmony of unearthly beauty ringing across the skies like an angel's anthem. That night, for the first time in months, they slept soundly and at peace, slumbering under palm trees.

The next morning Liam's sons wanted to go exploring. Liam called a halt to that until Fiacra and his sons returned with their reports. When they finally arrived, Fiacra revealed he had found a large, hidden valley filled with lush plants and waterfalls. It was less than two leagues from the beach. Liam told the eagle to show the valley to him.

Fiacra, hovering on the wind, led them through the jungle paths to the cliffs overlooking the valley. Liam stood on the shore of a huge lake that emptied out through a broad waterfall into the river that flowed through the valley. Looking down at this beautiful paradise, he knew they had indeed found a home. He knelt down in the grass, and everyone else did the same. Bowing his head, he offered a simple prayer of thanks to the One for guiding them to a safe place of refuge.

Rising to his feet, Liam looked upon the beautiful valley. It was wide, lush, and green, its walls filled with waterfalls. Liam knew this would be the last refuge of the Light Elves. He named it Nantuor, "Valley Where the River Begins."

The elves settled into a peaceful routine on the island, building and shaping their new home. Where the cliffs were too steep, they would carve out the large basin needed for the huge eyries of the Great Eagles. The eagle clan placed itself around the entire valley, settling especially in eyries on the cliff's face and around the upper lake, which allowed them to keep watch over the valley and the elves.

The idyllic existence on the island was marred by two deaths: Ranal's wife and son. His son had been stillborn.

Liam looked into his friend's tear-stained eyes. "Ranal," he said gently, "it is time. We must start the burial ceremony."

Ranal wept silently next to his wife's body. He hadn't stopped crying since her heart had stopped beating. She had died quietly in her husband's arms, her body worn out with age. He had loved this human for over a hundred years, but finally even Liam's healing skills weren't enough to save her.

"I can't bear to let her go," said Ranal softly. "She is the reason my heart beats." He turned to his king and asked brokenly, "How can I go on living if she is dead?"

"The same way you went on living when your unborn son died long ago, my friend," said Liam gently. "You will see them again, when this world is over and we are taken up into the bosom of the One. You will see them both." He laid a comforting hand on Ranal's head as Ranal bowed it and sobbed, his great warrior's heart breaking.

Over centuries, the elves cultivated the island to their use. They had brought their favorite plants, trees, and animals with them, many from the Realm itself. The lush valley was shaped into an elven fortress, including a farm across the river from the elven settlement and a sturdy stone bridge connecting the two. The farm flourished with elven horses, dogs, and all manner of farm animals needed to sustain Liam's people. The entire valley was filled with flowering plants, fruit trees, gardens, and intricate trellises.

The fortress was an elegant, many-tiered structure filled with delicate arches, beautiful fountains, and private gardens overflowing with jasmine, exotic flowers, and fruit trees. White deer from the

Realm, peacocks, and birds of paradise decorated the gardens and grounds. It was a land of unearthly beauty, its architecture something that appeared only in dreams.

They built three huge buildings to house military offices, a learning center, and medical facilities, all connected by covered walkways, halls, private gardens, and lush lawns that together made one huge, continuous fortress. There was a large building for the stables with several hundred elegant homes above them. Finally at the top of the huge tiered fortress was the Royal Quarters where Liam and his family resided.

After many centuries of cultivation, most of the inland part of the island was covered by a lush pasture of knee-deep grass or a thick forest filled with songbirds, peaceful glens with waterfalls emptying into lily-covered ponds, and streams stocked with fish. The elves had also preserved a large ring of thick jungle around their precious forest to give any intruders the illusion that they were on a deserted island.

It took many years to rid the island of the larger dragons. But thanks to the One and the precise caution of General Arth, not one elven life had been forfeited. The smaller dragons, which could be just as deadly as their larger cousins, had been hunted almost to extinction, though a few had eluded the elves in the caves at the island's south end.

Eventually men had come to explore the island. Liam drove them off with visions of ghosts and goblins or disturbing dreams. Rumors began to circulate that the island was haunted, and ships began avoiding the small beach on Brisal.

Finally, in the late 1700s, an old Marquis, and several farmhands built a manor house and a small farm on the island. Liam tried to entice the humans to move, but the old Marquis would not be run off. Elven guards were placed around the farm to ensure the humans did not move further inland. By human standards it was only a half day's ride to the elven settlement of Nantuor, and Liam wanted to keep safe what was left of his people.

One spring day, the elven guards observed the humans having their Sunday service. From nearby trees, they heard the Marquis telling the story of salvation. The guards could hardly contain their excitement. The humans knew about the One and the Redeemer.

They even mentioned the Holy Spirit. Unable to contain himself, one guard ran all the way to Nantuor with his happy news. They knew! They knew! There was great rejoicing in Nantuor that night.

The favors and gifts began to be exchanged one winter's eve. When the old man went into the house to fetch tools to fix a broken fence near his stables, an elven guard jumped from his tree and quickly bound up the fence, then returned to his post just as the old man was returning. Staring at the fence, the old man smiled and muttered to himself, "I knew it – Leprechauns." He returned to the house as the elf laughed softly. The man soon came back and placed a bucket next to the fence. Straightening up, he whispered "thank you" and hobbled back into the house.

The curious guard left his tree to look in the bucket and found a tankard of sweet red wine. Chuckling with delight, he took his present back into the tree and enjoyed its excellent taste as he kept the rest of his watch. He returned the tankard to the bucket with some herbs that would make a soothing tea to ease the old man's arthritis. The next morning the old man came out and found the tankard. Casting a warm smile at the trees around him, he murmured another "thank you" and carried his gift inside.

It was a strange friendship, not openly acknowledged by either side. Gifts of hot food and cool wine were left in various places about the farm, to be replaced by healing herbs or strange, sweet fruit.

One winter the elves had overheard the old man telling a servant that Christmas might be a little late because of the rough seas. The next night a farmhand heard a strange bird chirping in the trees. Intrigued by the sound, he followed it to the beach, where the elves had left an enormous trunk filled with gifts. He sent for the other farmhands, who together dragged the trunk into the house and opened it. Inside were clothes of fine fabrics, silver pens, elegant jewelry, fine leather boots, a silver sewing case with silver needles and fine silk thread of a multitude of colors, and other wonderful surprises. A second box at the bottom of the first contained an enormous ham with all the trimmings, along with boxes of candies and delicate pastries.

No one went without a present that year. Although the Marquis never mentioned it, he noticed that the trunk was somehow bone dry after washing ashore. That night he left out a barrel of his best ale for the guards, along with mugs, ham, baked bread and butter, and one of his wife's plum puddings. The old man had moved his wife and son to the island the previous summer. It was a merry Christmas for everyone that night.

This friendly arrangement continued for years, the farm finally passing to the Marquis' son. Liam had met the son when he was a small child. He had gotten lost in the jungle and Liam, drawn by his sobbing, had led him safely home. That had been the first of many adventures. The lad had sworn himself to secrecy about the elves, and he only broke his word once.

One day, the Marquis' niece, a beautiful young woman named Emily Remington, came to Liam's island and stayed with the Marquis' family. As Liam watched her, he realized how much he missed his wife, and how lonely he really was. What happened between them is a tale for another time. The journal she left, a treasure for another to find.

Finally, the humans moved off the island to North America. Things remained quiet until the twenty-first century.

Chapter 3

The Escape

Two thousand years had eased the formidable climate on Krewabrig. By the year 2000, it was not unusual for people to climb the mountain that legend said was a place of evil. But as the sciences advanced, man began to forget that sometimes legend and myth had some basis in fact.

The two hikers sat on adjacent boulders, catching their breath after reaching the mountaintop. The girl had been in a foul mood most of the day thanks to her boyfriend's incessant teasing. She wasn't happy when he started in again.

"You know why no one comes up here, don't you?" he smirked. "Because they're afraid of being carried off by elves,"

Alicia turned to him in disgust. "Come on, Brad. You know that's bull." She turned on her heel and started walking back down the hill.

Laughing, Brad picked up his backpack and followed her. "Where's your sense of adventure, Alicia?" he snickered. "Maybe it would be *cool* to be captured by elves."

"That will never happen," she retorted, waiting for him impatiently a few feet down the hill.

"And why is that?" he asked as he walked past her.

"Because everyone knows there are no such things as elves!" she shouted at his back before following him in a huff.

If they had stayed just a little longer, they would have heard a sharp clang shoot through the air, like the first crack in the ice on top of a pond before it collapses. Somewhere on the mountaintop, Braen looked up startled and then smiled to himself at the tiny break in the barrier.

Over the next few years, numerous groups of visitors went to the mountaintop. They frequently discussed old legends of the area being inhabited by evil elves, often resulting in arguments and someone shouting that there were no such things as elves. There would be a sharp crack in the air, followed by a stunned silence around the campfire. Then someone would laugh nervously and suggest they change the subject. Sleep would be fitful and full of evil dreams. Groups wasted no time leaving the next morning.

The place had an overwhelming aura of evil. It became stronger after each statement of unbelief by a human, until no one dared to venture there but those who had an aura of evil themselves.

That is how one spring afternoon a group of bikers came to the mountaintop. They had decided to make this last night in Europe their best. They searched out the most evil place they could find and prepared for a long night of debauchery. When they began trading opinions about elves, one dark-haired biker became enraged. His ears had been ringing since he had arrived, and it had begun to sound like whispers. His nerves finally got the best of him.

He got to his feet and drunkenly yelled over and over, "There is no such thing as elves!" Suddenly a cracking sound broke through the air like a lightening bolt. Then there was silence. The hair started to rise up on the biker's neck as he looked around nervously. Someone or something was out there in the dark, just beyond the firelight.

An evil laugh broke the silence. Everyone turned to see Braen and his elves surrounding the campsite.

"No such thing as elves?" he chuckled darkly. "I'll bet you'll believe in elves by the time I'm done with you."

A mysterious force froze the terror-stricken bikers in place. The Dark Elves moved into the firelight, each selecting a human victim and dropping a small, gray seed in their mouths. The elves' eyes flickered with an evil light as they muttered wicked words that hadn't been spoken in centuries. The light intensified and then shone in the eyes of their victims. Suddenly the humans became aware of a fire kindled inside them, as if they were burning from the inside out. They crumpled to the ground in agony while the Dark Elves laughed with delight. The screams continued late into the night, unheard by the townspeople far below.

Finally the humans were silent, stiff husks. Inside every body an evil thing squirmed. Each elf stepped forward to a human and gave the husk a firm kick. They broke open and out of each slid a slimy human sized reptilian form, hissing and striking at anything that moved. Hungrily, they started searching for food.

Braen watched the lizard like monsters quickly devour the bodies. By the time they'd finished, the monsters had already learned to stand upright. Morfran, his second in command, stood before him expectantly.

"We go to find Liam and his precious little Light Elves," said Braen. "The sooner we rid ourselves of them, the sooner we will be free to enjoy what this world has to offer." He jerked his head toward the path, motioning his troops to move out. They silently moved down the mountain, their shadows slithering behind them in the moonlight. Each Dark Elf was followed by a slimy, gray-skinned creature.

The bikes were found the next morning with no clue as to the whereabouts of their owners. It had indeed been their last night in Europe.

Natha sat at his desk going over the day's accounts. He made a good living as the mayor of Cluse. It was easy to get these weak-minded humans to vote him into office, requiring just a few midnight visits around election time.

He sat back in his chair and surveyed his plush home, the largest in the village. Surrounded by an enormous park, it offered a magnificent view from the study, which had large French doors on one side that opened out onto a huge garden ending at an ornate stone fence. With the doors open, he could hear the sound of the ocean beating against the cliffs below.

The other side of the study had a fine view of the village down the hill. Krewabrig loomed on the other side of the small village, its icy peak shining like a ghostly dagger in the moonlight. There was a churchyard and cemetery across the street. Most important, from here he could keep an eye on all the villagers' comings and goings.

Natha's house had been made up of stones taken from the scene of the Great Battle, each one having been stained with the blood of a Light Elf. The aged stains appeared as decorative dark streaks, causing many visitors to surmise that the stones were of some rare marble from a far away land. When they would ask if the stones came at a dear price, Natha would chuckle and reply, "A very dear price indeed."

He had hung about the village for two thousand years now. He would appear to live a normal life span, fake his own death, and then show up as his own heir and reclaim his holdings. He had exploited this trick during his campaigns for mayor, claiming he could trace his lineage back further than anyone else in the village. Over the centuries he built up a considerable fortune, allowing him to build his magnificent house in the 1400s.

Every time he saw hikers heading up the mountain, he would plant in their minds the suggestion that elves did not exist. He knew that enough statements of unbelief could weaken any barrier. He had even gone with a few of them to ensure the conversation turned to elves.

One morning, an old man from America stepped off the ferry and disappeared into the crowds gathering for the local festival. Natha saw him trudging up the road back to the docks near sunset, a nylon bag in hand. In his daily journal, Natha noted the arrival and departure of the unusual visitor. He had given his servants the weekend off for the festival, but it wouldn't be difficult to obtain the old man's comings and goings from them. These humans loved to gossip.

He sighed to himself. His servants would not be back for two days. Until then he would just have to make due, which meant pouring his own wine.

He rose from his desk and stepped to the ornate sideboard by the huge window in his study. It held a silver tray containing a wine decanter and several glasses. As he reached for a glass, he felt a touch of premonition – strangely, it felt like a premonition of his own death. He chuckled at the thought; he was a Dark Elf, destined to live for thousands of years. He had it made. He could eat, drink, and be merry, for tomorrow . . . He shivered and didn't finish the thought.

Just then a movement outside in the dark caught his eye. He looked closely. There it was again. He was sure he saw the toe of a boot just underneath the shadow of a large monument in the cemetery across the street.

"Natha, where are you my old friend?" a silky voice purred in his mind.

Braen! Natha swallowed thickly. He didn't know why a cold shiver went up his spine. He had done well by his old master. In two thousand years he had acquired considerable wealth and position. He would be a powerful ally for his king.

"I am here my king," he answered timidly, his heart beating like a hammer. "In the house across the road. I will be waiting for you at the door." He should be feeling joy, as Braen had promised great reward for his loyalty. Why then did he have such a feeling of dread?

Natha watched as a dark shadow flitted across the road to his home. He quickly walked to the door and opened it. Braen stood in the doorway, his cat-like eyes glinting green in the moonlight. With a slight scent of death, Braen stepped into Natha's study. He surveyed the rich decor as Natha hurriedly closed the door behind him.

"You have done well for yourself, my old friend," he intoned. "I can see you have not been idle in my absence."

"No, my Lord, I have not," said Natha meekly. He felt the warm room growing cold. "I feel I have done quite well by you. I hope to receive an ample reward for my efforts, my lord." Braen turned his jade-colored gaze toward him, pinning him to the spot.

"You feel you have done well, do you?" said Braen, smiling slightly. "Believe me my friend, your reward will be more ample than even you deserve."

Braen looked at a picture of Mt. Krewabrig on the wall. The wall safe was hidden behind it. He smiled at Natha. "Yes, you have acquired quite a bit in two thousand years. Such riches make me wonder why we were left to languish so long on that wretched mountain." His green eyes bored into Natha, sending another shiver through his body.

"My Lord," started Natha nervously. "I did the best I could. It was many years before I could even get the humans up on the mountain, much less plant suggestions in their minds. Their superstitions kept them away for almost the entire time. It is only recently that I was able to get them to go near it at all." He took a fearful step back, suddenly feeling in danger.

"Ah, Natha, my old faithful friend. I am frightening you. This is no way to greet you after all you have done for me. Come here and let me embrace you."

Natha stepped toward his master, trembling slightly. Braen smiled and gave him a warm embrace. Natha felt like he was being enveloped in a wall of anger. After a moment Braen released his captive.

"There now, Natha. You have nothing to fear from me. Did I not tell you that I would show you my gratitude for your loyalty?" Braen cast a bright gaze on Natha. He had seen that look before, having cast it often on the victims of his own ill temper.

"And now," said Braen as he moved to the front door, "let us greet the rest of your old friends. I'm sure you will have a lot to talk about. You haven't seen each other in a long time."

Braen opened the door, allowing shadow after shadow to slither into the room. Natha knew instantly his quiet life here had come to an end.

Braen's son Daman entered the room and took his place at his father's side. He had the same compelling green eyes as Braen, only it seemed to Natha that there was something even deadlier lurking behind them, as if an evil were hidden there, scratching to get out and unleash its insane fury on the world.

Braen watched as the rest of the elves and their gray warriors filled the entryway. He closed the door behind them and locked it.

"You have a wine cellar, do you not?" he asked, turning to Natha.

"Why yes, of course, my lord. I have the finest wine cellar in the area."

"Good," said Braen smiling. "I haven't had wine in two thousand years and I feel like celebrating." He ordered his soldiers, "Go upstairs and find rooms for yourselves and your pets."

He turned again to Natha. "Natha, go prepare some food at once. We are famished after surviving on what little that wretched mountain has to offer. And bring plenty of wine. Morfran will make sure you carry enough up for an abundant supply for our feast."

Natha turned to lead Morfran to the wine cellar. Now his precious collection of rare wines would be decimated by these ragged, dead-end warriors. One of the Dark Elves chuckled as Natha walked by him toward the cellar door.

Hours later, with all the unwelcome guests disgustingly drunk, Natha carried in another tray loaded with food. The gray warriors lay about on the floor fighting over the scraps thrown to them by their masters. Natha sighed and looked at his beautiful Kurdistan carpets. He doubted if he would ever be able to get them clean.

Exhausted and hungry, he approached Braen tentatively. "My lord, if you would permit me, I haven't had a thing to eat all night and I was wondering . . . ?" he trailed off without finishing his request.

"Of course, Natha old friend. What were we thinking? Our poor host has not eaten all evening."

Several Dark Elves snickered. Daman's cold face remained blank, but his eyes waited expectantly for his father's next move. Natha looked at the son and then the father.

"Of course, he won't mind bringing one more tray of food before he sits down to eat, will he?" smiled Morfran.

"Of course not, my lords, I will get it immediately." Natha hustled to the kitchen, dark laughter following him. In the end, he managed to procure a meager supper before finally going to bed.

He was rousted out of bed before daybreak by Morfran to cook breakfast for the entire household. As he carried one of many trays of food into the dining room he heard familiar voices in the foyer. He peeked around the doorway to see several members of the city council in the entryway. Perhaps he could escape by leaving with them. He started toward his friends but was stopped by a rough hand on his shoulder.

"You would better serve your king elsewhere Natha," Morfran warned in his ear.

Natha watched in despair as a smiling Braen appearing as an old man sent his friends on their way. He turned from the door and favored Natha with a faint smile.

"I told them you were far too busy with your duties here to talk to them, and that perhaps they should not return until they were sent for. I told them to pass the same message on to your servants. You don't mind, do you Natha?" Braen smiled at Natha's helpless anger.

"No my lord, I'm sure you know what is best," he murmured meekly. His heart welled with despair as he was shoved roughly toward the kitchen to retrieve more food.

He spent the rest of the day running here and there, fulfilling every whim of the rest of the Dark Elves. By late afternoon he was spent, having barely eaten all day. Sighing wearily to himself, he filled Braen's brandy cup. Braen, who was studying Natha's poultry pens containing his prize hens and rare pheasants, turned to Natha with a smile. "I think we will have roast hen tonight and perhaps pheasant tomorrow. You don't mind, do you old friend?" Braen's eyes glinted warningly. This was not a request.

"But my lord, those are my prize birds," he protested weakly.

"But what better meat to present to your king?" demanded Morfran with a mocking smile.

Braen didn't bother turning from the window. "Prepare the hens immediately Natha. We are hungry."

"Yes, my lord." Natha stepped into the kitchen and out the door to the pens. "I must get away from him," he thought despairingly. "He is ruining me with his greed and gluttony. He will surely kill me before this is over."

Braen laughed to himself as he watched Natha. He already knew Natha was planning to escape. What a pity the weak-minded fool would fail. Beside him, Morfran laughed to himself as well.

The next day Braen summoned Natha to the study. Questioning him extensively on his efforts to eliminate the Light Elves, Braen was not pleased to learn that Liam and his people had not only survived, but had disappeared from the shores of Europe. He was even more upset to learn that there was no sign of Liam anywhere on earth.

"What do you mean you can't find him?" demanded Braen coldly. He drew close to Natha, his hands clinched in fury.

Natha stumbled backward into Daman. Shivering at the icy look in his green eyes, he turned back to Braen with a pleading gesture.

"I am sorry my lord. But there is no sign of Liam or his elves anywhere. It is as if they disappeared from the face of the earth."

Braen's hand came down hard. Natha knew not to dodge the blow. It would only mean many more. He crumpled to the floor, clutching his bleeding cheek.

Braen raised his hand for another blow when something outside the window captured his attention. The ocean was shining in the sunlight, and a huge Great White shark was cruising not far from the shoreline.

Stepping outside to the cliffs, Braen called to the shark's mind. After a few minutes of conversation the shark swam off to search for Liam, with a good meal offered as its reward.

The next morning Braen was perusing Natha's journal as Marfach waited patiently. He looked up and his lieutenant began to speak. "My lord, I have heard rumors that a human from another land was snooping around the old caves near the Field of the Great Battle. I am concerned that he might have discovered some relic of our past. It would not do to have these humans aware of our existence."

Braen's eyes narrowed as he looked at Marfach. "Indeed it would not."

He glanced at the journal. "What day was the strange human here, Marfach?"

"The day of the festival, great lord."

Braen paged through the journal until his eyes lit angrily on the page he was seeking. The old man was an archeologist from a small university in Texas. Natha hadn't even bothered to find out where the man had gone or what he was doing in Cluse. An archeologist was probing around the only place on earth that contained physical evidence of his people, and Natha just let him slip through his fingers.

"That fool!" he muttered.

He looked up at Marfach, fire in his eyes. "Natha noted that the human was carrying a bag. We must find out what was in it and where he went."

"It will be done my lord," answered Marfach, smiling grimly. He had not killed a human in almost two thousand years. This would be delicious. "I will have Natha make arrangements for my journey immediately."

"Do not fail to have him inform you of the customs of this time," instructed Braen. "And tell him I want to see him before you leave to seek the human."

"It will be done," answered Marfach. He did not envy Natha his next visit to this room.

A few weeks later the shark returned with news of a large island in the Atlantic rumored to harbor an elven colony. Braen had Natha draw out a huge sum from his personal bank account to purchase a large yacht with a generous hold.

Within a week Braen and his elves were ready to follow the shark to Liam's island. He left a small contingent of elves at the house and forced Natha to sign the estate over to Daman along with his bank account.

Braen then took Natha to the cliffs that bordered the estate. Braen stood in the evening breeze and called to the Great White. It quickly swam to the bottom of the cliffs and waited expectantly.

Natha stood on trembling knees before Braen, his body wasted and scarred from Braen's beatings. He watched as the shark circled below the cliff, waiting for Braen to push him into the water. He shuddered as he felt Braen's hand stroke his face.

"Natha, old friend," Braen purred. "You have done so much for me."

"And you repay me with torture," snarled Natha.

"Yes, but I didn't mean it," Braen said softly. "I have been upset and frustrated lately. And it's all Liam's fault. He has hidden himself far too well these past years. I was wrong to take it out on such a dear friend." Braen sighed sadly as he looked at Natha. "Truly my friend, I didn't mean it"

"Then why did you?" spat Natha.

"You seem surprised, old friend," smiled Braen. He paused, looking down at the shark. "Have you ever heard the story of the scorpion and the frog?"

Natha shook his head.

"Well," continued Braen, "it seems there was a scorpion who wanted to get across the river. On the bank nearby, he spied a frog. He asked the frog to carry him safely across the river. The frog said, 'Oh no, you'll sting me and I'll die.'

'No, no, I promise,' said the scorpion. So the frog agreed and off they went across the river. Halfway across the scorpion stung the frog. The frog said, 'Why did you do that? Now we are both going to die.'

The scorpion just shrugged and said, 'What did you expect, Frog? I'm only a scorpion.'"

"You said you would reward me for helping you," protested Natha.

"And so I shall," replied Braen. Smiling, he shoved Natha's ragged body off the cliff. The elves laughed with delight as the shark devoured his reward.

Chapter 4

The Usurpers

After putting the finishing touches on her auburn hair, Ginger Carter went downstairs to help her best friend Alta Morgan with her six year old twins. Ginger and Alta had promised Alta's girls a day at the zoo. Having not left the Texas ranch in two weeks, the little blonds were thrilled.

They begged to take along their doctor's kit, claiming it might be needed to help the animals, but Alta talked them out of it by noting they might hurt the feelings of the vet at the zoo. To soothe their feelings, Ginger's grandfather Felix gave them each a $50 bill to spend on their outing. The little girls squealed with delight and hugged the tall old man, smothering him with kisses and 'I love you's'.

Grinning from ear to ear, Felix walked to the front hall, put on his Stetson, and went out to join the rest of the men in the barn. They planned to finish repenning a few horses and then spend the rest of the afternoon at the auction barn looking over potential bucking stock.

Returning through the living room, Ginger spotted a coffee table buried under a pile of coupons with a large pair of scissors on top. She smiled to herself as she headed into the kitchen. Alta really knew how to look for bargains.

Alta was in the kitchen. She had finished curling Cheyanne's hair and was starting to work on Casey.

"Momma, I don't want my hair curled. I don't like it, comb it out," Cheyanne pleaded.

"Just a minute baby, Momma's busy," Alta responded distractedly as she continued with Casey's hair.

Cheyanne gave up and disappeared into the living room. Alta soon finished with Casey's hair and looked around for Cheyanne.

"Ginger, where did Cheyanne go?" she asked.

"I saw her headed toward the living room. I guess she's watching TV."

Alta went into the living room. After a moment of dead silence, her horrified voice rang out.

"Cheyanne! What have you done?!?"

Ginger hurried into the room to find a shocked Alta staring at Cheyanne. The girl had taken the scissors and cut all the curls out of her hair except for a single one on top of her head. The rest of her blond hair was lying at her feet.

Alta led her into the kitchen and trimmed her hair to make it as presentable as possible. Then she bundled the twins in the truck and set out with Ginger for the zoo. Ginger drove. Alta was quiet on the ride there.

"Mom, are you stressing again?" asked Cheyanne.

"Yes," she replied quietly as she sat back against the seat with her eyes shut.

"Does that mean you lose your nerve?" asked Casey.

"No, that means I lose my patience"

"Oh," said the girls.

When they arrived at the crowded zoo, Casey immediately got her head caught in a rail fence while trying to get a good look at the ducks. A crowd stared in bemusement as Ginger and Alta worked to get her free. After Alta finally extricated her, Ginger suggested they go to the petting zoo. What could happen there?

Almost as soon as they got there, a goat bit Cheyanne's hand, drawing a good deal of blood. As the embarrassed attendant apologized profusely, Alta and Ginger gathered up the girls to take Cheyanne to the hospital. Running to the car, Casey fell and hit her head on the tile sidewalk. The blow left no scratches on her head, though it cracked the tile.

Hearing her sister fall, Cheyanne began running back across the parking lot. She only got a few steps before she was knocked down by a slow moving car. Suffering nothing worse than a few bruises, she quickly stood up and announced, "I'm fine. It only knocked the breath out of me." The driver, however, trembled and cried as she jumped out of her car and went to check on Cheyanne.

After ensuring Cheyanne was unhurt, Alta turned to the driver and shouted at her, shaking her finger in her face. Alta was stunned to realize afterward that in her shock, she had scolded the driver entirely in German.

There was a traffic jam of people driving into the zoo so Ginger decided to drive the girls to the hospital herself. She had to drag Alta back to the four door Ford truck with Cheyanne and Casey. A block from the hospital, a woman ran a stop sign and hit the back of the truck. Ginger's seat belt jammed, trapping her in the truck, so she reached in her pocket for her Swiss army knife to cut herself free.

Meanwhile, Alta jumped out. She was hyperventilating so badly she couldn't speak, so she silently shook an angry finger at the other driver and pointed to the stop sign she ran. The woman was badly shaken, thinking Alta couldn't breathe because she'd been severely injured. A police officer soon appeared and had Alta place her hands on the trunk of his cruiser. It looked like she was being arrested, though he was simply trying to help her catch her breath.

A passing motorist yelled out his car window, "Hey, she's the one who got rear ended. What are you doing?"

With the officer staring at his expired tag, the driver quickly moved on.

When Alta finally got her breath, she glared at the other driver and repeatedly gasped, "Didn't you see the stop sign?"

Two ambulances arrived. Alta and Ginger rode in one, with Alta's pager going off the entire way. The other ambulance took the twins, both of whom were on small backboards, much to their delight.

"Casey," whispered Cheyanne excitedly. "We're going to the hospital!"

"I know!" Casey whispered back. "This is great. Wonder if they'll let us be doctors when we get there. Doc already taught us how."

The EMT smiled.

When they arrived at the hospital, he and the driver carried them in. The girls stared in wonder at the instruments and uniformed people. The men gently set them on a bed just beside the alcove where Alta had been placed.

"Mom!" said Casey.

"Yes baby, I'm here."

"Do you want a drink of water or anything?" asked Casey.

"No baby, Momma's fine. Are you two alright?"

"No," replied Cheyanne anxiously.

Alta tensed. "What's wrong, honey?"

"I need to go to the bathroom."

Alta relaxed. Her pager went off again. She rolled her eyes and silenced it. Several nurses took all three of them for X-rays. The results were good – no broken bones, just a few scrapes and bruises. Cheyanne's hand had a large band-aid on it with a happy face sticker.

Left alone in her alcove for a moment, Alta breathed a sigh of relief. Suddenly the twins came running in, each waving a sheet of paper.

"Momma, Momma," they exclaimed at once.

"What is it, babies?"

"We just signed these papers so we could get out of the hospital. Just like real doctors! Doc will be so proud of us!"

Alta examined the papers. Sure enough, each release form had been signed by one of the twins. They had carefully printed their first names at the bottom of the page.

"Oh Lord," Alta sighed, leaning her head back on the pillow and shutting her eyes.

"Would you like some water Momma?" asked Casey.

"Sure honey," Alta replied without opening her eyes. "It's over there on the table."

When no one answered, she opened her eyes to find the room empty except for Ginger. The twins had dashed out the door to get her some water.

"Oh Lord let this day end soon," muttered Alta.

"Amen to that," said Ginger from the next bed.

Twenty minutes later an impatient-looking nurse led the twins back in. As she turned to leave, Casey blurted out, "But we only wanted to help."

"Where were they?" asked Alta, dreading the answer.

"Dr. Harrison was performing an appendectomy when two very short nurses in scrubs, caps, and yellow rubber gloves showed up in the OR."

Ginger tried to stifle her laughter.

Alta's pager went off again. She angrily shut it off and dialed the phone next to her bed.

A man's voice answered.

"What do you want?!" spat Alta.

Her husband asked irritably, "Where are you? We are waiting on you to fix lunch."

"I was in an accident and I'm in the hospital," she answered quietly. Then her voice rose. "Quit paging me!"

After a moment of shocked silence he replied, "Oh heck. I'll be right there!"

Alta hung up. She and Ginger lay for a moment with their eyes closed. Then Ginger quietly asked, "How long do you think it will take him to get here?"

"Oh, he'll probably come 'charging to the rescue' in about twenty minutes," she said.

"When he does, he gets to keep the twins for the rest of the day," remarked Ginger.

"You got it, honey," Alta smirked.

"I feel better already," smiled Ginger.

True to Alta's prediction, her distraught husband rushed into the room twenty minutes later. They were released two hours after that. Her husband reassured her on the way to the truck that she wouldn't have to fix lunch – he would buy barbecue for everyone. Unfortunately, he couldn't take the twins with him to the auction barn, since they'd been banned for, as they explained it, "releasing" several valuable bulls into the "wild."

When they got home the twins were in a rush to go to their room.

"Where are you going in such a hurry?" Alta asked.

"We want to check on Mr. Fuzzy. He had a headache last night so we gave him some Tylenol."

As the twins went to check on the hamster, Alta and Ginger looked at each other and grimaced.

"Oh Lord," Alta murmured.

"Thank heaven for little girls," quipped Ginger.

A moment later the girls came running back into the room. "He's okay," Casey reassured her mother. "He's asleep and he has this big grin on his face."

Alta looked at Ginger and nodded at the stairs. Leaving the twins, they quietly went upstairs and found the hamster was dead.

"Oh well," said Alta stoically, "at least he went with a smile."

Ginger elbowed her in the ribs.

Alta went back downstairs and fixed each girl a large bowl of ice cream. It was an adequate distraction as Ginger stuck the hamster in a bag and quickly buried him outside in a flowerbed.

Later, as Ginger and Alta sat at the kitchen table drinking coffee, the girls ran in with the inevitable announcement.

"We can't find Mr. Fuzzy Momma," said Cheyanne.

"Uh girls, Mr. Fuzzy had to go on a long trip. He didn't say when he'd be back," Alta told them.

"Yeah, he went west," (which is cowboy for 'he died'), said Ginger under her breath. Alta kicked her under the table.

"Why don't you girls go check on that new batch of kittens out in the barn?" suggested Alta.

And with that, the twins ran excitedly straight out to the barn.

"You are so bad," said Alta.

"I know," answered Ginger, sighing tiredly. "Well, maybe tomorrow will be a little quieter," she added.

"You going back to work?" asked Alta.

"Yeah, I've had all of this vacation nonsense I can handle. I want to get back to work and finish up some files."

"Well, try not to get shot doing it, okay?" said Alta.

"Shot? Me?" asked Ginger. "My job is a walk in the park."

"Oh yeah, being a Texas Ranger is a real quiet job," retorted Alta, smiling.

"I'll try to stay out of trouble." Ginger grinned as she took a sip of coffee.

"I'll believe that when I see it," murmured Alta.

Ginger went to work early the next morning. By afternoon she was chasing down a drug dealer.

Rafael raced down the city street and turned right at the first corner. His boys on the other hand drove through an old warehouse to cut corners and save time. They also meant to block Ginger who was in hot pursuit. Their effort ended tragically for them. "Have you lost your mind?!" demanded her partner Harry, as the black van was pinballed into an oil pit. Ginger continue through the old warehouse in order to cut Rafael off on the other side.

"You don't want him to get away do you?" she asked with a grin as she pushed the truck to its limit.

"I want to live to read him his rights," protested Harry, shaking his head as Rafael's Maserati shot past outside the warehouse exit on the street.

"Do you want to live forever?" smirked Ginger as she slid in behind Rafael's car.

She hit the gas and bumped the suspect's right rear fender. It slid and spun out of control into a pile of barrels. Rafael struggled furiously to escape past his airbag as Ginger and her partner got out of the truck and approached him.

"Here, let me help you," Ginger chirped as she pulled open the door.

She grabbed Rafael by the arm and jerked him from the car. He swung at her with his fist. Ginger caught his arm and used his momentum to throw him to the ground, knocking the breath from him. She pounced on him like a tiger and cuffed him.

Harry pulled him to his feet, and began reading from a small card. "You have the right to remain silent. If you give up that right anything you say can and will be used against you in a court of law. You have the right . . ."

"Oh shut up," snapped Rafael. "I know my rights better than you do."

"I'll just bet you do," Ginger replied. "However, we don't want you to get lost in the land of legal red tape, now do we?"

Harry finished reading the South American his Miranda rights. Ginger patted down the suspect, producing a wallet, a passport and two semi-automatic pistols. She began leafing through the passport.

"Well, well, well, what do we have here?" she said. "Why, according to this your passport has expired. Shame on you, Rafael. And here we have a South American driver's license. And here's a picture of you with your father and friends. I see one drug dealer from New York and two New York Mafioso with their own little hit man. Why, there's even someone who resembles a known terrorist from the Middle East."

She showed the picture to Harry, then turned back to Rafael.

"My, my, what a handsome man your father is. And rich-looking too. Take a gander at that huge house he is standing in front of. Why, that must be Mt. Villa Rosa in the background. That's some expensive real estate. And so secluded."

Everyone knew Rafael's father was the richest drug lord in South America and that he offered sanctuary to terrorists. But no one knew where he was – until now.

Rafael stood looking at the ground in sullen silence.

"And all those important guests that no one has seen for years. And take a look at that fella there. He looks just like a terrorist the Feds have been absolutely wild to capture."

She smiled grimly at Rafael. "And look at your father's arm around his shoulders. He must really be somebody big. I wonder who it is. Don't *you* wonder, Rafael?"

Rafael's eyes smoldered with anger.

"I just love it when the bad guys get mad, don't you?" she asked Harry.

"I think you like it a little too much," he said ruefully.

"Oh, Rafael doesn't mind my poking sticks at him, do you Rafael?"

He remained silent. No one had ever dared to talk to him like this. She would be sorry.

Several state troopers pulled their cars to a stop and got out.

"Sheesh Ginger, ya' think you'd have left us a taste," remarked one tall trooper, his handsome face spread in a wide grin.

"I left you guys a taste inside the warehouse," smiled Ginger. "The rest of Ol' Rafael's boys are pinned in a black van."

"It seems someone ran them into an oil pit," added Harry, nodding his head slightly at Ginger.

Several of the cars went inside the warehouse to snag the rest of Rafael's boys. She watched as two stout troopers deposited Rafael in a patrol car. Looking through the window at Ginger, he squinted his eyes, smiled menacingly, and blew her a kiss.

Ginger knew she'd just been marked for death. She wasn't impressed. "Go ahead and try it Bubba," she barked. "I'll send you runnin' home to your Mama."

Rafael kept his eyes fixed on her until the patrol car he was in drove off.

"That boy really needs an attitude adjustment," Ginger muttered. She figured he might get one when he's locked up far away from his father's money and influence. She grinned at the thought of pampered Rafael sharing a jail cell with some huge guy named Tiny. Hearing a door slam, she looked over her shoulder at Captain Hays.

"Officers Carter," he looked at Ginger, "and Benson." Harry nodded pleasantly. "Does the word 'backup' mean anything to you?" he demanded, trying not to smile. This was a major bust that would save a lot of lives. Still, he had to go through the proper motions.

"I seem to recall you mentioning it to me this morning," Ginger commented. "However, Rafael and his little friends wouldn't wait."

Her captain shot her an aggravated look.

She frowned. "They were going to get away! I called you guys before I took off after him."

"Oh, well then, that makes everything alright," said her boss. "Next time wait for backup or start thinking about working the truck scales down by the highway!"

Ginger rolled her eyes heavenward. She was just doing her job. One riot, one Ranger.

"Don't you roll your eyes at me young lady," Hays warned, "or I'll have your grandfather exile you to that island of his."

Everyone laughed quietly and got ready to head back to the station, where Rafael and his cohorts were being booked. Rafael used his one phone call to inform his father's law firm what had happened. Mr. Hale, one of his father's lawyers, soon arrived to meet him. Rafael gave him one sheet of paper containing a concise set of instructions. Hale read the paper with a grim face. He responded simply, "It will be done." He left soon afterward.

Ginger spent the rest of the afternoon writing out her report. Then she and Harry picked up her grandfather Felix at the ranch and headed back to town to celebrate their bust with a steak dinner.

Two hours later, after a great meal, the trio came strolling out of the steakhouse laughing and chatting. Harry got in the car and started the engine as Felix settled into the passenger seat and Ginger stepped into the back. Suddenly, there was a horrific explosion and the car was engulfed in flames. Ginger was thrown onto the pavement with savage force. Before she lost consciousness, she caught a glimpse of her grandfather and Harry, both dead, already burned beyond recognition. A tear coursed down her cheek and everything went black.

The explosion injured Ginger's back so severely that it took a year of therapy before she could walk normally again. She resigned from the Rangers, refusing Captain Hays' pleas to accept a desk job. She needed to get away from all the bad memories for a while.

She never left the ranch now. She hardly even went out to the barn to see her BLUE STAR stallion Ibby. The gray Arabian probably thought she had forgotten him by now anyway.

It was Christmas day in Texas. The weather was sunny with just a hint of coolness in the air. Doc and the rest of the ranch hands tried to cheer her up for the holidays by showering her with gifts, and Alta had outdone herself cooking. All their goodwill over the past year had had an effect. She had grown closer to these people. She loved them dearly. They were her family now.

After lunch, Alta settled Ginger in her grandfather's old study in front of the warm fireplace. She set a tray with coffee and chocolate cake beside Ginger's chair, then returned to the dining room to join the rest of the ranch hands. Ginger had asked to sit alone for a while.

She sat thinking about her visit to her grandfather's lawyer the year before. She had sat quietly as he read her Felix's will. She barely heard that she had inherited twenty million dollars, her grandfather's ranch, and his mysterious island off the Texas gulf. All she could process was that the two most important people in her life were dead.

She knew she shouldn't blame herself. Rafael had a reputation for avenging even the smallest slight. Maybe if she hadn't mocked him while arresting him, Harry and her grandfather would still be alive. She sighed, knowing he probably would have put out the hit just for arresting him.

She looked out the window at the sunny Texas landscape. Her heart ached with memories of her grandfather's smiling face. Wherever she looked, she saw something they had built or planted together.

"Merry Christmas Grandpa," she thought as a tear rolled down her cheek.

Everywhere she looked were memories. She felt a stab of pain as she saw a picture of her standing on the front porch with her grandfather and Harry. She couldn't stay at the ranch much longer. The pain was becoming unbearable. She had to get away somewhere. But where?

And what about Doc and the others? They depended on her for a living. What would they do if she picked up and left? Doc had worked for her grandfather most of his life. Heck, Grandpa put him through vet school. When he graduated he went to work for her grandfather as the ranch veterinarian. If she left how would they live?

Well heck fire, she could always take them with her, she mused. But where? You don't just ask folks to pull up stakes and follow you to who-knows-where. Her eye lit on a map of her grandfather's island tacked on his office wall. She walked over to take a closer look. The name on the map sounded strange, foreign.

Most of it looked like dense jungle and rocky mountains, but in one small part of the island there was an area that seemed to have been cleared. There was a smaller map of this area beside the first one. It showed a large house with a garden, some barns, and a few cleared fields.

Her stockman's eye ran over the map. It wasn't big, she thought, but it might hold all her grandfather's prized bucking stock. There were already barns for the livestock, and she certainly had enough money to construct whatever else was necessary to turn the farm into a working operation.

She shook her head at her own crazy imagination. What was she thinking? Doc and the others wouldn't leave Texas for some remote island in the Atlantic. Maybe she could just move there herself. She wanted to be alone with her ghosts anyway, didn't she?

She was interrupted by Doc's voice behind her. "I was wondering how long that map was gonna hang there before you saw it."

She turned to see him and everyone else in the house crowded into the study. She turned her curious gaze toward Doc, who glanced at the others. His look was answered by terse nods. He turned back to Ginger and cleared his throat.

"It's like this girl. You're keeping to yourself too much and there's not one of us that hasn't figured out that you need a change of scenery. And you need it pretty quick."

Alta spoke up. "What about spending some time on that island of your grandpa's? We could all move in and make it a real running operation. Maybe it would help you take your mind off your troubles for a while."

"One thing we ain't gonna do," Doc said firmly, "is let you stay here and grieve yourself to death the way you're doing now. Maybe it'll help if you go to this island and get away from all these memories for a while. You can always come back to Texas when you're ready."

His heart warmed at the grateful smile in Ginger's face.

After supper they sat around the dining table making plans for the move to Brisal.

Liam was not pleased to learn of his new visitors.

Quin and Madrun were idly sitting at their post in the trees overhanging the path that led to Nantuor. Even here there was paperwork, sighed Quin as he sat on a broad limb making an entry into his watch journal.

Suddenly he looked up from his journal. The sentry listened carefully. "What is that noise down the trail?"

"It sounds like King Liam's sons coming back from their hunting trip," answered his companion Madrun. "I can hear their voices."

The two guards watched as Liam's sons came into view.

The guards smiled at the sight of the young princes, but their smiles faded as the four brothers come into full view. They were as tall as their father, but their frames were bent in pain.

"Oh no, not again!" groaned Madrun. Their emerald green tunics were torn and bloody, and their beautiful faces were haggard with pain. Their hair was tangled, and they were scratched and bruised from head to foot.

Owain was supporting the oldest, Teagan, whose right leg was wrapped in a bloody bandage. With Teagan's right arm around his shoulders, Owain helped his brother down the trail. Teagan's dark brown hair covered his blue-gray eyes as he bowed his head to concentrate on keeping on his feet.

Owain's dark hair hung about his face and his gray eyes had a slightly feverish look to them. His left forearm sported a blood-stained bandage.

Handsome Barram's golden head was wrapped in a bandage, and his steps were a bit unsteady. His bright blue eyes were slightly unfocused. The youngest, Rigalis, was at his elbow steadying him with his good arm. Rigalis' left arm was bound in a sling. His dark hair was disheveled, his gray eyes were fierce with pain.

Looking like a young version of Liam, Rigalis was twenty five hundred years old. His brothers weren't much older: Barram was twenty eight hundred years old, Spokesman Owain was three thousand, and fiery Teagan was thirty two hundred. By human standards they would be eighteen, nineteen, twenty, and twenty-one.

The guards jumped from their post in the trees, whistling an alarm to the guards further down the path.

"Shall I call for a cart my lords?" asked Quin, eyeing the bloodied princes with concern as he put his watch journal back into his pouch.

"No," muttered Teagan wearily, his breath shallow from pain. "We will make it to the house on our own, thank you."

"Indeed you will not!" said a stern voice from the bushes.

The brothers looked up to find their father's Chief Counselor, Tiernan, gazing down on them from his horse. He dismounted and stood in the middle of the path, blocking the young elves' way. His sleek brown hair hung about the shoulders of his dark green cloak. He wore a dark brown tunic embellished with golden leaves set in elegant embroidery. His gray eyes were dark with worry at the sight of the battered princes. They had not kept their promise to come back uninjured.

He was displeased. "I have just ordered the cart to be brought. Wait for it to arrive."

His voice was stern but his eyes were filled with concern. He loved the young elves like a father. His eyes swept quickly over their bandages. He tried to assess their injuries as the cart, pulled by an elven horse, came into view. Fortunately, none of them seemed at death's door – this time. He breathed a quiet sigh of relief.

The brothers grimaced when they saw the cart. They wanted to walk to the house on their own, not be carried there like wounded soldiers from the battlefield.

"You have only yourselves to blame," said Tiernan, guessing their thoughts.

He motioned to the attendants accompanying the cart. "If you didn't persist in coming home bloodied and battered from your adventures, the cart would have stayed at the house. As it is, however, I have decided that whenever you go out from now on it will be stationed near the trail for your convenience."

He smiled grimly at them as the attendants helped them into the cart. "Your father and I agreed that it would save so much more time that way." He quietly mounted his horse and turned him toward Nantuor.

Teagan sighed at the mention of his father. What was he going to think when they came home injured again? They had promised to be careful on this hunting trip. And now every one of them had an open wound, and he and Barram probably had broken ribs.

"We had no idea there were dragons on that part of the island," insisted Rigalis as the cart started back to Nantuor. "It was not our fault."

"It never is," responded Tiernan, riding alongside the cart.

"We came upon that she-drake unexpectedly," protested Rigalis.

"And how were we to know she was nesting?" added Barram.

"We just wanted a closer look," grumped Teagan defensively.

"And I really had no intention of stepping on one of her eggs," explained Owain.

"Nevertheless, I doubt your father will let you out of Nantuor for a while," said Tiernan. "Certainly not until you heal up this time."

"We were well enough to go hunting, Tiernan," Owain sulked. "Athair said so."

"I doubt whether your health will be a factor in his next decision to loose you upon the isle of Brisal," said Tiernan, a wicked twinkle in his eye. "You will be fortunate indeed if he lets you do anything more dangerous than walking the Royal Gardens."

The young elves groaned. They hated to admit it, but Tiernan was probably right. Every time they went on an expedition, at least one of them got hurt. As if proving the point, the numerous elves along the road appeared unsurprised and uninterested at their condition.

One of the elven guards in the main courtyard motioned to another as the cart passed. Grimacing and shaking his head, the second guard reluctantly handed over a few silver coins. The first guard dropped them in his pouch as they both moved to follow the cart. Silver coins covertly changed hands all around the courtyard and a treasured golden dagger found a new home as the cart made its way to the front steps of the huge elven complex that housed the medical facilities.

They rolled to a stop in the main courtyard and watched their father descend the front steps of the main hall and approach his sons.

Liam looked them over for a moment.

"Just once I would like to see all of you arrive home under your own power."

Sighing deeply, he helped Tiernan and the attendants unload the princes, sending a flow of healing energy into each son as he was lifted from the cart.

He looked at the attendants and their charges. "Gentlemen, I believe you know the way to my healing rooms by now," he said with an elegant motion of his hand. The elves moved up the steps to Liam's medical facilities.

He followed his sons into the house, giving instructions to the attendants as he went. It would be a long time indeed before he let his sons out of the house again.

Liam worked for some time repairing torn flesh and starting broken ribs to mending. He saw to it that his sons had a hot meal and then took a moment to speak to them before sending them into a deep healing sleep.

"My sons, I understand your yearning for adventure. You are young and seek excitement. That is only natural at your age."

They smiled hopefully.

"However, times are difficult, and I have no time for binding up avoidable wounds. Until I determine how much of a threat these new humans are, you are to stay in Nantuor."

Dismay was clear on the faces of his sons. "But Athair . . ." started Teagan.

"Until further notice," said Liam sternly, fixing his sons with a regal stare.

There was no use arguing. "Yes Athair," came the reluctant chorus from his sons.

"Good," said Liam satisfied. "Sleep a blessed sleep my sons. And may you awake basking in the blessings of the One."

His sons smiled at his benediction. It was said with love and respect.

"Thank you Athair," they mumbled, already yawning sleepily.

Liam quietly sent them to sleep and turned to go. He found General Arth at his elbow.

"How are they my lord?" he asked, somewhat amused as he followed his king out into the hall.

"No worse than they usually are after these jaunts into the forest," replied Liam, ruefully shaking his head. They had far too much of their grandfather in them, he decided.

Arth smiled to himself. More than once he had to go after the young princes himself. How they found so much trouble in such a well-guarded forest was beyond his kin. He looked at his king and his face grew grim.

"I have the new reports from the human settlement my lord," he told Liam. "It is not good."

"Summon the High Council and then come into my study and give me your reports," Liam commanded.

An hour later Liam sat at his desk looking over the reports.

"It's an invasion my lord, nothing less," frowned General Arth. He was flanked by his commanders. There was Kendhal, Commander of the Swordsmen; Gildas, Commander of the Archers; and Ahern, Commander of the Cavalry. Arth had left Commander Trahern, his second in command to watch the house with Captain Brennus and his warriors.

Liam raised an eyebrow at the number of humans at the ranch complex. And Arth had told him of even more on the beach unloading huge machines, equipment, and supplies from large ships. There were also many animals including horses. What were these humans up to? It did indeed look like an invasion.

He looked up from the reports as his three counselors entered his study. He silently motioned them to sit down and continued reading the reports. A she-elf brought a tray with a wine decanter and glasses. She poured the wine and then discreetly left the High Counsel to its deliberations.

The elf lords settled themselves in the chairs in front of his desk and quietly sipped their wine, waiting patiently for him to finish reading.

Finally he finished the last page. He set the reports to one side and leaned back in his chair.

"There are over three hundred humans on this island at present. And Fiacra and his eagles tell me of yet another ship approaching, one carrying several hundred more."

He looked up at the members of the High Council.

"In addition, the humans have enough horses for a small cavalry. Gentlemen, we are outnumbered."

Ahern spoke up. "It is true, my liege, that they have many horses, but at least half of them are not rideable. They buck like a fury at any rider. I have even seen some humans reward them with treats whenever they throw someone."

"Most curious," commented Tiernan with a puzzled frown.

"And a most inconvenient way for a cavalry horse to behave," smiled Ranal.

"I wonder . . ." uttered Egan, deep in thought.

"What is it?" asked Kendhal eyeing his brother.

"It's just this," said Egan thoughtfully. "The humans act as though it is a game. What if they *want* the horses to buck?"

"Now, why would they want something so foolish?" asked Tiernan. "The riders could be seriously hurt. You know how frail humans are."

"Perhaps it's sport," answered Egan. "I have seen humans do stranger things. I was in the first scouting parties to the humans' new settlement. I have seen them watching a box called television at night and many other inexplicable things. I have seen people riding bulls . . ."

"What?" interrupted Gildas. "Why would they want to ride cattle?"

"They seem to see it as a challenging sport. Perhaps these bucking horses are kept for sport, too."

"Perhaps," intoned Liam. "That would certainly cut down their cavalry to a more manageable size."

"And so far I haven't seen many weapons," added Arth. "They have a few guns, but they have no archers, no swordsmen. Perhaps it is just their intent to settle here, not to go to war."

"If they settle here there will surely be a war, whether they seek one or not," said Liam, his eyes dark with worry. "I will not allow so many humans to stay on Brisal. They must be convinced to leave."

He turned to General Arth. "Have your scouts observe what the humans are doing and look for weaknesses, anything that can be sabotaged without harming them. I would prefer to evict them peacefully if possible. If not . . ." His voice trailed off as his eyes grew dark with conviction. "In the meantime, I will go to the human's house and see what is going on."

Liam quickly made arrangements to ride to the old farm. He frowned as General Arth led him through the jungle to the ranch complex. He followed Arth up a large oak to Captain Brennus' observation post. Standing on a huge limb, Brennus and Trahern peered through the thick leaves at the construction going on below. Trahern turned and gave Liam a respectful bow.

"My King, the humans have wasted no time moving into the old manor house. They are also preparing large barns and many pens for their animals."

Liam looked through the leaves at the activity below. What he saw gave him a knot in his stomach. Enough books and magazines had washed up on shore through the years to give Liam a good idea of what he was witnessing.

The humans were busily putting a new roof on the manor house next to the old rose garden. Workmen were moving in and out of the house installing electrical wiring and plumbing. Huge crates full of furniture and appliances sat in the largest barn, waiting to be moved into Ginger's new home. A huge generator was being installed behind the house.

Numerous machines were working to smooth areas across a large cleared space. His serious eyes turned dark gray as he took in the size of the area being cleared – it was as big as a small town. This must be stopped – soon.

He turned toward a woman's voice he heard in the distance. He frowned slightly at the sight. This island was no place for a frail human woman.

Ginger sat on Ibby, an elegant gray stallion, watching the construction workers. Liam thought she looked small and quite pretty, though there was a paleness in her features. Her auburn hair caught the afternoon sun as it filtered through the trees. Her hazel eyes caught the light, making them appear as green as the surrounding jungle. She looked in Liam's direction and his heart skipped a beat. Brennus noticed his king staring at the woman.

"My King, that is the human who is in charge of this construction. She has been directing everything. She seems quite forceful."

Brennus looked back at Ginger. "She was riding through the old rose garden to the old manor house and almost found the trail to the main road. Lt. Niall mocked the cry of a leopard and made rustling noises in the branches of a tree to frighten her away. She didn't run though. She simply pulled out a weapon and started firing into the tree. Lt. Niall was nearly shot and barely escaped into the jungle without being hit. She is apparently a good marksman. Difficult to distract, too."

"Oh yes," said Liam absently, temporarily mesmerized by her penetrating eyes. "Very distracting."

"My king?" Brennus said, puzzled at Liam's answer.

Frowning at his own inattention, Liam cleared his throat and turned serious eyes to Capt. Brennus. "She seems aggressive. It would be better not to use a predator to try to frighten her away, as it seems she is not easily frightened."

"I agree," said General Arth. "Perhaps a few construction mishaps will discourage them from settling here."

"Yes. But we will have to be certain that no humans are harmed. Come Arth, we will return to Nantuor to devise our battle plan."

He took one more look at Ginger. There was something disturbing about her. He didn't like the way his heartbeat had quickened at her gaze. The sooner she was gone from Brisal, the better for everyone, he thought to himself.

The ranch complex was completed despite Liam's best efforts to run off the humans. After one sabotage attempt on their equipment resulted in a human injury, Liam ended all attempts to chase them off. The remaining animals were moved in, the exotic deer being the last shipment.

Liam breathed a sigh of relief when he learned that most of the humans had packed up and left the island. Only Ginger and her small group of ranch hands remained.

Captain Brennus reported there were several small children on the ranch as well – a pair of twin girls who couldn't have been more than ten years old. They carried an old medical bag with them and were always on the prowl for something or someone to "patch up."

Leroy and Chad gave Captain Brennus a bad moment when they saddled up to go exploring. They were only one hundred feet from the main road to Nantuor when the Captain and his guards managed to lure them in another direction using the sounds of two large cats fighting.

Intrigued by the noise, the two young ranch hands followed the sounds until Brennus and his elves led them back to the ranch complex.

This incident caused no end of consternation on Liam's part. He ordered Captain Brennus and his troop of elves to stay at the ranch to keep the humans from finding the way to Nantuor.

Chapter 5

The Deer Incident

Liam's sons sat fidgeting in their chairs, waiting for their father to finish his breakfast. Teagan leaned over to Owain. "Ask him."

"You ask him," Owain whispered back.

The brothers grew impatient. Finally Barram took a deep breath. But before he could utter a word, Rigalis blurted out, "Athair, could we go to the humans' house today and explore?" He was promptly speared by a look from his three older brothers. This was not their idea of using subtlety to convince their father to let them go someplace he considered unsafe.

Liam cocked an inquisitive eye at his youngest son. He could not protect them forever, much as he would like to. They were growing up, and like their grandfather, they longed for adventure.

He realized Rigalis was waiting for his answer.

"My son, what have I told you before?" he asked gently.

Rigalis frowned at his brother's snickers, kicking a foot under the table at Barram. He sighed in resignation. "You have said that humans almost hunted us to extinction once, and it is not safe to have contact with them." At his father's look he continued. "But Athair, maybe these humans are different . . ."

He was interrupted by Teagan. "They are not different, Rigalis. Oh, Athair, I'll bet he doesn't even remember how it was when we had to leave on the ships."

"I do too remember," declared Rigalis indignantly. "I was there."

"But you were only a thousand years old then," pointed out Teagan. "You were only a baby."

"I still remember Teagan," Rigalis said. He turned to his father. "I just want to go see the humans. I promise I will stay out of sight. Please Athair." He pleaded in a voice that had often softened his father's heart.

The rest of his sons looked expectantly at him. Obviously, they all wanted to go see the new humans.

His father smiled wearily. "Well, I suppose I will get no peace until you have seen the humans for yourselves."

Smiling broadly, his sons jumped up from the table.

"However," he added quietly, bringing the boys to a standstill.

Liam's eyes grew serious. "Remember, even though we were appointed as the humans' comforters and helpers, they nearly destroyed us. When you arrive, have Captain Brennus find you a safe place to observe them. And keep your distance and don't let them see or hear you. I want no more injuries for a while – a long while. Understood?"

Liam raised a stern eyebrow at his sons. They knew he meant business. Crowding around their father, they each gave him a farewell kiss on the cheek before leaving. He nodded and they stampeded out the door, stopping by the huge dish in the hall to grab a handful of fruit for the trip. He heard their laughing, shouting voices long after they disappeared from sight.

Ranal came in and poured himself a cup of coffee as he sat down beside Liam. "Your sons are off on another adventure I see," he said with a smile.

"Let us hope it doesn't turn out to be too much of an adventure. Send a scout to follow them and make sure Captain Brennus finds them a safe place to observe the humans. I don't want them spotted and hurt."

Ranal nodded. "It will be done, my King." He finished his cup and rose to go, chuckling.

"What is so funny Ranal?" asked Liam, looking perplexed.

"I seem to remember another elf going to the old house for adventure and finding a very fetching human maiden."

Liam smiled at Emily's memory. "Yes, she was one of the best things that ever happened to me. She is sorely missed – by all of us," he said, looking at his son's empty chairs.

"Then why don't you find another wife?" suggested Ranal with a smirk. "Perhaps another trip to the old house is in order. It worked the last time." He scampered out of his friend's reach. "I promise we won't tease you half as much as we did last time," he laughed as he ran out the door.

"Half as much is still too much, you scoundrel," grinned Liam as he chased his friend out the door.

Ginger looked up and squinted at the noonday sun. The old manor house stood by an ancient rose garden filled with huge old trees and overflowing with roses and jasmine. The old garden's sweet perfume filled the tropical air.

She would be glad to unload the last of the livestock and finally get settled in. Chad backed the trailer up to the gate leading to the pens for the exotic deer. This load of big English deer included Old Trouble, a buck that had been slamming himself around in the trailer like a fool the entire trip from the beach. Ginger shook her head. She had seen people like that. Nothing better to do with their time than cause trouble any way they could. She walked around the front of the truck to help unload her livestock.

The four brothers sat in the tree assigned them by Captain Brennus. The tree, a huge oak with plenty of concealing branches, stood amid a mass of trees, giving the young elves plenty of cover. They sat contentedly munching on some fruit supplied by the Captain, idly watching the humans as they prepared to unload the deer.

In the next tree their guard sat trying to catch his breath. They had played a long, hard game of follow the leader when they discovered their escort. He was scratched from head to foot from all the precarious places through which they led him. The scout sighed in frustration at the snickers that came his way from the next tree. He looked over at the four princes as they stifled their laughter and turned again to watch the humans.

"What are they doing?" asked Rigalis curiously.

"It looks like they brought some deer with them," replied Barram around a mouthful of apple.

Rigalis peered through the leaves intently. "But why should they do that? We already have plenty of deer on the island." He frowned at his older brother, perplexed.

"Don't ask me to try to explain human behavior," Barram interjected. "Even Athair hasn't totally figured them out yet."

He heard laughing from the branches below and looked down at his other two brothers.

"What is so funny, may I ask?"

His two older brothers' faces grinned up at him from the branches below.

"I wouldn't ask you to explain anything after some of the ridiculous answers you gave on Tiernan's examination last week," chuckled Owain. "Not to mention the poor score you received."

As Owain lazily lay draped over the large limb, Barram casually swung his foot down toward his face. Owain deftly swung out of the way and moved to a safer place further down the limb. His older brother Teagan sat laughing on the next limb over. This earned him a glare from his younger sibling.

"You're one to laugh, Teagan. Your score was just as poor. I heard old Tiernan wonder how anyone could do so badly without actually doing it on purpose." It was Barram's turn to duck as Teagan frowned and took a swipe at him.

"Now, now, gentlemen. Is that the proper conduct for a member of the Royal House?" asked Owain sternly. His mockery of Tiernan's voice was so perfect it made Rigalis jump and look around nervously.

"Ah, see there," scolded Barram. "Now you've scared our baby brother." He was immediately shot a withering look by his sibling.

"I am not afraid of Tiernan," insisted Rigalis. "At least not any more than the rest of you," he added impudently.

The brothers gave each other an annoyed look.

"You know he gets more like Athair every day," Owain remarked.

"More like Tiernan you mean," said Teagan. He quickly ducked as Rigalis swung down off his limb and came at his older brother, thoroughly incensed.

"I do NOT!" he said angrily, pushing his brother.

Teagan laughed as he fended off his youngest brother's indignation. From their own branches, the other two brothers watched the conflict with amusement, suddenly oblivious to what was happening at the ranch.

Back there, Leroy was stepping to the rear of the trailer to help unload the deer.

"Boss lady, you might want to warn Leroy to be careful opening that gate," warned Chad. "Old Trouble is wanting to get out."

Ginger started toward the back of the trailer and called out, "Hey Leroy, be careful, don't let the . . ."

Just then the buck slammed through the gate Leroy had just unfastened, knocking him down. The deer jumped over him, shot past the group of ranch hands, and bolted toward the jungle.

"...deer out," Ginger finished lamely. "Oh well, I never liked that deer anyway," she commented as he disappeared into the jungle.

Ginger looked at Leroy's shocked face as he lay sprawled, though unhurt, in the grass. She smiled at him sympathetically and said, "Well, at least out there he can't make a nuisance of himself." Famous last words.

"Look," said Owain. His brothers stopped fighting at the urgency in his voice. The group peered through the leaves at the ranch hands as the huge deer bolted away from them.

"Stupid humans," snorted Teagan. "They can't even handle one deer." His comment drew derisive laughs from his brothers.

"Come on," implored Barram. "I'm bored. The most entertaining thing happening around here is a loose deer. Why don't we go hunting?"

The four brothers jumped out of the tree and, waving at Captain Brennus in the next tree, melted into the jungle. The guard tried to rise to follow them, then sat back down with a tired sigh. Captain Brennus motioned for him to stay put. Liam's sons should be safe enough on the road back to Nantuor. They were only going back to the house. What could happen?

The buck ran quickly down the jungle path, relishing its freedom. Soon the jungle faded into woodland, and the buck found himself running through lush meadows. Slowing down, he walked down a steep embankment to drink from the stream at the bottom.

Suddenly his feet slipped on slick mud and he fell the rest of the way down to the stream. As he tumbled to a halt, his left hip slammed against a sharp rock, cutting a gash. He lay there for a moment stunned and then quickly tried to get to his feet. Pain shot through his hip, hampering his movements. He tried to climb the embankment but found the sides were too steep and slick. He frantically tried jumping up the embankment but fell back sprawling into the stream.

He struggled for hours to get out of the water, growing tired and weak. As the sun began to set, the stag lay in the cold water, panting heavily. He heard footsteps approaching and bucked violently a few more times.

Liam's sons stood at the top of the embankment and stared down at the helpless stag.

They tried talking to the deer to calm him, but he was having none of it. He struggled some more and weakened himself further.

Finally Barram took out an arrow and lifted his bow.

"What are you doing?" asked Rigalis.

"Putting it out of its misery," replied Barram.

"The poor thing is suffering," remarked Teagan.

"No! Don't!" Rigalis struck down his brother's bow. "We could help him."

"Have you taken leave of your senses, Rigalis?" reprimanded Owain. "That animal is in pain. He would be impossible to handle in this condition. Getting him out of there would also be impossible. It would be cruel to allow him to suffer."

"But we could heal it," insisted Rigalis, always on the lookout for excuses to practice what his father had taught him.

"Rigalis," said Owain patiently, "I know you love animals, but it would be more merciful to put it out of its misery. What if its leg is broken?"

"We are a family of healers," Rigalis protested. "Why can't we heal him?"

Barram was skeptical, eyeing the stag's huge rack. "And how do you propose that we get close enough to treat him without being torn to pieces by those antlers?"

Rigalis smiled. "I saw a bottle of oil of poppy seed in our emergency kit. We can pour it on some sweet berries, feed them to him, and put him to sleep. Then we can take him home and treat him," he finished triumphantly.

Barram rolled his eyes at his youngest brother's latest crazy scheme. "Rigalis, Athair would never let us take a stag into the house unless we were going to cook him," he explained.

As if to plead his case, the stag bleated helplessly from the water.

All four elves looked down at the deer's large, dark eyes and then at each other. They sighed in resignation.

"Alright Rigalis," said Teagan as they stepped down the embankment. "But if Athair asks, this was your idea."

Getting the stag to eat the oil of poppy-soaked berries was no problem. In fact, the ravenous deer nearly took off one of Teagan's fingers along with the berries he was feeding him.

"Hey!" Teagan scolded. "Watch what you are doing!"

The stag continued drowsily munching the berries. After the deer nodded off, the brothers carted him out of the stream and up the embankment. They took turns carrying him back to the house – Rigalis went first, since this was his idea. When they reached the forest near the Royal Quarters, they decided to wait until just before dawn to haul the deer into the house – it would probably be better if no one saw their odd undertaking.

When the time was right, they approached the courtyard and shifted the stag to the oldest, Teagan, who usually carried in the kill after a hunt. He flung the sleeping stag over his shoulders as though he had taken it in the hunt and strode swiftly toward the house, praying to the One that his father was asleep. Although his brother had promised that the deer would stay asleep the entire time it was inside, he couldn't help but worry about bringing a live stag into a house that was decorated with a lot of ancient relics.

The four conspirators walked in the front door and pretended to head for the kitchen with their prize. Barram went ahead and peeked into Liam's study. Good, it was empty. Keeping an eye out for any unwelcome witnesses, he motioned for his brothers to bring the deer into the study. They quickly disappeared through the doorway. Barram took one last look around and saw Tiernan coming down the hall. What was he doing up at this hour? Barram tried to duck inside but it was too late. He had been seen.

"You missed your afternoon lesson, your highness." Tiernan grumped. "If you had bothered to come to your lesson, you would have learned a great deal about wind and weather and how it affects our crops."

Barram could barely keep from rolling his eyes. The biggest wind he knew was the one coming from Tiernan's mouth. Anyway, he would much rather be out in the cool woods than sleeping through another one of Tiernan's boring lessons. Besides, Tiernan always woke him so rudely – a rap on the head with a riding whip was just not necessary. And then there was his brothers' snickering – they never warned him, preferring the entertainment of seeing him nearly fall out of his chair.

"I am very sorry, my lord," Barram said in his most courtly manner. "I shall endeavor to be on time for the next lesson."

Tiernan was instantly suspicious. Barram seemed to be using his body and the partly-closed door to block the view into the study.

"What are you doing?" Tiernan asked with a raised eyebrow.

"Oh," responded Barram lightly. "My brothers and I are studying."

"You're lying." Tiernan replied. He knew these four young princes never studied, though they devised crafty ways to earn high marks. Twas a pity that they dedicated so much of their talent and intelligence to causing mischief.

"Oh no, my lord, I'm not." Barram gave Tiernan his most sincere look.

His father's Chief Counselor scowled back at him.

Suddenly there was a loud bump in the study.

"What was that?" Tiernan demanded.

There was another, louder bump.

"What are you doing in there?" he scowled, stepping closer to the door.

Barram thought quickly. "Lord Tiernan, don't you remember last week's lesson on field dressings?"

Tiernan stared at him.

Barram took a deep breath and continued. "Well, we are practicing field dressings."

Tiernan looked into his sincere blue eyes.

Just then Rigalis appeared impatiently at the door holding a roll of bandages. His eyes widened at seeing Tiernan.

"Oh, alright," Tiernan sighed, as if disappointed that he hadn't caught them at something. "Continue your studies. If you need any help . . ." he offered.

"No, my lord," answered Barram quickly. "We will be fine. We would like to do this on our own."

Tiernan bowed and left, suspicions still nagging at him.

The two brothers swiftly shut the door. Everyone breathed a sigh of relief.

"What took you so long?" asked Owain.

"Tiernan." The brothers grimaced.

"What was that bumping sound I heard?" asked Barram.

His brothers pointed behind him. Barram looked and saw the stag standing on wobbly legs. He was aghast. He turned accusing eyes on his younger brother.

"You said you gave him enough oil of poppy seed to keep him asleep until we could get him out of here!"

"Well, I may have napped a little through that lesson on dosages," Rigalis answered sheepishly. "You know how boring Tiernan's lessons can be."

"I also know how severe Athair's temper will be if he sees a stag loose in the Royal Quarters!" retorted Barram.

The stag snorted feebly at the four young elves as it stood swaying on the carpet.

Teagan went to rummage around his father's huge medicine cabinet. He came back with a small red jar and handed it to Owain. "Here, put this healing ointment on the stag. The label is faded, but I am sure that is the right jar."

Owain looked at the jar and then handed it to Rigalis.

"Alright," said Rigalis doubtfully.

Teagan turned and eyed the defiant stag. "Owain, Barram, and I will hold him. Rigalis, you tend the wound." He exhaled deeply. "Let's get this over with, shall we?"

The stag looked up as the four elves approached. He tried to point his antlers at them and almost toppled to the floor.

The elves pounced and pinned him to the floor. Owain sat on top of him while Teagan and Barram held him by his antlers. Quickly stepping to his hindquarters, Rigalis scooped out a huge lump of the red ointment to salve over the wound on the deer's hip. As he did so, his fingers tingled.

"This must be potent medicine," he thought as he spread the thick ointment firmly into the wound. The moment the ointment touched him, the stag froze. Then suddenly he came alive. With a mighty leap and a loud squall, he jumped out from under the elves. Just then a she-elf entered the room with a tray laden with teacups, an afterthought of Tiernan's. The stag bowled over the startled servant and bolted down the hall. Cups and saucers went rolling across the floor and hot tea lay steaming into the plush rug.

For a moment the brothers were too stunned to move. Then they exchanged frantic looks. Finally, Teagan and Owain ran down the hall after the escaped deer while Barram and Rigalis tended to the servant.

Barram quickly knelt beside the she-elf.

"Are you hurt?"

"Oh no, my lord," she answered. Her breath caught in her throat as she looked up and realized who was tending to her. "I . . . I am quite all right, your highness," she whispered, her heart pounding at being so close to the handsome elven prince.

"What happened?" she asked shakily.

"You didn't see?" asked Rigalis hopefully.

"No, your highness," answered the she-elf shyly as she pushed her golden hair behind a delicately pointed ear. "My eyes were on the tray." She looked at the two brothers questioningly. Rigalis looked at Barram.

Barram turned his most charming smile toward the she-elf. "We really are going to have to give Teagan and Owain a firm scolding for being so clumsy," he said, showing her his most captivating look. "You do forgive them, don't you?" he asked as he took her in his strong arms and helped her to her feet. Rigalis stood watching, openmouthed.

She breathed deeply. Prince Barram was the most handsome elf she had ever seen. If he said the sky was falling, it must be so. "Of course, your highness. It was nothing really."

Barram quickly produced a beautiful flower from a nearby vase and pressed it into her hand as he kissed it fervently. The elf-maid almost swooned.

"Oh forgive me, my Prince," she said, remembering her duties. "I must get back to the kitchen."

"Oh no," Barram jumped in front of the door, blocking her path. "I wouldn't dream of it. You stay right here and rest until you have recovered from your horrible ordeal. As your Prince, I insist. You stay right here, while Rigalis and I go seek my two brothers. Believe me, we shall not rest until we find them." He put his hand behind his back, motioning his younger brother from the room.

With that, he gave her a courtly bow and quickly swept out of the room, shutting the door behind him. He and Rigalis breathed a sigh of relief and then ran down the hall in search of their brothers and their unwanted guest.

The four brothers spent most of the early morning hours chasing the errant stag through the laundry, storage areas, and other empty parts of the huge elven palace. Plastered in flour and other debris, he even had one of Liam's silk nightshirts entangled in his antlers, a souvenir from the laundry area. Around five in the morning he managed to slip past the youngsters and get into the more inhabited parts of the house.

Earlier that evening Liam had sat thoughtfully, drinking his tea. He had quite a busy day dealing with the new humans. Repeatedly, some of the new arrivals had wanted to go off exploring and almost discovered the road to Nantuor. That caused a few tense moments for everyone until Brennus and his guards lured the humans back to the house. Liam could feel the tight muscles between his shoulder blades sitting like a sailor's knot. A good night's sleep was what he needed, so he had prepared himself a sleeping draught.

Leaving Tiernan in charge, he retired to his room to drink the potent tea. Liam finished the concoction and set his cup down on the bedside table. He lay back against his pillows, anticipating a deep sleep.

Unfortunately he had a restless night, troubled by the sound of thundering hooves and running footsteps that recalled the wars he had fought in his long life. His dreams turning to ancient battles and cavalry charges, he became entangled in his bedcovers. Suddenly he lifted his head off his pillow. What was *that*? He listened intently. Nothing. He settled back down under the covers.

There it was again. What was that noise? Just then he heard voices in the corridor – the voices of his children.

"Stop him. Don't let him get into Athair's room."

"What do you think I'm trying to do?"

A loud crash caused Liam to bolt upright in bed.

"Are you crazy? He almost killed me."

"Would you rather he get into Athair's room?" The voice was fiercely protective.

"Hurry! He's going to get away."

"We've got to stop that lunatic before he kills someone."

The voices faded down the hall.

"My children!" thought Liam. Extricating himself from the covers, he grabbed his sword and headed for the door. In his haste he hit his big toe on the seat at the foot of the bed. He hopped the rest of the way to the door muttering to himself, then hastily swung it open and sprang out into the hall, sword at the ready. The hall was empty. He stood listening. All was quiet.

Perplexed, Liam looked down at his nightshirt. A dream – it must have been a dream. It seemed so real. Shaking his head, he went back to bed, grateful that no one had seen him looking so ridiculous.

Later that morning, as Rigalis ran down the corridor after his brothers, he saw the edge of Barram's cloak disappear around the corner at the far end of the hall. He went charging down the hall after them. Just as he passed his father's study, the door flung open and

Liam called his name. He slid to a graceless stop and turned innocent eyes to his father.

Liam had seen that look before, usually when his rambunctious sons were up to no good. He fixed his son with a regal gaze and said calmly, "Good morning, Rigalis. You seem quite out of breath. Why such haste?"

"Oh, good morning, Athair," Rigalis said, his heart pounding with anxiety. "I was just on my way to find my brothers." A small muscle in his face twitched involuntarily.

Liam's sharp eyes didn't miss it. Now he knew they were up to something. Rigalis shifted uneasily under his father's glare. Liam gave his son a slight smile as he took him by the arm.

"Perhaps we can find them together. You four are inseparable, and it disturbs me to see you in such anguish as to their whereabouts."

"Oh no, Athair," Rigalis replied with a smile. "That won't be necessary. I can always find them later."

Liam smiled back. "Good. Then perhaps you can keep me company while I prepare my report for the Council of Elders."

Liam knew his son had urgent business with his brothers, probably related to some kind of mischief. Helping his father with a report right then would be torturous. Liam sometimes felt a twinge of guilt at tormenting his children like this – though it usually disappeared when he discovered what kind of mischief they had actually been causing.

Chapter 6

Consequences

Rigalis was led into his father's study. Liam closed the door behind them and turned to his son.

"Would you care for something refreshing to drink? This will take quite some time." Liam didn't miss the slight widening of his son's eyes. Perhaps he could sweat the information out of him. His smile crinkled the corners of his eyes. "Tea?" he asked, motioning toward an elegant silver teapot in the shape of a swan.

Rigalis nodded. He stood uncertainly, feeling like a trapped animal. Liam poured the fragrant tea into an ornate cup and set it on the table next to him. He then poured himself another cup and resumed his seat behind his desk.

Picking up a quill, he began to write on a piece of parchment. Without looking up he said, "No need to stand, my son. Please make yourself comfortable." He glanced at the chair behind Rigalis, who sighed softly and sat down, his tea untouched. His mind was racing, wondering where his brothers were and how he was going to find them. And where was that blasted stag?

Continuing to write, his father noted his anguish. "So, what mischief have you been up to today?" he asked casually.

"W . . . what?" stammered Rigalis, his face pale.

Liam hid his smile. "What have you been doing for amusement?"

"Oh, just following my brothers around, my lord." Rigalis grabbed the teacup and took several swallows.

Rigalis' nerves were giving him away. "Why are you so apprehensive my son? Is something amiss?"

Rigalis inhaled when he should have swallowed and began coughing violently. As Liam rose from his desk to come to his son's aid, he heard snickering from the other side of his study door. Stepping quietly to the door, he swiftly swung it open to reveal his other sons. Owain was vainly trying to silence Teagan's laughter with a hand over his mouth. When Liam swung open the door, they both tumbled into the room. Liam stepped past them and into the hall.

"Barram, where are you going in such haste? Attend me." The elven king didn't raise his voice. He seldom needed to. But it held the ring of command nonetheless. In a moment Barram reluctantly walked into the room still breathing hard from his run, and Liam shut the door behind him. Teagan was pounding Rigalis on the back to stop his coughing. They all looked a bit out of breath. He said as much.

Owain was usually the group's spokesman. He gave his father his most dazzling smile and opened his mouth to speak. Liam cut him off.

"There have been reports this morning of an apparition of sorts sighted at different intervals on the grounds and about the house. It even made an appearance in the kitchen, scaring the cook and kitchen maids half to death." Owain's mouth snapped shut.

Liam smiled. "Have any of you seen this apparition?" His darkening gray eyes captured those of his sons.

Owain took a deep breath. "Actually Athair, we were looking for such an apparition ourselves."

"Really? Any luck?" He pinned them to the spot with his stare.

"Not yet," replied Barram sadly. "But we will try our best to get to the bottom of this." All four sons nodded vigorously. Rigalis was almost recovered from his coughing fit.

Liam knew they were up to something, but he didn't know what it was – yet. He grinned again. "Very well, my children. Please continue your hunt." He motioned toward the door.

They walked out of the room impatiently, then stopped at the sound of their father's voice.

"Please keep me informed on your progress," Liam said sternly. "This apparition has disturbed the tranquility of my household quite long enough."

His sons weakly returned his smile and walked as casually as they could down the hall in the direction the buck had last taken.

One hour later Rigalis hastily brushed the few remaining leaves from his shirt and walked apprehensively into Liam's study, his tall frame slightly hunched. "Uh . . . Athair? Do you have any wound ointment?"

The King of Nantuor looked up from the ancient text he was perusing. His son did not appear to be injured. But knowing Rigalis . . . He rose from behind his desk, one eyebrow cocked and one finger marking his place in his book. "Have you injured yourself Rigalis . . . or perhaps, has someone else?"

There was a long pause as Rigalis gulped hard. Assuming his most innocent look, he asked meekly, "What makes you think that, my lord?"

"Well, you have just asked me for some wound ointment, which would lead me to believe that someone, perhaps yourself, has a wound that needs attention." Liam moved around the desk to confront his son. "Rigalis? Was it perhaps someone else?"

Losing his nerve, Rigalis replied, "Perhaps I don't need it after all. I'll just go to my room." He stepped away to leave.

Liam stared at his wayward youngest son. Surely he was not afraid to show him his injury if there was one? But perhaps he should look into this further a bit later.

"Alright, Rigalis, if you are certain you do not need the ointment." He returned to his chair behind the desk and looked into his book, asking, "If there is nothing further then . . . ?"

Rigalis hesitated. His brothers would kill him if he came back without the ointment. But how was he going to explain to his father that his brothers had just been run over by a stag? Or that they had hoof prints on their faces? Or that the stag was still loose in the house?

"Athair, perhaps I need that ointment after all. Couldn't I just take it to my room?" he asked hopefully.

Liam looked up, trying to keep the smile out of his eyes. Rigalis or someone else obviously needed the ointment badly, but Rigalis was reluctant to explain why. He rose again and went to the large cabinet behind him that housed some common medical supplies, bringing out the jar of ointment and a handful of clean cloths. Raising an eyebrow at his son, he handed the items to him. "The ointment, Rigalis. If you need any help . . . ?"

About to return to his studies, Liam turned to his son with a sudden thought. "And if you should happen to see your brothers, please remind them I expect to see them at the midday meal. We will be eating out on the terrace."

"Yes Athair," Rigalis replied and quickly made his escape.

Liam stared at the closed door. As the sun rose in the east, he knew now that all his sons were involved in something. But he also knew if something was terribly wrong, Rigalis would have asked for the ointment without any hesitation or monkey business.

The elf-king half rose out of his chair again and then shook his head as he sat back down. He would wait until noon to see his sons again. This gave them a few hours to clean up whatever their mess was. He looked at his medical cabinet. Perhaps it would not hurt to make sure he had plenty of extra medical supplies . . .

Meanwhile, Rigalis ran to the barn with the supplies. Just as he got to the barn door, an arm shot out and jerked him inside. All three of his brothers' faces had at least two distinct hoof prints on them.

"What took you so long?" demanded Teagan. "My face is killing me."

"I tried to hurry," Rigalis replied as he handed over the jar. "It took some doing to get the ointment from Athair. He wants us to have lunch with him!"

"Oh great," fumed Owain. "Now what do we do?" He paused. "Do you think he suspects anything?"

Before Rigalis could answer, Barram turned to him. "You are going to have to think up some excuse to get us out of lunch."

"Me? Why me?" demanded Rigalis.

"Because this whole mess was your idea," retorted Teagan.

"But you insisted on using that ointment," Rigalis protested.

"Just do it, Rigalis," ordered Owain as he smeared some of the ointment on his face. "You will be in just as much trouble as we are if Athair finds out we let a stag loose in the house."

Sullenly, Rigalis began devising a plausible excuse for his brothers' absence from lunch.

The noon bell sounded as the stag bounded up the back stairs – for the third time. The boys stopped with a groan.

"Not again!" exclaimed Rigalis wearily.

The brothers stood listening as the bell continued to chime. The three older brothers turned their gazes toward Rigalis.

"What?" he asked.

"Athair is expecting us to have lunch with him, remember?" Barram reminded him.

Rigalis' shoulders sagged. It had been a long night and an even longer morning chasing the stag. Luckily for them, many inhabitants of Nantuor were camped out along the river for the spring festival. Most of the house was deserted as the elves made ready for the celebration of springtime.

"You have to go stall Athair," Owain told Rigalis.

"Me?" asked Rigalis, his eyes wide.

"Yes, you," said Teagan as he shoved Rigalis toward his father's study.

"But what will I say?" he protested.

"Say whatever comes into your mind," Owain told him. "You have a pretty good imagination. You imagined we could handle this stag didn't you?" he said sourly, pushing Rigalis down the hall.

Rigalis frowned, punched his arm, and moved quickly down the hall out of his brother's reach, wondering what in the world he was going to say when he got to his father's study.

Liam sat out on the terrace, enjoying the light breeze and the faint scent of jasmine in the air. He looked down at his cooling soup.

Well, perhaps the boys were merely delayed covering up that last bit of evidence. Looking at the four table settings opposite him, he smiled. They were young, and mischief seemed to follow them like a rainbow after a storm. Well, perhaps that was not the right analogy. He slumped slightly . . . more like carrion crows after a battle!

Rising abruptly, he went to the edge of the terrace and looked out over the early spring landscape. He scanned the crowd of elves busily putting up arbors and setting up tables for the festival. He saw no sign of his boys. By the stars! If they thought they could just dismiss his request all because of a childish mishap . . .

Hearing the inner door to his suite open, he turned expectantly.

Rigalis nonchalantly entered his father's study. With a cheery "Hello Athair," he sat down at the table, trying not to betray his nervousness. Perhaps Athair wouldn't buy the idea of his brothers having left on a quest. Well, they were on a quest of sorts – just not a very dignified one. He smiled at his father again and studied the landscape, hoping his brothers would hurry up and catch that blasted stag before someone spotted them.

"Well, it is nice to see *one* of my sons has joined me for lunch."

Liam immediately knew Rigalis was hiding something. "Are your brothers on their way? The soup has already gone cold."

Rigalis stared at his father, his mind racing. So much for buying time.

"Perhaps they have been delayed," he offered. He hoped Liam hadn't noticed the slight hitch in his voice. "Should we start without them?" he asked hopefully.

Liam was silent for a moment. "Rigalis, let us go together and determine the reason for your brothers' delay. I would like to finish my meal sometime before the sun sets."

Grabbing Rigalis by the elbow, Liam hauled him out of the chair and headed to his suite. Enough was enough!

"Athair," Rigalis pleaded, "I don't think you will find them. They said something about a pair of drakes being sighted in the pass near Nantuor. They were going to go investigate and track them down. They went alone, as it was only two small dragons. The area is so large they will probably be gone for some time."

Liam stopped just inside the door leading to the outer corridor. He turned to his youngest son in disbelief. "Drakes. They've gone to hunt . . . drakes."

Liam's eyes captured the young elf's, turning dark gray and then almost black. They reached a terrible intensity as he spoke.

"They have suddenly, with no word to me, the Lord of Nantuor last I checked, decided to take it upon themselves to hunt . . . drakes."

Liam leaned closer to Rigalis. "Rather sudden, is it not Rigalis?"

Rigalis quailed and blinked rapidly. Liam drew back, shuttering his power. "I think I deserve an explanation, Rigalis – a real one, without fantasies and prevarication. Come, let us go back and you can tell me while we eat."

Rigalis wondered why in the world he had mentioned drakes. As his father sat him down in the chair, he realized that Liam had grown tired of his games. Maybe he could tell him what happened in the way least damaging to his brothers. He took a deep breath and started to explain.

"Well Athair," he began, "we were out hunting and there was a slight 'accident' with a stag. And it may have run over my brothers. Nothing serious, just sort of jumped over them. And we may have made a few unwise decisions. N . . . nothing terribly serious, just rather unwise. And . . . well . . . my brothers may have gotten a few hoof prints on their faces . . . just a few. . . and they would like to perhaps not be seen too much in public until their faces look a little more normal," he finished breathlessly.

There. He sat and waited for his father's reply – his understanding, loving, patient father – while hoping his brothers had finally caught and evicted the stag.

Liam sat back and looked at his son, his mouth open. Then, he bent over and laughed until tears were streaming down his face. When he finally composed himself, he wiped his eyes with a napkin. Seeing his son's shocked expression almost sent Liam into another fit of laughter. Taking a breath, he leaned back in his chair and took a deep swallow of wine.

"Rigalis, I beg you, it is so much easier to tell the truth than to take all this time and creative energy to come up with such an elaborate hoax! Think of all the anxiety you could have saved! Come, let us finish our lunch and then we can go find your brothers."

Rigalis breathed a sigh of relief. With his appetite suddenly restored, he finished his lunch with the gusto of a hunting hound. He knew he'd eventually have to tell his father about the stag, but for now he was too relieved to worry.

Back in Teagan's quarters, the boys had managed to trap the stag in the bedroom. He stood at bay by Teagan's bed, his flour-caked head lowered, threatening to charge. The ragged remains of Liam's nightshirt still hung in tatters on his antlers like a burial shroud, giving the stag an unearthly look. The eggshell and flour plastered to its hooves and chest added to the ghostly appearance.

"Grab him," said Owain.

"*You* grab him," retorted Barram.

Suddenly Teagan jerked around toward the door, thinking he heard something.

He gasped out loud. What was that? Owain quickly clamped his hand over Teagan's mouth. They all listened intently. Nothing. They breathed a sigh of relief.

Seeing his opportunity, the stag bowled over the elves and made for the balcony railing. Barram managed to grab one hind foot while his brothers lunged at the beast. It shook them off and hopped over the railing.

Outside their door, Liam and Rigalis were walking toward the family quarters to replace Rigalis' shirt, which Liam had noticed was torn. Hearing a sudden thump from Teagan's room, Liam opened the door just in time to see his three sons climbing over the railing. Startled, they turned toward him, giving him his first look at their imprinted faces.

Not wishing to surrender his dignity yet again, the elf-king spent a minute swallowing and suppressing his mirth. His poor sons! Their faces, now shiny with his ointment, reminded him of deer trails he'd seen hunting outside the valley.

"Surely the front door would be easier to use my sons. There is no need to sneak out of your own home like thieves in the night." He went to them smiling and softly touched Teagan's reddened brow.

"I imagine this deer hunting episode has an interesting story behind it. And you Owain? Barram?" He smiled at them, taking note of all their injuries. Fortunately none looked too severe.

"It seems the three of you were involved in the same . . . situation? Come," he pulled Teagan by the elbow back onto the terrace, "you still have not had lunch. You too, Barram. Come have your lunch and then I will see to your . . . wounds."

As they walked out of the room, Barram gave Rigalis a quizzical look. Rigalis motioned him to silence.

As Rigalis turned to close the door, he saw the stag below bounding off toward the water lily pond in the far end of Liam's private garden. He fought his instinct to go after it, took a deep breath, and shut the door.

After lunch Liam took them to his study and administered more wound ointment, placing his hand on each cut and sending a warm flow of healing energy into each.

Smiling at his sons, he placed his medical supplies back in the cabinet. "I hope this apparition will not be as troublesome as the deer you encountered," he told them.

Liam noticed that Rigalis stopped breathing for a moment. "I imagine you are anxious to continue the hunt," he said.

"Yes, of course we are," replied Owain, looking at his brothers. "We really should be going now, Athair." He motioned to his brothers. They rose from their seats and headed for the door. Their father's voice stopped them at the doorway.

"Be careful my sons, that you do not get into more trouble than you can get out of."

They smiled at him. "Of course not, Athair," answered Teagan. They bowed respectfully to their father and bolted out the door.

Liam stood thoughtfully for a moment. Whatever was going on, they were surely punishing themselves much more right now than he ever could. Satisfied, he returned to his desk and continued to study the ancient parchment before him.

The brothers moved quickly down the hall and stopped at the large balcony overlooking the gardens. Desperately looking for the stag, Rigalis spied handsome Ranal strolling through the vast garden with several simpering elf-maidens. With his blond head tipped to one side, he was entertaining his enchanted audience with one of his stories, his hair flowing down his tunic front like spun gold. *All hanging on his every word I'll bet*, Rigalis thought to himself.

He finally spotted the stag wandering near Ranal's entourage, Liam's nightshirt still hanging on its face, its front still plastered by flour.

"It looks like a wraith," snorted Barram. "No wonder the kitchen maids were terrified."

As they watched, the buck bounded toward a gap in the tree line bordering Liam's garden. The brothers heaved a sigh of relief. But just then the deer swerved and headed for Ranal's group. The elf-maidens shrieked and hid behind Ranal.

The golden haired elf-lord stood his full height. "Begone!" he reprimanded. He swiftly reached for the clasp on his cloak.

Rigalis gasped in dismay.

"Ranal, no . . . don't!" The last word faded into a plaintive squeak. His brothers stared at him.

Ranal swept his cloak from his broad shoulders in one swift, graceful movement and swung it at the apparition, shooing it away. It swerved from him, moving away from the gap. The four brothers watched openmouthed as it came bounding back toward them and disappeared under their balcony. They leaned over the railing to watch it go. Rigalis groaned as they heard it clip clopping back into the house.

"What are you scoundrels up to now?" demanded a stern voice behind them.

All four nearly jumped out of their skins. They turned slowly to find Tiernan looking at them suspiciously.

"Nothing," replied the brothers at once, each looking wide-eyed and innocent. By now the hoof prints on their faces had vanished. Tiernan heard the faint, receding sound of the deer's clip clopping .

"What is that?" he demanded.

"What is what?" asked Rigalis.

Everyone listened intently. Silence.

"I don't hear anything," said Barram softly.

Tiernan stared at them – he knew they were up to something.

Teagan leaned against the balcony railing, brushing imaginary dust from his sleeve. Owain seemed busy working out a tiny tangle in his long hair. Barram was trying to remove a loose thread from his trousers, and Rigalis simply sat on the railing staring at his hands.

Luckily for him, Tiernan couldn't see the drop of sweat running down his cheek.

Tiernan remembered how just the previous week the brothers had hung his underclothes out all over Liam's garden. Some people had no respect for other people's personal belongings.

After a long moment Tiernan finally relaxed. "Well, at least you are staying out of trouble," he said begrudgingly.

The brothers smiled at him weakly. "We are trying our best, my lord," responded Owain softly.

"Well, alright then. Well done." He gave them a little smile. Tiernan didn't smile at them often – and when he did it was frightening.

Weak smiles returned his own. Tiernan then retreated down the hall and turned the corner. As soon as he was out of sight, the brothers stampeded down the stairs in search of the buck. They slid to a stop at the foot of the stairs. There was no sign of him.

"Where is he?" worried Rigalis, frantically looking up and down the hall.

"He could be anywhere by now," grumbled Teagan fiercely.

Just then there was a shriek from near the kitchen.

"Oh, there he is," said Owain sardonically.

They charged down the hall toward the kitchen, running past a surprised elf-maid with a tray full of food. As Rigalis ran past her, he accidentally caught his boot in the hem of her skirt. They both went tumbling to the floor amid a rain of bread and pastries.

"Rigalis, come on," Teagan urged impatiently.

"I'm trying to," responded Rigalis as he staggered to his feet and helped the elf-maid up. Helping her pick up the scattered bread, he told her, "I'm so very sorry. I didn't mean to . . ."

"*Rigalis*!"

He quickly handed her a broken loaf of bread, half of it hanging precariously toward the floor. It had a large boot print down the middle of it.

"I'm sorry," he apologized again. Just then Tiernan came around the far corner of the hall. Rigalis panicked and ran toward his brothers, accidentally knocking over the elf-maid again.

As they ran toward the kitchen, they heard Tiernan scolding her.

"What are you doing sitting in the middle of the floor? Get up at once and clean up this mess. And then go about your duties. No, no, I don't want to hear your excuses. Now go!"

The brothers decided to stop running and formulate a plan for trapping the deer. Rigalis suggested using poisoned darts. He reminded his brothers of Tiernan's lesson a few weeks before on ancient history, which included accounts of people using poisoned darts to bring down their prey. Agreeing to the plan, Owain went back up to his room with Rigalis in tow and found his healer's kit while Teagan and Barram began fashioning darts and a blowpipe. Everyone met up in Owain's room, where Owain ensured the dosage was strong enough to bring down the stag. Then they painted concentrated oil of poppy seed onto the tips of several darts.

It was decided that Teagan would handle the blowpipe. Packing up their new weapon carefully into a small pouch, they headed back out the door in search of their prey.

They found him quickly – he had somehow gotten into Ranal's apartments. They came charging into the room as the stag was munching on a vase of roses. He wheeled and charged toward Ranal's bathroom with the boys in hot pursuit. Teagan loaded up the blowpipe and shot a dart at the stag. The animal jumped into the hot bathing pool that took up half the room, spraying water all over the room. Teagan frowned as the dart missed its target and bounced off the wall.

He turned and called to his brothers, who were still in the bedroom. "What are you doing in there?" he asked irritably. "Help me before he gets away!"

Barram stuck his head in the door. "You should see Ranal's bedroom! And his wardrobe! No wonder it takes him so long to get dressed."

Teagan rolled his eyes. "Get in here and help me with this stag!" he demanded angrily.

His three brothers walked reluctantly to the doorway. Ranal's room was almost more luxurious than their father's was – and he was king!

Rigalis looked back into the next room. "Teagan, you should see some of the things Ranal has in his room. He . . ."

"If we don't catch this stag, all we'll be seeing is the inside of *our* rooms, probably for the next twenty years!" scolded Teagan. Sobered by the thought, the brothers ran into the room to assist. They stopped in their tracks when they saw the stag standing in the warm bubbling water, his antlers at the ready.

Teagan's grim voice got them moving again. "Which would you rather face – the stag or Athair?"

The three brothers pounced on the waiting deer. They tried to hold him still to give Teagan a clear shot, but he fought them furiously. Finally Teagan had to pocket the blowpipe and jump in the pool to help his brothers. They had almost wrestled the beast into submission when Teagan suddenly stopped and looked around the room.

"Where's Owain?"

He and Barram stared at each other, then dove under the water. They brought up Owain choking and sputtering. The stag took the opportunity to jump out of the pool. Teagan made a grab for him but only liberated his father's shredded nightshirt.

"You idiot!" Owain shouted. "He's getting away!"

"Ingrate," Teagan responded.

"Elf-fop," retorted Owain.

Their nerves frayed from being up all night, they began brawling. Barram and Rigalis quickly separated them.

The two younger brothers finally yelled out, "Hey!"

They turned to Barram and Rigalis. "What?"

"The stag!" shouted the brothers, pointing into Ranal's bedroom.

"Oh!" Owain and Teagan barreled out the door, Teagan readying the last dart.

He saw the stag shoot out the bedroom door and into the hall, knocking an ancient vase off its stand. Teagan let the dart fly.

Just then Tiernan, having seen the stag knock over the vase, leaped and caught the antique just before it hit the floor. Unfortunately he also caught Teagan's dart in his rear end as the stag bounded away down the hall.

The boys had to leap over him to get out the door. Rigalis tripped over one of his brother's feet and fell face first onto Tiernan's chest. He found himself nose to nose with his teacher.

Tiernan's eyes were blazing with anger. Rigalis quickly rolled off his chest and ran after his brothers. Tiernan missed grabbing his cloak by inches.

"I might have known," Tiernan grumbled as he drifted asleep, cradling the vase in his arms.

"Well at least we know it works," Owain smirked to himself as they ran.

As Liam sat at his desk, trying to make sense of his sons' bizarre behavior, a deer bounded past the open doorway to his study. He did a double take. Watching in astonishment, he saw his wet sons run past the doorway. Understanding dawned in his face.

He stepped toward the doorway, his eyes raging. "Halt!" His voice cracked like a whip.

The four elves skidded to a stop in the hall – and so did the deer. Several hearts skipped a beat. The Lord of Nantuor stood in the hall, displeased.

"A . . . A . . . Athair?" Teagan began uncertainly.

"Silence!" Liam thundered.

A pin drop could have been heard in the hallway. Five sets of eyes were fixed on Liam, each of them as big as saucers. All movement and conversation abruptly halted, inside the house and out. Liam had had enough.

The elf-king's eyes were so dark they were almost black. They glittered as he stepped past his sons to look the buck in the eye.

"Get out of my house!" he ordered. The animal turned and ran, jumping out the nearest window. It dashed at top speed for the safety of the trees.

Liam turned to his sons and showed them a smile that made their blood run cold.

"Come with me," he said quietly. They reluctantly followed him into the study as if they were going to their own execution. After they shuffled in, the Lord of Nantuor closed the door behind them.

A moment later a she-elf came down the hall with some daily reports for Liam.

"Have you lost your minds!" thundered Liam's voice from the other side of the door. The she-elf could feel waves of power emanating under the door.

She stopped in her tracks, almost dropping the papers. *Perhaps I should return later*, she thought. She quickly turned and beat a hasty retreat, Liam's angry voice following her down the hall and around the corner.

He shouted at his sons for an hour, reminding them of their duty as members of the royal family. He shamed them for abusing the scout he had assigned to escort them to the humans' house and for submitting the rest of the household to their antics. He reminded them of all his hard work to create a serene haven for them, and admonished them for disturbing that serenity.

Finally it seemed to his sons that he was running out of steam. Liam, however, wisely saw no reason to punish himself with exhaustion when he could punish the guilty parties instead.

He looked at them as they shifted uneasily. *I think my young bulls would bellow more softly in another pasture,* he thought to himself. His eyes met theirs.

"I don't like that glint in his eye," Owain whispered to Teagan.

The next morning the four brothers walked slowly down the steps, conscious of their father's stern gaze boring into their backs. Exiled! They had been exiled to guard duty at the humans' house, the most boring job on the entire island!

Rigalis turned back to his father. "Athair, you could visit us if you would like," he said. "We would take great joy in your company." He smiled hopefully.

His Athair smiled back. Owain spotted a familiar, unsettling gleam in Liam's eye as he replied, "I shall indeed be with you, my son – in spirit."

Rigalis' face fell.

Barram put a reassuring arm around his youngest brother's shoulders. "Come Rigalis. We might as well make the best of it."

Sighing, Rigalis walked down the steps with his brother.

They met a group of their friends coming up the steps from archery and fencing practice. They were accompanied by Chief Archer Captain Gildas and Captain Kendhal, Liam's Sword Master. Having heard of their exile, their friends were coming to see them off. Their closest friends, Wyn, Malven, and Llyr, led the group.

Teagan favored Wyn with a smile. He was about to thank them for their kindness when Wyn spoke.

"You idiots have really done it this time," he smirked. Teagan slapped him on the back of the head as he passed him on the steps.

The four exiles got sympathetic looks from Kendhal and Gildas as they passed. The two older elves smiled at their younger counterparts, recalling their own impetuous childhoods.

As Liam watched his sons go, he suddenly felt alarmed. Though his elven senses weren't as strong as they had been before the Great Battle, he distinctly felt something was amiss.

Perhaps he was just apprehensive about the prospect of not seeing his sons for two months. He sighed deeply. They were growing up. He would have to learn to let go sometime. At least he would see them one more time in a few days during the spring festival.

The four princes reluctantly mounted their horses and joined the rest of the troop that would relieve the detail at the humans' house. They turned and looked at their father. He smiled and waved.

Liam put aside his concerns and chuckled softly as he watched the four sullen princes ride out of the main courtyard. He felt a brief twinge of pity for Captain Brennus when his sons would arrive at the guard post.

On the south side of the island, Braen and his elves swam silently toward the cliffs, camouflaged by a huge mass of seaweed and wood. They had left the yacht anchored miles away at an island so small it didn't even appear on the maps. It was safely tucked away in a tiny lagoon hidden by towering palm trees.

They were searching for a cleft at the bottom of the cliffs. Braen's shark had told them about it –a narrow entrance to the caves on the south side of the island that led up to the labyrinth of caves at the top of the cliffs.

After finding the passageway, they quickly climbed up the cliffs. As they rested in the dark of the cave's entrance, Braen caught a familiar scent blowing on the breeze. Humans!

He didn't expect to find humans on Liam's island. "Now *that* should make things interesting," he smirked. Just like the old days, running Liam on a merry chase as he tries to protect his precious humanity. And he hadn't tasted human blood in at least a few weeks.

Smiling, he gave the order to move north.

Chapter 7

Guard Duty

Ginger stretched and put her pencil down. After working on horse pedigrees for two hours, it was time for a break. She got up, headed for the back porch, and stepped out into the sunshine, stopping and letting it warm her face. She started to relax.

Suddenly alarm bells went off in her head – she was being watched. She had had this feeling since the day she moved to the island, but she had assumed it was the animals. This time, however, the feeling was stronger. She looked toward a large clump of oak trees at the edge of the yard. Liam's sons pulled back slightly from their hidden vantage-point behind a wall of leaves. She stepped toward the trees, the feeling growing even stronger as she did so.

She pulled out her Desert Eagle. As she stood looking intently at the young prince's hiding place, she pulled back the hammer cocking the gun.

Brennus was immediately concerned for the young prince's safety. He quickly sent for Fiacra. Flying over the treetops to distract Ginger, the giant eagle climbed high in the sky and then flew off in the direction of the beach. Ginger was so startled by his size that she didn't shoot.

"Dang, that's a big eagle," she muttered as it disappeared over the treetops. She turned back to the oak trees. Brennus sent a bird of paradise flying out of the shrubbery. It flitted to a fence post near

Ginger and preened its elegant feathers. It was quite beautiful, with long, brightly colored plumes. She smiled and put her gun away, feeling safer as Brennus quietly sang a song of comfort and peace. He sang at a frequency she could hear but was not overtly aware of.

Replacing the Velcro flap across her pistol, she grinned at the elegant bird. "You really should make more noise. I almost shot you." The bird stopped preening and stared back uncomfortably. She paused before going back into the house. "You're kinda pretty though. Hang on a minute and I'll bring you some apple."

She went into the house and returned with some apple slices on a plate, which she set on top of her pickup hood. As soon as she went back on the porch, the delighted bird flew to the hood of her truck and began enjoying his gift. She chuckled and went back into the house.

"You talking to animals again?" asked Alta from the sink, where she was peeling potatoes.

"You say that like it bothers you," smirked Ginger.

"Just as long as they don't talk back," replied Alta. Ginger had talked to animals all her life. She supposed she wasn't going to stop now.

Ginger went back to her study to continue working on horse pedigrees.

Later that night Captain Brennus heard a male drake singing courting songs at the bottom of the steep cliffs near the manor house. He was raising quite a ruckus as he roared and splashed in the water, trying to attract the females on the island. Brennus rolled his eyes in disgust. This was all he needed. The humans would surely hear it and go investigate, possibly stumbling upon the road to Nantuor or placing their lives at risk from the deadly predator.

He turned to send Lieutenant Niall and some archers to kill the animal when he heard the kitchen door open. Ginger stepped out into the moonlight carrying a double barrel shotgun. She walked to the barn and came back out riding Ibby. Brennus raised an eyebrow when he discovered she rode without a saddle or bridle, yet the Arabian stallion moved as if under full tack. He watched in dismay as she rode toward the cliffs to find the source of the racket.

Brennus took a squad of elves to follow her in case she got into trouble. Arriving at the cliffs, Ginger dismounted and walked to the edge. Ibby didn't like the scent, so he stayed close to protect Ginger. The sound was coming from the sea. As she looked down, the full moon shone brightly on the water. She thought she saw a large form swimming toward the cliffs.

"What the heck is that?" she mumbled. Ibby felt the growing threat and moved closer to Ginger.

The two companions looked down as the form reached the edge of the cliffs. A large reptilian head emerged from the water. It was attached to a long, snake-like neck. As seawater flowed off its green scales, she saw the rest of its body climbing out of the water onto the rocks along the cliff. The thing was a good thirty feet long. She was speechless, not realizing she was gazing upon an adolescent green drake. Was she hallucinating? Ibby's warning snort at the thing reassured her that he saw it, too. The drake lifted its head, its yellow eyes glinting in the moonlight as it caught sight of the woman and her horse on top of the cliff. It licked its lips at its prospective meal.

The creature climbed swiftly up the cliff directly at her. It was already halfway up the hundred-foot cliff by the time she jumped on Ibby's back and turned to go. As she grabbed a handful of mane, she heard the thing scrambling over the edge of the cliff onto the grass. It snapped at her. Ibby sprang away just in time, and the drake's jaws snapped shut on air. Snarling, it gave chase, moving at a rolling gallop after the swift Arabian. Seeing a turn in the path, it quickly scrambled straight through the trees and placed itself on the path just as Ginger and Ibby were galloping around the bend. Ginger immediately spun Ibby around, and they headed back toward the cliffs. The thing went back through the trees and jumped back on the path directly behind Ibby. They slid to a stop at the cliff's edge. The drake came slithering back down the path as Ginger realized there was nowhere else to go.

Her face grim, she raised her shotgun and pulled back both hammers. Ibby pinned his ears flat against his head, preparing to fight the strange attacker. The drake slowly approached the two, anticipating a rare opportunity for something other than venison. He instinctively knew that humans gave more sport. He growled low in his throat, hoping to make Ginger run. She and Ibby stood their ground. She aimed her shotgun at the thing's throat. Just as the drake raised its head to shower them both in flame he heard the most unexpected sound.

Several she-drakes were trilling a courtship song. The notes were so sweet the drake couldn't resist. He took one last glance at Ginger and hurried down the path. The trilling grew fainter as did the sounds of the drake's huge body pushing through the vegetation. Suddenly there was an astonished roar from the drake. The elves had opened fire, showering it with arrows. The sound quickly cut off and then all was quiet.

Ginger shivered. What the heck had she gotten into? What kind of creatures lived here? Was she dreaming? She looked down at Ibby. His ears were pricked forward as he stared at the jungle directly ahead. Hearing the sweet notes of a bird in a nearby tree, Ginger drifted off to sleep as an elf slipped out of the bushes beside her and caught her before she fell. He gently set her upright on Ibby's back.

The elf gave Ibby a reassuring pat on the neck. "There now friend, let's get her to safety, shall we?"

Ibby answered with a friendly nuzzle to the elf's chest.

Brennus slipped up behind Ginger and held her securely in front of him. He rode Ibby back to the house and had Lieutenant Niall put him away while he returned Ginger to her bedroom. He lay her gently down on her pillow. Then he covered her with a blanket and brushed her hair from her face.

The elf stood looking down at the human woman. *What a brave little soul,* he thought, *to take on a drake all by herself.* Smiling, he bent down and gently kissed her forehead.

"Sleep a blessed sleep little one," he whispered. "When you awake you will believe this was all a dream." He turned and silently slipped back out the window.

Hours later the morning sun shone down on Alta as she fed the ducks and chickens in front of the barn.

"Here chick, chick, chick," sang Alta as she threw grain to the birds surrounding her. Then a movement caught her eye.

Two black ducks were running toward her from opposite sides of the corral fence. As they neared the fence's corner post, they both took flight toward the grain. They collided violently in midair and dropped to the ground, stunned.

"Oh Lord," muttered Alta. First the airplane broke down last night, then the ham radio in the main barn, now this. She turned to Doc, who was by the barn ordering Leroy and Chad to dig postholes today.

"Doc, you and Leroy better revive those two before the twins find 'em. They won't have a feather left between 'em."

Doc looked at the groggy ducks and shook his head. "By Neds, don't they ever learn?"

He and Leroy picked up the two ducks, walked them over to the water trough, and began splashing cold water on their heads to wake them before the twins could triage them.

Their latest patient sat nearby on the roof of the barn. The poor calico cat had brightly colored band aids all over her body. She had jumped off the porch railing, prompting the twins to "bandage" her. Doc looked up at the cat sympathetically. "I sure feel sorry for you when those band aids come off." Sadie meowed plaintively.

Alta looked at the cat and frowned. She figured she would spend at least a good hour clipping the band aids off – that is, if the cat would allow herself to be caught. She went into the house to look for the scissors and a can of tuna to entice the cat from the roof.

Liam's sons sat in their tree a few yards into the jungle and watched as Leroy and Chad began digging postholes. Having been there two days already, they were bored to death. Aside from the drake the previous night, the most exciting thing that had happened was a midair collision between two hungry ducks.

"Now what are they doing?" Rigalis asked.

"They are digging holes in the ground," replied Teagan. "Tiernan may now rejoice that all his hard won training of the future heirs of Nantuor has come to fruition. We are safely in place watching humans dig holes in the ground."

Rigalis frowned and moved to another limb for a closer look. With their heads down, both humans were working away at the hole.

Teagan crouched in the branches to get a better look at their activity. Suddenly he was aware that he was being watched. He looked down and found himself face to face with the twins. With them stood Jake, the black Great Dane who had refused to leave the twins' side since the previous afternoon. Perhaps it was a portent of things to come.

"Whatcha doing?" asked Cheyanne as she stared up at his perch.

Teagan froze. How had she seen him? Fearing the girls would draw more attention to him, he looked nervously toward the ranch hands. They were too engrossed in their work to notice what the twins were doing. He breathed a sigh of relief. It was short-lived.

"I said whatcha doing?" shouted Cheyanne.

How could such a small child make so much noise? thought Teagan frantically. He motioned her to be quiet as he heard Captain Brennus moving in the next tree for a closer look at what was going on.

"Why do you want Cheyanne to be quiet, mister?" yelled Casey.

Teagan waved frantically at them to be quiet. His brothers hurried over to his limb, their eyes widening when they saw the twins staring up at them.

"Hey, who is that with you in the tree?" yelled Cheyanne.

"In the name of all that is good, will you please stop shouting?" whispered Teagan, looking around anxiously. Leroy and Chad remained focused on the posthole.

"Why don't you want us to talk to you mister?" asked Casey. "Are you trying to hide or something? You better not be a burglar. Cause if you are we're gonna tell on you. Right now!"

Both twins took a deep breath, preparing to sound the alarm. Suddenly Rigalis appeared out of the lilac bushes with some fruit in his hand. He smiled at them reassuringly as he held out the food, the bushes concealing him from the ranch hands. The little girls looked at the fruit suspiciously.

"We are elves. Please do not tell on us little ones," Rigalis pleaded softly as he handed them the fruit. "We are afraid of the adults, and we fear they might harm us if they know we are here."

Casey and Cheyanne looked back at Leroy and Chad as they began work on another post hole.

"Aw, don't worry about them," said Cheyanne grinning. "They're pushovers. Just let 'em think they're the boss and you can do anything you want."

"Hey, why are your ears pointy?" demanded Casey. "You look like something in the movies."

Rigalis was nonplussed for a moment. What was she talking about? He smiled at her kindly. "Please don't tell on us little ones. The adult humans tried to wipe us out many years ago. We fear they may succeed if they find out we are here." He looked imploringly at the girls. They looked at each other and nodded.

Cheyanne and Casey stepped closer to Rigalis. "Don't worry," whispered Casey, "We won't tell on you. You'll be our secret."

Rigalis breathed a sigh of relief. Suddenly he found himself the object of severe scrutiny.

The twins looked at him curiously. "Are you an animal or a people?" asked Casey. "We are going to be vets and if you're an animal you probably need a splint or something." She and Cheyanne rummaged around in their medical bag and came up with some bandages and tape.

Rigalis grew uneasy. "Why don't you practice on your kitty?" he suggested. "I'm sure she would appreciate your kind attention."

"But she won't let us catch her anymore," said Casey frowning. "The last time we got to treat her was when Mama gave us a package of band aids. We used most of 'em to practice patching her up after we saw her jump off the porch. Doc says a major fall can cause all kinds of cuts and 'brasions so we put band aids on her. She didn't like it when we tried to pull them off, and now she won't come down off the barn roof. She's what Doc calls a difficult patient."

Not liking the way the girls were looking at him, Rigalis backed into the shrubbery.

"Wait a minute," said Cheyanne. "We're not through talking to you yet."

Rigalis looked up at his brothers for help. Teagan was giving him a stern stare as he motioned for him to return to the tree.

"Rigalis, come back up here this instant!" ordered Teagan.

Cheyanne looked at Teagan. "Hey you, stop fussin' at our friend!"

Teagan gave her a royal frown. He was the crown prince, and no one ordered him about. His eyes widening, he moved quickly to avoid a rock that Cheyanne threw at him. It narrowly missed his head.

"Why you little snip. Stop that this instant!" he commanded.

"Don't you yell at my sister!" shouted Casey as she let fly her own rock, just missing Teagan.

"Now see here," scolded Owain. "You can't just keep throwing stones at us."

"Oh yes I can," replied Casey as she bent to pick up another rock.

"Stop throwing stones at me!" ordered Teagan.

"Say please," demanded Casey.

Teagan raised his royal head proudly in refusal, but thought better of it as he watched Casey pick up a particularly jagged rock.

"Please!" said Teagan quickly as she drew her arm back for another throw.

"That's better," responded Casey. "Do you surrender?" she asked, still holding the rock.

Teagan's jaw tightened. Shooting her with an arrow was out of the question, but he was beginning to see why the cat stayed on the roof.

"A Midir never surrenders," he said stiffly.

"Okay then," said Cheyanne. She turned to her sister. "Let him have it."

"Alright," interjected Teagan quickly. "Perhaps we can negotiate."

"Well, then you'd better come down so we can talk," replied Casey with a frown. She took no prisoners when it came to trespassers.

Teagan wondered how safe this was. He looked at Rigalis, who was grinning broadly at him. Answering his smile with a frown, Teagan jumped lightly to the ground. The twins immediately started looking through their bag.

Cheyanne grabbed him by the sleeve. "You'd better lie down mister. That was a major fall." She turned a serious face to her sister. "He will probably need to be triaged – like kitty."

Teagan quickly stepped back into a more defensible position beside his brother. These human children were more dangerous than the adults.

He decided to try a little diplomacy. "Little one, would you mind very much fetching me a drink of water? I am terribly thirsty." He gave her his most winning smile.

"Okay," said Casey good-naturedly. "You stay right here and we will get you a drink. Heck, we can bring you lots of things – snacks, toys, bandages."

At the mention of bandages Teagan tensed up. "Uh, just water will do."

"That's not good Texas hospitality," said Casey. Cheyanne nodded in agreement. "Back in the old days, if someone came to your ranch you had to take them in the house and feed 'em."

She grabbed both the elves' hands and started to drag them out from behind the lilac bushes.

Teagan thought quickly. "We can't leave here little one. This is our post. Couldn't you just bring us a cup of water?"

By this time Rigalis had slipped unnoticed into a nearby tree, leaving his brother at the mercy of the twins. He snickered as he watched his brother trying to talk his way away from them. He finally convinced them to go into the house for some water.

Teagan heard his laughter and looked up in annoyance. "I ought to shoot you," he muttered as he fingered his bow.

In a few minutes the two little girls came tearing out the back door, their hands full of snacks and cold drink pouches. Cheyanne even had an old Pacman game under her arm. They raced down the back steps with their loot. They stopped just after they got off the porch. Cheyanne frowned. "We don't have our medical bag. You better go get it. I'll carry the rest of the snacks to the you-know-whats."

Rigalis wasn't sure he liked being called a you-know-what, but the snacks smelled delicious. He waited impatiently in the tree as Cheyanne headed for Teagan's tree. Darting into the house, Casey quickly re-emerged with the medical bag and ran to the edge of the group of trees in search of her sister.

Cheyanne was halfway to the elves' tree when Casey stopped in her tracks near some bushes. She had taken a wrong turn and was a little too far into the jungle for safety. Concerned, Rigalis moved toward her, stepping lightly through the trees.

Casey heard her name whispered on the wind. She stopped walking and looked curiously into the jungle. She couldn't see anyone at first. Then a shadow moved and a beautiful elf stepped into the sunlight. With his dark brown hair and brown eyes, he was more handsome than anyone she had ever seen, except maybe Rigalis. He smiled reassuringly as he stepped toward her.

Maccus licked his lips. He hadn't killed a human child in several thousand years. This was going to be delicious. He had spent most of the night helping the rest of Braen's scouting party do mischief to the humans' equipment at the ranch. The Dark Elves had destroyed the electrical system on their airplane and their radio. There was no one to help them now. He looked back at the rest of the scouting party. With Braen nodding affirmatively, he turned and started toward Casey.

As he neared her, the Dark Elf smiled his kindest smile. "Would you like to see something pretty, little one?" he asked softly, enticing her closer. His hand reached into the pouch at his side and lit upon a brightly colored snake no bigger than a worm. He held it concealed in his hand.

Casey hesitated. Her mother had taught her not to take things from strangers. He sure was pretty though. His eyes captured hers and she stood still, unable to move. He smiled and stepped toward her, holding out the snake.

"Soon you will be dead, just like the rest of your miserable race should be," he hissed savagely.

A tear rolled down Casey's cheek, and her lower lip quivered.

He moved the snake within striking distance of Casey's arm. He whispered to it and it opened its mouth, striking at the little girl. But just as it reached her arm an arrow flew through the air, impaled it, and knocked it from Maccus' grasp. Its fangs barely scrapped her flesh, injecting a minimal amount of poison that was still enough to kill her in a few days.

As Casey lost consciousness, Maccus looked up and locked eyes with Rigalis. The young prince's eyes were blazing with elven fire as he quickly sent another arrow flying straight into Maccus' heart. The Dark Elf fell to the ground and lay in a twisted heap.

Braen cursed with rage and sent an arrow of his own flying at Rigalis. It lodged itself close to his heart, knocking him out of the tree down into the thick jungle.

As Captain Brennus saw Rigalis fall, he caught sight of the markings on the dark arrow imbedded in his chest. Dark Elves!

The Light Elves were jolted with the realization that their ancient enemies had arrived. The jungle became alive with Light Elves surging to rescue their prince and with Dark Elves racing to finish him off.

Arrows filled the air. Characteristically, Braen quietly left the area without notifying his troops. He could see the Light Elves would wipe out his small scouting party, and he had no intention of sharing their fate.

After the Dark Elves were quickly dispatched, all Light Elves were on full alert, looking for their enemies.

Teagan held Rigalis in his arms. He looked up at Captain Brennus, his eyes filled with tears.

Captain Brennus saw Rigalis take a shallow breath. "He lives!" he exclaimed. "Quickly, we must get him to the king."

Captain Brennus whistled for Fiacra, and soon the sky was filled with eagles searching for Dark Elves. Fiacra's oldest daughter Iona landed lightly beside Teagan and Rigalis. Carefully breaking off the arrow and quickly binding up his wound, Teagan climbed onto Iona's back and took his brother from Owain.

"Stay here," he commanded. "Make sure there are no Dark Elves left to harm the humans. And see what can be done for the little girl." His heart heavy, he raced for Nantuor and his father.

Several eagles landed and took off again carrying archers ready to send arrows through the heart of any Dark Elf foolish enough to remain in the area. Brennus issued shoot-on-sight orders to several of these airborne teams tasked with watching the perimeter of the ranch complex.

Fiacra sent one of his sons to report to Liam at Brisal and to send for more troops. When they arrived, Captain Brennus and Owain quickly formed several search parties. Brennus set half of them around the perimeter of the ranch to ensure no more Dark Elves approached the house. He and Owain then took two squads each and began to search for their enemies.

Meanwhile, Barram paced uneasily on the huge tree limb outside Casey's bedroom window. He had immediately sent Jake to bring Doc to assist her. The snake, which was still dangerous when dead, had been quickly removed from the scene by Barram. Doc had done all he could for Casey, but that wasn't much, since the humans had no antidote. Without a functioning airplane or radio, they could only try to make her comfortable and pray.

Hours later Owain and his troop stopped in a small glen and looked around. It was almost noon and the sun shone in the plush glen like a blessing.

They were far from the house now but there was still no sign of Braen. Owain told his elves to sit for a moment and refresh themselves with some fruit and cool water. In his mind he was considering several more places to search, but his heart was full of grief and concern for his brother. He had sent up a fervent prayer to the One when Rigalis was shot, and he knew his youngest brother was in His hands now. Pushing aside his grief, he stalked quickly to the middle of the clearing.

He spotted Fiacra cruising above them, searching out the enemy. Owain sent a sharp whistle into the air. Fiacra dropped down closer, hovering above the glen.

"Yes my lord," the great eagle called down.

"Any sign of the Dark Elves?" Owain asked.

"Not yet my lord, but not all my children have reported back in."

"Very well, report to me when they have."

"Aye my lord." Fiacra wheeled away and continued his search. He had the sharpest eyes in the Realm – and any Dark Elf he spotted would be in deep trouble on this day.

His oldest son Eirnan found a lone Dark Elf who, like Braen, had run from the attack on the scouting party. Eirnan attempted to capture him alive so he could be questioned. But the Dark Elf tried to take Eirnan's head with his sword, forcing Eirnan to defend himself. As the Dark Elf raised his sword again, Eirnan broke his neck with one blow of his mighty wing.

Brennus had him take the body back to Nantuor to be seen by Liam as the squads continued searching for Braen.

Fiacra had spotted him running further into the forest, but Braen quickly lost the great eagle by slipping from shadow to shadow, rendering himself a mere dark presence in the shade of the trees. He moved like a dark ghost through the forest and left the area before Fiacra could bring back several elves to search under the trees.

Teagan strode into his father's study followed by several members of the Royal Guard. His father had doubled the guard around the valley, and quickly readied his operating room. Teagan swept into the operating room and gently set his brother down on the table.

Liam and Teagan turned and washed their hands in the steaming bowls of herb water provided by Liam's nurse Aili.

Liam quickly cut away Rigalis' bloody shirt and examined the wound, his face grim. He could smell the poison from the arrow as it seeped out of the wound. Gathering his strength, he commanded the poison to become impotent and fade away. Originating in the Realm, the Dark Elves' poison was strong, and it took a good deal of Liam's strength to overcome its effects. Liam gave a weary sigh as he finally felt the poison dissipate. Then with a tender touch he laid his hand on his son's forehead and sent him into a deep healing sleep.

Handed a slender knife by Aili, Liam made several incisions in his son's chest. As he and Teagan worked, Liam prayed to the One for the strength and skill to safely remove the arrow that lay near Rigalis' heart. He felt the One reassuring him that his son would live. Struggling to hold back tears of gratitude, he sang a song of thanks to the One as he finished his work. He set the evil arrow aside and turned to Teagan, who had stepped back from the table.

"Come here Teagan." he said gently. "The poison will severely hinder any healing. We will both need to pray in earnest to close the wound." Teagan hesitated and then came to his father. Liam was puzzled.

"Why do you hesitate, my son?"

"It was my responsibility to keep my brothers safe," Teagan said. A tear slid down his face as he looked down at his youngest brother. "I failed Rigalis," he whispered. His grief bore down on him like a mountain. "I failed them all."

"My precious child, you can't know all things. That is for the One. Do we not pray for our safety every morning and night? Do you not watch over your brothers night and day?" Liam put his arm around his oldest son's shoulders. "It is not your fault. There is only one doorstep on which the blame lies, and it is not yours. Help me now to heal your brother's wound. I will need your extra strength to ensure his recovery."

Teagan drew a deep breath and stepped to his father's side. "I will not fail you this time, Rigalis," he whispered. He and his father placed their hands on the spot where the arrow had entered Rigalis' body. They prayed to the One for Rigalis' recovery, sending healing energy into his body and feeling strength from the One surging into him as well. The wound began healing from the inside out, slowly closing as if sealed by an invisible hand. Finally the skin came together completely. It was soft and unscarred, as if there had never been a wound.

Tears filled their eyes. "Thank you Mighty Father," whispered Teagan.

Rigalis moaned quietly and opened his eyes. He broke out into a bright smile at the sight of his brother and father.

"Here, what is this? I take a nap for a moment and the both of you are in tears," he jested softly, his weak smile lighting up his beautiful face.

Liam kissed his son on the forehead. "My precious, precious son, you gave your father quite a scare." He put his arm around Teagan's shoulders. "Your brother as well."

Teagan leaned forward and gently laid his hand on Rigalis' shoulder. "Never again will I accuse you of being a child. You have done the part of a warrior this day."

Rigalis' smile shone in his eyes at his brother's praise. Liam placed his hand on his son's forehead. "Yes, you have indeed. You must rest now, precious one."

"But what about the little girl?" Rigalis protested weakly. "I must see if she is alright."

Liam stroked a stray wisp of hair from Rigalis' forehead. "You have been through much in a short time. Sleep a blessed sleep, my son." Rigalis sighed and slipped back into peaceful slumber.

Liam carefully moved Rigalis from the table to the recovery bed in the next room. He and Teagan stood for a moment watching Rigalis sleep. Then Liam motioned for Teagan to follow him into his study as Aili cleaned up the surgery.

Pouring them both a small glass of wine, Liam motioned for Teagan to join him in front of the fire. He had often talked to his father there, relating his problems or just telling him about his day. This time Teagan explained all the events leading up to the attack. The twins' knowledge of the elves was of little consequence. It would be dismissed as children's imagination. And if not, Liam could make the humans forget the elves existed.

"What is being done for the little girl?" asked Liam quietly as he stared into the fire.

"Barram is caring for her, Athair," replied Teagan.

Liam nodded absently, his face full of worry.

"Athair?" said Teagan. "Rigalis will be alright. The One heard our prayer. The wound is healed."

Liam nodded tiredly. He managed a smile at his oldest son. "Get some rest, Teagan. As soon as I talk to General Arth we must decide what to do. The Dark Elves are back."

"Yes Athair. But please do not worry about Rigalis. His wound is no more." He looked at his father in concern.

There would be no wound if I had not put him into danger in the first place, thought Liam, but he kept this to himself and smiled at his son. "Go now. Sleep a blessed sleep, my precious son."

Teagan kissed his father's cheek and left for his room. Liam, waiting for General Arth to return from his investigation at the ranch, sat quietly in front of the fire, fighting with his guilt. His thoughts were interrupted by a soft voice beside him.

"Does the king of Nantuor not believe his own words? You tell your son not to feel guilty but your face is covered with sorrow and guilt."

Liam turned and saw his councilors standing behind him. They had just arrived from a trip to the ranch. How had he not heard them come in? It was Ranal who had spoken. He turned back toward the fire.

"Was it not I who so coldly sent them to the ranch despite their protests?" asked Liam tiredly.

"Was it not your sons who let a stag leave a trail of destruction through the house?" pointed out Tiernan.

Egan stood thoughtfully. "The king is right. It was he who sent his sons to guard the house."

He smiled at the shocked looks from the other two councilors. "Is this not true, my king?" he asked quietly.

"Yes," replied Liam sorrowfully. "It is true. I sent them there."

"And since Rigalis started this whole chain of events by bringing the stag here, I think he should take the blame for the little girl's injury, especially if she dies." Egan's face was stern.

Liam was aghast. "Egan, how could you say such a thing?"

"The little girl may die, highness. Should he not answer for his misjudgment?"

"No!" said Liam vehemently.

"And why not?" asked Egan coldly.

"Because he had no way of knowing she would be hurt. Only the One has access to such knowledge."

"Indeed your Majesty?" responded Egan, looking Liam in the eye. "Then why do you blame yourself for the same thing?" He smiled in triumph at the shocked look on Liam's face. It was rare that he or anyone else outwitted the king. It was a sweet victory.

Liam stared at Egan for a moment and then sighed in defeat. He smiled fondly at the tall, red-haired elf. "Thank you my friend. It is sometimes hard to distinguish between the things we can control and the things we cannot."

He looked at his grinning counselors. "I am indeed fortunate to have such friends."

"Just remember that when we tell you something you *don't* want to hear, my friend," remarked Ranal.

Liam turned to business. "And now, to the matter of Braen and his Dark Elves."

"An eagle arrived a few moments ago carrying a message from General Arth," responded Tiernan.

"What does General Arth report?" asked Liam.

"Only that there was a scouting party of Dark Elves near the ranch. The rest of them are not to be found." Tiernan paused. "Braen disappeared when our guards moved in to defend their prince."

"Naturally," muttered Liam in disgust. "In his mind, why risk his precious hide when he can let others take the arrows meant for him while he escapes to safety."

The three counselors agreed. This was the way of the Dark Elves.

Ranal poured himself some wine and then paused. "My king, what about the caves at the other end of the island? Remember the caves along the shore near Cluse? Could they not hide there as they did in the Great Land across the sea?"

Liam nodded. "It is possible. If the drakes can elude us in those caves, why not the Dark Elves? They are more cunning than a hundred drakes." His face was grim. "Start search patrols throughout the island. Alert every animal ally. Have every inch of this island searched, especially the cave area."

"It will be done my lord," said Tiernan. He, Egan, and Ranal bent over a map of the island sitting on Liam's desk. Stepping quickly to the door, Liam spoke to the young guard in the hall. "Have General Arth sent here immediately upon his arrival."

The startled guard blurted out, "It will be done my lord" and hurried off toward the courtyard to alert the guards there.

Back at the ranch complex, Barram waited patiently outside Casey's window until everyone had left the room but the girl's mother. He put her to sleep with a soft song, then quickly moved into the room. Stepping to Casey's bedside, he put his hand on her feverish brow.

He knew he had inherited healing powers, but they rarely came into full strength for elves so young. Praying to the One for help, he concentrated on the poison that was attacking Casey's small body. With all of his strength and mind, he willed the poison to become impotent.

After a few moments Casey yawned and opened her eyes. They were clear and bright. She smiled up at Barram. He gently stroked her face and whispered, "You will be alright now, little one. The One has allowed my gift to mature when I needed it the most. Rest now, precious one." He gently kissed Casey's forehead.

Casey yawned again. "I don't want to go to sleep," she murmured before drifting into peaceful slumber. Barram looked at her sleeping mother. She seemed exhausted with worry. Barram reached over and stroked her face gently. "Sleep a blessed sleep precious one. When you awake you will feel rested and refreshed."

Alta sighed and slipped into a more restful sleep. Barram adjusted her head on the pillow and then, kneeling on the carpet, he offered a prayer of thanks to the One for sparing the little one's life. He prayed for a deep, comforting sleep for both humans and then rose to his feet. After listening for a moment to their slow, even breathing, he slipped out of the room.

He stood watch outside the window until just before sunrise, when Doc came to check on them both. Nodding to the guards in the nearby trees, Barram got his horse and sped back to Nantuor.

Doc woke the entire house with the news that Casey would be all right. There was a celebration at the breakfast table that day. Casey drew laughs when she said it was like Christmas morning.

The elven guards outside the windows heartily agreed. Word was quickly sent to Liam, who immediately went to tell Rigalis that the girl would be fine.

Chapter 8

Rigalis' Recovery

When Liam entered his study Rigalis was in the next room trying to dress himself. Liam moved quickly to his son and pulled off the robe he had just placed around his shoulders.

"Rigalis you are in no condition to be on your feet yet," he said as he moved to help Rigalis back into bed.

"I am alright Athair," Rigalis protested. "I need to get back to help protect the humans."

His father gently but firmly pushed him back down on his pillow. "As your Athair, I am extremely proud of you for your concern for humans. But as your healer, I must insist that you rest for a few more days. Your wound caused considerable blood loss, and you need to build your strength back up before you enter the fray again."

"But the little girl . . ." protested Rigalis.

". . . will be alright," Liam finished for him.

Liam's eyes twinkled with amusement and pride at Rigalis' relieved smile. He turned to a small bedside table and began mixing herbs into a silver goblet. Dropping in a large dollop of honey, he filled the glass the rest of the way with sweet cherry cordial.

"What's this?" purred Barram's voice. "Our brother, still in bed at this hour? Rigalis, you keep the hours of a court fop."

Rigalis smirked back at his smiling brothers. "Well, I see the secondary troops have arrived. Come to pay homage to your fallen hero?"

Barram snorted in amusement. "Rigalis really, it is not our fault if after two thousand years you still haven't learned to duck." He himself then ducked to avoid the pillow Rigalis tossed at his head.

His brothers approached the bed. With the image of his bloodied body still fresh in their minds, it was good to see him sitting up and smiling.

"So," drawled Owain, "how long do you intend to lay about Athair's study while the rest of us do all the fighting?"

His father sighed wearily. "Gentlemen, your brother is to rest for the next two days."

Owain opened his mouth and then shut it again at the sharp glint in his father's eye.

"Those are my orders as king," Liam said quietly.

His four children nodded, recognizing that tone. Their father never reminded them of his kingship unless he was serious.

"Now, out with you while I give your brother his medicines," commanded Liam with a smile.

Rigalis started to protest, but was stopped by his father. "You will recover more quickly if I give you the necessary nutrients to help your body strengthen itself."

He handed Rigalis the silver goblet and watched him drink it down. Rigalis handed it back to his father with a grimace. "Athair, that drink would have done well with some honey. It tasted terrible."

"I did add honey," his father informed him. "Otherwise you wouldn't have been able to drink it at all."

Rigalis sank back into his pillow wondering what horrible concoction his father had given him. In a few moments he yawned and quietly fell asleep.

When he awoke late in the morning, his brothers had prepared a chaise for him on the sunny terrace outside their father's study. They sat there together until noon, laughing and chatting. When lunch was served, Rigalis' brothers moved the table beside the chaise and the family talked happily for several hours.

Finally Liam went back to his desk and his sons gathered round Rigalis, each trying to keep him entertained. Barram juggled apples until Owain asked him to dance and sing as well. He did, much to Rigalis' amusement, until a group of giggling elven maids walking the gardens caught his eye. Blushing, he quickly returned to his seat beside his laughing brothers.

A glance from their father quieted them a little. "Don't get your brother too stimulated," he cautioned. "He needs his rest."

"Yes, Athair," they responded.

Barram could still hear the elf-maids laughing in the garden below. He looked at Owain indignantly.

"Did you see them walking in the garden?" he demanded in a fierce whisper.

"Of course," snickered Owain. "Why else would I ask you to do something so ridiculous?"

Barram's blue eyes blazed. "I was planning on asking one of those maids to take a walk with me this evening. Now she will probably laugh me out of the dining hall."

"I doubt that brother," responded Owain. "All you have to do is look at her with your big blue eyes and she will fall into your arms."

Barram smiled shyly.

"He is getting to be as bad as Ranal," smirked Teagan.

"I beg your pardon young prince," said a raw silk voice at the terrace doorway. "If your brother chooses to emulate me, well, he could do worse."

The brothers looked over and saw the tall, golden-haired elf-lord smiling at them. He was flanked by Egan and Tiernan. Ranal's blue eyes were dancing with amusement at Teagan.

Teagan blushed faintly. "I beg your pardon Lord Ranal. I meant no offense."

Ranal gave him a kind smile. "No offense was taken, young warrior. I was quite flattered actually."

Teagan's face lit up at the title Ranal had given him.

"You are right about the title, Ranal," Tiernan said. "These young princes have far surpassed my expectations. Their quick actions not only saved a young child but their courageous brother as well. I am very, very proud of them." Their old teacher's smile brought warmth to their hearts. Here was a side of Tiernan they had not often seen.

"Thank you my lord," said Rigalis. He hesitated a moment. "Your kind words are generous, but we only did our duty."

Tiernan's face lit up in a kind smile. "You did much more than that, young prince. You put yourself at risk when you could have just as easily called Captain Brennus to come help. If you had not acted as quickly as you did, the little girl would be long dead by now. She owes you her life."

"She owes her life to the One, great counselor," said Rigalis. "It was an honor to help her." His brothers nodded assent. Their father had taught them long ago that it was an honor to help humans.

Liam's counselors smiled like proud fathers. It seemed that the four princes were growing up. It made Tiernan's heart swell with pride to know they harbored such a deep love for humanity, something some of the younger elves at times neglected to nurture.

"It seems, my friends, that we will have to treat our young princes with more respect," declared Egan. "They have certainly earned it."

The four brothers looked at each other. Teagan nodded to Owain. "My lords, that is not truly accurate," Owain said. "There were times when we were childish and disrespectful, especially to Lord Tiernan. For that we humbly ask his forgiveness."

"Forgiveness has been obtained long ago, little one," replied Tiernan softly as he looked at the young elves with the loving eyes of a foster father. "There is no need to even ask."

Owain turned to Rigalis. "I know for a fact that Lord Tiernan sat by your bedside last night until just before dawn, watching over you in your sleep. For that alone he has my utmost respect."

Rigalis looked at Tiernan for a moment. "You . . . you sat with me all night? I did not know." He was speechless. He recalled all the pranks he'd played on his teacher and every belligerent word uttered to him. He looked down in shame. "You are kinder than I deserve Lord Tiernan." His voice softened, a tone of respect replacing his usual petulance.

"There is no need to feel shame, Prince Rigalis," responded Tiernan kindly. "You know as well as anyone the words of the One: 'When I was a child, I spake as a child'. You are a warrior now and I am very proud of you." He looked at the other princes. "I have always been proud of all of you, as proud as if I were your father."

He left the rest of his words unspoken. He had never told Liam that he too had courted their beautiful mother Aife. He had stepped aside after seeing the light in Liam's eyes when he introduced the two. He helped watch over their children all those years, and he fulfilled his promise to her to continue to watch over them. It was a promise he would never break.

He smiled down at his four charges. For once they were at a loss for words. He suppressed a chuckle and assumed the familiar air of teacher. "We have been standing here for some moments, gentlemen, and have not been offered a place to sit or even tea." He raised a stern eyebrow.

Three young elves scrambled to offer their seats to the counselors. They fetched cups of tea for their guests while Tiernan sat beside Rigalis and ensured he remained on the chaise.

Inside his study, Liam watched and laughed to himself. They were indeed growing up. He felt a twinge of panic at the thought and then reprimanded himself. He should be glad they were becoming adults. And yet he felt . . . a sense of loss. His children were no longer children, and he missed them already.

Outside on the terrace Barram's voice caught his attention. He was singing for Rigalis. Tiernan had made Rigalis lay back on the chaise to rest. He slowly drifted off to sleep listening to the sweet tenor of his brother's voice. Tiernan covered him in a light coverlet and turned his attention to Barram's performance. When the last note faded he smiled his approval.

"Well done, Prince Barram," he said. "Very, very well done. Your voice can do nothing but improve." He cocked an amused eye at Ranal. "I suspect you will soon rival Ranal in that respect."

Barram smiled broadly at the praise. Ranal shook his golden head. "Do not give him ideas, Tiernan. I will not have an elf-maid left to my name. Then I will have no choice but to dash myself upon the rocks of Brisal."

The three counselors burst out laughing at Barram's distressed look.

"Do not be alarmed, Prince Barram," Chuckled Egan. "I will make sure Lord Ranal does not do himself any mischief in his grief." He gave Ranal a playful wink as he laughed at Barram's wry grin.

"Many thanks, old friend," responded Ranal, flashing his bright smile. "It will not be the first time you have saved my life."

Barram joined in the two friends' laughter. For the first time he felt part of the adult conversation. For most of his life he had only talked to adults when he had to, except his father of course. Now, he took a certain pleasure in talking to the two elves.

Teagan and Owain were grinning at each other, instantly arousing Barram's suspicions.

"And what may I ask is so funny?" he demanded. They both burst out laughing. A chuckling Teagan motioned toward the gardens. The same group of elven maids had stopped underneath a tree to hear his singing. They were gathered under a huge oak tree, sound asleep.

"Well brother, I guess your singing was so astounding that their hearts could take no more and they fell asleep in self-defense," snickered Teagan.

Barram's handsome face was creased into a frown. "For your information, I was singing a song to put Rigalis to sleep."

"Well it worked," interjected Owain, "in more ways than one." He laughed as he looked back at the sleeping she-elves.

The king's counselors stared at the toes of their boots or out into the garden, trying to control their mirth. None of them wanted to embarrass Barram. Finally Barram good-naturedly joined in the laughter.

"Quietly my sons," said their father as he came out on the terrace and gently took Rigalis in his arms. "Do not wake your brother." When he turned to go back into the house Tiernan reached for Rigalis.

"I would be happy to carry him to his bed, my lord."

Liam turned away defensively, his son clutched protectively to him. "I can carry him Tiernan, thank you."

Tiernan smiled. "I seem to remember a conversation like this on the night of his birth."

Liam raised an eyebrow at his friend and took his son back to his bed.

Tiernan's eyes twinkled with amusement. Liam had driven everyone to distraction with his fretting before Rigalis was born. When his son was an infant, Liam hovered over him like a lion, barely even allowing the nurses to change his diapers. He had been like this with all his children. With a shake of her pretty head, his wife gave up trying to change him after his second son was born. Liam's friends and counselors had observed all this with great amusement.

Liam was writing up the farm accounting when he heard a sigh in the other room. He looked up to find Rigalis deep in thought, his eyes full of sadness and his young face serious. This struck deep into the heart of his father, who immediately put his pen down and went to his son.

He quietly sat down on the bed. "What troubles you, little heart?" he asked, using an old childhood endearment.

Rigalis stirred himself. "I was just thinking of the Dark Elf I shot." He looked up at his father, his piercing gray eyes bright with concentration. "His eyes were so full of hatred. Athair, what could humanity have done to garner such evil hatred?"

Liam smiled sadly at his youngest son. "Nothing, Rigalis. They hate for hate's sake. They have never forgiven the One for spending so much of his boundless love on these precious little creatures."

"But they also are loved by the One, even though he hates their evil deeds. They could gain forgiveness as easily as anyone else if they would but ask. I just do not understand, Athair."

"And I hope you never do, precious one." Liam wrapped his arms around Rigalis and bathed him in a warm glow of comfort and love.

His other three sons came sauntering in and flopped down on the bed. They looked from their father to Rigalis, concern in their eyes. Teagan tried to lighten the mood. "Another nightmare about final examinations, Rigalis?" His gray eyes held a wicked glint.

Rigalis pulled himself from his father and assumed a dignified air. "I have not had those dreams for five hundred years, Teagan. When are you going to let me forget them, you scoundrel?"

His brothers chuckled at his impudent smirk.

Liam looked at his sons for a moment, his heart full at having them together, alive, and well.

"It is time for nightly prayers, my children," he told them.

The family clasped hands and bowed their heads in prayer.

"Mighty Father, we ask that you forgive us our sins and keep us safe this night, watch over us as we rest or are at our watches in the night. Watch over elf and human and animal alike, and let us see the morning light as we praise You once more. We ask in the name of the Blessed Redeemer Jesus. Amen"

Liam rose to his feet. "It is time for you to go to bed, children," he said, suddenly relishing the words. It would probably be one of the last times he would utter them. His sons were entering adulthood.

His sons crowded around him, giving him hugs and goodnight kisses. "Good night Athair. I love you," each told him in turn.

"And I you, little ones," he whispered as they left his study. "Sleep well," he called after them, his eyes a bit misty.

He turned to Rigalis, wanting to do this one more time before he was too old. "Sleep a blessed sleep, little one." He kissed his son on the forehead and sent him into a peaceful slumber full of beautiful dreams, just as he had when Rigalis was a small elfling.

Tucking the covers carefully around Rigalis, he started back toward his desk. He stopped halfway across the study, realizing his heart was not in any more work that night.

Liam turned and stepped out onto the terrace, breathing in the scent of jasmine and the heavy perfume of roses. He looked out over the vast valley of Nantuor. It was bathed in soft moonlight that sparkled like diamonds on the dew, the river, and the waterfalls that fell along the walls of the valley. He saw several of Fiacra's younger sons wheeling around as the moonlight shone on their broad wings. Several more huge eagles kept watch above the perimeters of the valley.

He was surrounded by elven laughter and soft singing. Meanwhile, the eagles' rich voices echoed the songs back down into the valley, both groups filling the air with a soothing melody that beckoned its listeners with the promise of sweet dreams. The tunes mixed with the sounds of nightingales and crickets as the valley and its people settled in for the night.

The sound of familiar laughter caught his attention. He looked down and saw Tiernan and Ranal chatting beneath a huge apple tree. They did not see him watching. Smiling faintly at the rare opportunity, Liam lowered himself down from the terrace railing and landed silently on the ground.

He moved noiselessly toward his friends in the dark. As he got closer he could hear their conversation.

"This time has been rather hard on him," commented Tiernan. His eyes were filled with concern.

"Yes," answered Ranal. "I hope he will survive it unscarred."

"Rigalis is very strong, gentlemen," Liam suddenly pronounced. "He will survive. He is a Midir."

Ranal turned away to hide his silent laughter. Tiernan looked at his friend for a moment, his eyes twinkling with amusement.

"I was speaking of *you*, Liam, and you surviving your sons' growing to maturity."

Liam stood silently, his mouth open in surprise. His look drew hearty laughter from his friends, who put their arms around his shoulders and led him down into the gardens to enjoy the rest of the evening. The words of an elvish love song rang from Ranal's lips until all three were singing as they walked through the moonlit garden.

Liam's sons smiled as they lay on their pillows listening to their father's strong voice in the night. They soon drifted off to pleasant dreams of slaying dragons and rescuing beautiful maidens.

Puzzled, Ginger counted again. Twelve deer. Last night there had been sixteen. She walked to the back of the pen to ensure she hadn't missed any, and then back to the loafing shed near the gate. There she found Ol' Trouble cowering in the back of the shed. Frowning, she slowly approached him to see if he was hurt. He shivered and gave a plaintive bleat. For once he seemed glad to see her.

She gently offered him the bucket of oats she carried. He dipped his muzzle in and started to eat, then nearly jumped out of his skin when Leroy came into the shed. Ginger calmed him with a soothing voice and gentle strokes on his neck.

"Hey boss lady, what's happening around here?" Leroy asked. "Did you know we are missing some deer? And a couple of those Brahmas are missing too."

"What?!" Ginger was getting miffed. "I knew we were short four deer but bulls too? Is there a break in the fence anywhere?"

"No ma'am. That's the first thing I checked. Fences are fine and all the gates were shut. I don't even see any tracks leading away from the pens, at least not cattle or deer tracks. Some kind of animal was near the pens, but it looks like it was just walking away. Couldn't figure out what kind of animal either. It looked like some kind of big lizard or something."

"Could it have eaten the animals?" Ginger inquired.

"No ma'am, there would have been blood and leavin's."

He was right. If a large animal had eaten the deer or cattle, there would have been blood and pieces of the carcass left. If the animal had dragged the carcass off, it would have left drag marks. Ginger scratched her head in bewilderment.

"Well, turn on the hot wire around the pens and see if that doesn't keep it out. And from now on everyone carries at least one gun and no one goes out alone for any reason."

"Yes ma'am," answered Leroy. He followed Ginger outside the pen and headed for the bunkhouse to tell the rest of the crew. Ginger shut the gate and was headed for the house when she stepped on something that stopped her in her tracks.

She bent and picked up a six-inch piece of what looked like dried cornhusk. Holding it up for a better look, she nearly dropped it when she realized it was deer hide belonging to one of the missing does. She remembered having sprayed a cut with gentian violet the night before. Sure enough, there was a spray of purple across the piece of husk. What was going on here? Nothing could have dried out the hide so quickly. And where was the doe?

Shaking her head in frustration, Ginger looked around the ground and found several more pieces of husk scattered around the fence. She carefully gathered them and headed for the bunkhouse. *There's going to have to be a meeting of the minds to try to figure this one out*, she thought.

Unnoticed by Ginger, her young elven guard immediately left to report the news to Captain Brennus: the Dark Elves were using the farm animals to make Gray Warriors.

Brennus dispatched scouts to search the area for more husks. They located some near the ranch and many more farther into the island. The captain put his soldiers on alert and sent the husks to General Arth along with a detailed report. Arth immediately went to Liam, finding him standing at a large table in his study looking over a map of Nantuor.

"It is true my lord," said Arth spreading out the husks on the table. Liam saw pieces of hide from leopards and deer, and one piece from the hide of a drake. That piece worried him above the rest. A Gray Warrior hatched from a drake would be a formidable opponent indeed.

"Has there been any sign of the hatchlings?"

"No my lord," answered Arth. "They must be well-hidden if Fiacra and his clan cannot find them."

"The only place they could still be hidden is in the caves," said Liam thoughtfully. A disturbing thought came to his mind. The white deer of the Realm were very powerful. If the Dark Elves used them to make Gray Warriors . . .

"Have the white deer brought into Nantuor immediately," Liam ordered. "They are from the Realm. With their special abilities it wouldn't do to have them turned into hatchlings."

"Captain Brennus had them gathered on his way here," replied Arth. "They are safely in your Royal Gardens."

Liam smiled. Captain Brennus never missed anything.

Just then Fiacra landed lightly on the terrace and silently settled onto the ornate stones.

"Hello old friend," said Liam, "have you anything to report?"

"Yes," replied Fiacra, his eyes dark with concern. "Braen has been testing your troops' defenses as he scouts the lay of the land. I believe he is trying to locate Nantuor. If he finds it, there will be an attack."

"Yes," agreed Liam. "If he is going to survive in this world, his primary concern would be us. If he can rid himself of us, this world would be at his mercy."

Fiacra knew better but held his peace, waiting for his friend to work out this battle of faith for himself.

Shaking his head, Liam frowned at his own lack of faith. "The One forgive me. What am I saying?" He lifted his head and looked at his old friend. "The One will always be stronger than some evil beast of prey, even one as cunning as Braen. He will not leave or forsake humanity; He promised that long ago. He will not forget his promise. And we will not forget ours: 'To the last elf.'"

Liam's eyes shone with the old determination as he repeated the ancient promise to humanity.

Fiacra was satisfied; he knew his friend would come to the right answer eventually.

"Whatever strike Braen is planning, we will be ready," announced Liam. He turned to Fiacra. "Summon the High Council to my study."

"Aye, my Lord Liam." With the lightness of a sparrow, the great eagle turned and flew from the terrace. He looked back and called out, "And whatever you have in mind for Braen, may the One have him slide neatly into your hands."

It wasn't long before the Council was ensconced in Liam's study reviewing plans for defensive action against the Dark Elves. Several Elite units were placed in strategic areas around Nantuor, with some ordered to patrol the island disguised as regular patrols and hunters. The best archers were mounted on Fiacra's sons to go on patrols of their own. Painfully aware of the Dark Elves' love for the taste of human blood, Liam doubled the Elite guard around the ranch house. All units had the same orders: attack any Dark Elves you find, leave none alive.

The unit at the ranch took out one of Braen's scouting parties before the day was out. Liam frowned as he read the report. Having attempted to sneak past the guards and get into the house, the Dark Elves were wiped out, with one exception: as usual when things looked bad, Braen made his escape, leaving his troops to be slaughtered.

Liam set the report on his desk and leaned back in his chair. He knew Braen well enough to know he would not be deterred from attacking the humans. His lust for death was too great for that. No, Liam expected he would be lurking around the area looking for his opportunity while his troops scouted out Nantour's defenses.

Chapter 9

The Storm

As Ginger and Ibby moved down the trail they could hear the calf bawling. They found him at a turn in the trail, his legs tangled in vines. Ginger dropped her loop over his head and secured the rope to the saddle. She dismounted and quickly cut the calf loose.

Remounting, she turned Ibby back toward the house and settled into an easy walk. Halfway back to the house Ibby stumbled and fell to his knees, pitching Ginger forward onto the trail. Quickly recovering, she scrambled to her feet to check on the animals. The calf was alright but Ibby was holding his left front foot off the ground.

Her heart in her throat, Ginger quickly picked up his foot and saw the shoe dangling down. She pulled it off and did a quick once-over on his leg. She breathed a sigh of relief. She could see nothing broken, and when she let his foot down again he rested it on the ground. However, after leading him a few steps she detected a slight limp. Looking along the trail, she saw a root sticking out of the mud where they had slipped. She would need to remove it so no one else would fall. It was a perfect tripwire courtesy of Braen. He had seen her on the trail and slipped ahead to prepare his ambush.

Looking up at the approaching storm clouds, she sighed and looked at Ibby. She sure as heck wasn't going to ride him back and risk more injury. She took the slicker off the back of her saddle, reached up, and lovingly stroked the Arabian's elegant face.

"Ibby, I want you to go on and take the calf to the house. I'll be there in a little while. I need to cut this root out of the trail before somebody else falls. And don't forget to show Chad that you're limping."

The gray stallion nickered softly and nuzzled her hand.

"Go on now, I'll be fine. You need to get that baby calf to the barn before this storm hits."

Ibby nickered again, then turned and moved down the trail with the calf, matching its pace. Ginger watched for a moment as she shrugged into the slicker. Pulling her knife from her pocket, she went to work on the root. It took a while before it was cleared. By the time Ginger was finished the wind was up and small drops of rain were spattering in the trail.

Ginger adjusted her hat firmly and set off down the trail. Before long the rain was coming down in sheets, the wind driving it into her face. She continued walking, wondering if she could find a place to wait out the storm.

Chuckling under his breath, Braen waited for Ginger to draw closer to his hiding place. When she was in just the right position he released the limb he'd been holding. It swung out and knocked her from the trail, sending her tumbling down an embankment. She cried out in pain when her left foot connected with a tree trunk. She finally tumbled to a stop at the bottom and lay there in the mud feeling the raindrops pelting her body.

Ginger opened her eyes and looked around. She was lying against a tumble of rocks at the bottom of the twenty-foot embankment. Her head was spinning from hitting it on the rocks, and a white hot pain was shooting through her left ankle.

Oh great, she thought. *Now Ibby and I will both be crippled up.*

She tried to struggle to her feet but collapsed back into the mud with an anguished cry at the excruciating pain in her ankle.

With a strong gust of wind, the storm suddenly turned violent. Lightening cut across the sky in jagged streaks followed by deafening claps of thunder. The driving rain beat down mercilessly as the sun began to set.

Braen stood at the top of the embankment, enjoying every moment of Ginger's pain. Perhaps he would go down in a minute and see how much more pain she could take.

"Dang it all," Ginger yelled as she reached for a nearby tree to help herself up. She felt anger welling up inside her. It was bad enough to be wet and hurt, but she wasn't about to drown at the bottom of a gully to boot. Stubbornly she tried to put her weight on her injured ankle, only to cry out and collapse again in the mud, her head whirling from the effort.

There was a deafening lightning strike nearby and a horrendous clap of thunder. Ginger looked up, startled. On the small hill facing the embankment, she saw the silhouette of a man standing in the wind and rain. He was dressed in black with a sword hanging at his side, his dark green cloak blowing around him. Ginger blinked and shook her head, a motion that sent a wave of dizziness over her. She must have really hit her head hard if she was seeing men in cloaks with swords. She looked again.

The apparition was walking toward her, his dark, waist-length hair blowing in the wind. His handsome face was slick with rain. He was tall, she thought groggily, her police training taking over. He had to be at least six foot seven.

He moved toward her with an easy grace, even in the driving rain. There was a presence of great power about him, like being near a raging river. She felt she could almost reach out and touch it.

His dark gray eyes held a peculiar light. They intensely fixated on Ginger as she lay helplessly in the mud. She decided whoever this stranger was, she wasn't going down without a fight.

"Who the heck are you and what the heck are you doing on my island?" she demanded.

Liam smiled as he knelt beside her. "Don't be afraid, little one," he reassured her. "I'm not going to hurt you." He covered her with his cloak to keep out the rain.

"You're dang right you're not," Ginger retorted defiantly. She tried to rise again and collapsed, clutching her ankle.

Liam gently removed her boot and examined her ankle. He wrapped his hands around it, sending an inquiring thought into her body. He smiled at the response. No major breaks, just one small fracture in her ankle and a slight concussion. It wasn't as bad as he had feared.

"Ow!" spat Ginger, shoving his hand away. Liam tore off the left arm of his shirt, revealing a heavily muscled arm. He quickly wrapped her ankle with the cloth. Then, placing his hand on her ankle, he sent a warm flow of healing energy to ease the pain. Ginger stared at her ankle in shock. The pain had faded. *How did he do that?* she wondered. Things were happening too fast here.

Liam gently touched the bump on her head, sending healing energy to that spot as well. Then he quickly wrapped his cloak around her.

"Stop that," she ordered.

Raising an eyebrow at her commanding tone, he smiled, gathered her into his arms, and picked her up. She felt herself being enveloped in some immense power. Her head was spinning and her heart was pounding in her chest.

The elf-king smiled kindly as he carried her back toward the house.

"Hey you, put me down. Now!" she ordered, slightly alarmed at what she was feeling from him.

She didn't know this guy from Adam, and she had already been warned about what modern day pirates do to people. Was she being kidnapped? *Now without a fight, Mister!* As Liam continued walking, Ginger's eyes flashed and the little spitfire slugged him across the face as hard as she could.

The sting brought a frown to Liam's handsome face. His stern eyes turned dark, stormy gray as he looked down at her. Her stubborn hazel eyes stared defiantly back. As she glared at him, his eyes seemed to grow darker and more intense. Ginger felt herself being drawn into them, their immense power pulsing like a thunderous heartbeat. She couldn't seem to tear her eyes from his. She blinked a few times, and then with a frown and a sleepy "You . . .," she drifted off into oblivion.

The elven king chuckled softly as he started for the ranch house. She was certainly spirited. But far too foolhardy, running about by herself in a storm. Perhaps he would have to talk to her about that.

Braen watched from the darkness of the rain-soaked jungle as Liam tended to Ginger. Hidden behind a large rock, he saw Liam send her to sleep and pick her up to take her back to the ranch. He laughed to himself. *So Liam, you haven't changed much*, he thought. *You are still the same pathetic do-gooder you always were*.

He looked Ginger over. She would be quite amusing to play with. When he tired of tormenting her he could always kill her. He licked his lips, relishing the memory of the taste of human blood. Smiling to himself, he followed Liam through the storm back to the ranch house. He watched from the bushes as Liam quietly talked to Ginger and worked on her injured ankle. He noticed Liam glancing at her when he thought she wasn't looking. Smirking to himself, he settled down and waited.

Liam got her back into the house through the outside stairway that led to the upstairs balcony. He used the French doors to enter her room – he knew his way around from the scouts' reports. Gently laying her on her bed, he examined her ankle, which definitely had a small break along the bone. She moaned and began to shiver. Reaching into her mind, he gently woke her up as he reached for a small silver flask in his healer's kit. She groggily opened her eyes, and he poured some of the contents into her mouth. The cordial took effect immediately, warming her whole body. The shivering stopped.

Liam gently covered her with a blanket and continued examining her leg.

"Who are you?" Ginger asked sleepily.

"My name is Liam," he said as he checked her knee joint. No muscle tears – good.

"Does the other leg hurt, mistress?"

"No," she said, trying to keep her eyes open. "Just my left ankle." She paused, looking at him as he turned back to her ankle. She noticed the beauty of his face once again. His hair moved, revealing his pointed ear for the first time.

She gaped in shock. "What are you, some kind of leprechaun or something?" she asked incredulously.

With laughing eyes he replied, "I am an elf, mistress."

He gently held her ankle between his hands, a golden light shining from them enveloping her injury. He sent a strong wave of healing energy deep into the ankle. *This might take a few minutes*, he thought. Not only was there a break to repair, but the muscles in the ankle had tiny tears in them. The energy flowed from his hands into her ankle.

"What are you doing?" Ginger demanded.

"I am repairing the fracture in your bone as well as some small tears in the muscle."

"Thank you," she mumbled, yawning sleepily.

"You are quite welcome," Liam responded as he continued to work.

"What are you doing on my island?" she asked.

"I live here mistress. And this is *my* island." He gave her a regal smile.

"The heck it is," she frowned. "How long have you been here? How many of you are there anyway?"

Liam only smiled and continued working on her ankle. When the silence became too awkward, Ginger ventured another sleepy question.

"You don't mind me asking all these questions do you?"

Liam looked at her, slightly smiling. "No, I do no mind at all, Mistress, because in the morning you will remember none of this."

Ginger frowned. "Why not?"

"Because I will make you forget before I leave." Liam put the finishing touches on her damaged ankle.

And to add insult to injury, he has the gall to smile, Ginger thought.

"That is so wrong," she scolded grumpily.

His eyes turned a dark, stormy gray as he raised an eyebrow. "No, it is not. Sleep well Mistress." He reached out and touched her forehead.

"Don't you dar . . ." she began, and with that, she drifted off to sleep.

Liam laid his hand gently on the large bump on the side of her head and sent another wave of healing energy into the wound. He then reached into her mind, removing any memory of his encounter with her. Tucking the blanket around her and brushing a wisp of hair from her forehead, he caught himself staring at her face. *She was certainly quite beautiful for a human*, he thought.

His head snapped around at the sound of footsteps in the hall. An instant later two small girls came charging into the room followed by Alta.

"See?" exclaimed Cheyanne. "I told you she'd be in her room."

"Alright you two," said their mother. "Be quiet and go back downstairs. I need to call Doc. Everybody was about to go out in the rain and look for her after poor Ibby came in lame."

The girls stampeded down the hall as Alta quietly shut the door, never seeing Liam just outside the window. He headed for the barn, thinking he may as well tend to her horse's leg while he was there.

Braen waited outside until Liam left and then slithered in through the window. He stood at Ginger's bedside looking down at her long, auburn hair and long lashes. He would enjoy mutilating that lovely face. Reaching down and gently stroking her cheek, he relished the feel of the soft skin. He brought his fingers to his mouth and licked them. Her flesh tasted sweet. Her blood should taste even sweeter.

Braen reached out and took hold of her now healed ankle. Exerting his will, he told the bone to re-fracture. But even in his weakened state from healing Ginger, Liam's power was too strong, and Braen barely produced a hairline fracture. He could crush her ankle with his hand, but that would raise suspicions before the time was right. Cursing under his breath, he was suddenly struck by a thought: If Liam had a liking for this human, maybe he could use that to torment his old nemesis. He turned his hand and stroked her cheek again. *No, not yet. I'll make your life pure misery first. Then . . .*

He leaned down toward her again, intent on ripping her mind as she slept. But a sudden knock on the door sent him scowling into the closet. The twins stuck their little heads in the door, whispering fiercely, "She's still asleep, Momma."

Alta smiled behind them. "I can see that, sweetie. We'd better let her rest. She looks pretty tired."

She guided her small daughters back down the hall toward the stairs. "Come on. Let's see if we can't find some more of that chocolate cake." The twins' quiet giggles echoed down the hall.

Braen reemerged from the closet and stood over Ginger again. He listened intently to the movements of the humans in the house. There was too much risk of discovery right now, so he'd have to put off his amusement. Looking down at Ginger, his face twisted into a disappointed frown. He reached down and put his hand under her neck, exerting just the right amount of pressure on the nerves and then releasing her. In the morning she would wake up with a stiff neck. He couldn't risk taking time to do more damage. There would be plenty of opportunity later to torment her. For now, this was a good start.

He turned to go and then paused, thinking he might as well start her entrapment now. He was here anyway, and it would only take a moment.

Placing his hand across her forehead, he planted a faint image in her dreams – it was him, his face barely discernible. He sent an overwhelming feeling to her that the image was pleading for her help and solace. She moaned in her sleep, a tear of pity rolling down her cheek.

Good, Braen thought, *snaring human women is so easy. All you have to do is appeal to their sense of compassion. Such a useless sentiment*. He paused. *Or perhaps not. It has proved quite useful when hunting humans. Either way, I have planted the seed. Now I simply have to cultivate it. This will be the first of many visits, each one allowing me to tighten my grip on this woman. Soon she will be under my control.*

He slithered back out the window, the darkness reaching out to envelope him as if he were part of it.

The next morning Ginger awoke with a start, the sunlight pouring in the window onto her face. She stretched and yawned. Then suddenly she sat upright with a gasp. The muscles in her neck felt as if they were tied in a knot. What had she done to it? The last thing she remembered was riding after the calf. And she seemed to remember a storm. And then . . . nothing. How did she get back here, on her bed, covered with a blanket?

She got up, showered, and put on another pair of jeans and her favorite green shirt. The smell of steak, bacon, and eggs greeted her as she walked into the kitchen. Ginger yawned and gave Alta a sleepy "Good morning."

"Good morning yourself, sleepyhead," Alta smiled, cooking at the stove. "You sure got your beauty sleep last night."

"What do you mean?" asked Ginger as she poured herself some coffee and sat down at the table.

"We got worried when Ibby came in with the calf and went looking for you. Cheyanne and Casey finally checked your room and found you sleeping like a baby. Girl, you must have been really tired to go to bed at 7:00 without even putting your own horse up." Alta put Ginger's breakfast on her plate and brought it to the table. "It's nice to see you get some rest for a change. It wouldn't hurt you to sleep late more often."

"How's Ibby's leg?" Ginger asked as she started to eat.

"Nothing's wrong with Ibby's leg. He's sound as a dollar," said Alta, perplexed.

Ginger looked up from her eggs in surprise. Well, maybe he hadn't been hurt as badly as she thought. She glanced at her wrist. Dang, she forgot her watch. "What time is it?" she asked.

"It's 10:00," answered Alta from the kitchen counter.

"What?!" Ginger started to get up to go get her hat and head for the barn, but Alta stopped her.

"You might as well just sit down and finish your breakfast. The boys are already out working stock. It won't do you any good to go charging out there on an empty stomach." Alta poured herself a cup of coffee. "Besides, they can handle all that heavy work today. Why don't you relax and take a day off? You know the doctor told you to take it easy."

Ginger reluctantly sat back in her chair. "I won't tell him if you won't," she muttered as she reached up and rubbed her neck.

"What's wrong with your neck?" asked Alta.

"I slept really lousy and when I woke up I had a stiff neck."

Alta moved behind Ginger and massaged her neck.

"Thanks. That feels good."

"Well, I guess all those years as a nurse come in handy every once in a while," Alta responded. "Besides, I promised Dr. Hunter I'd look after you. Good Lord girl, what did you do to get such a stiff neck? These muscles sure are all in a knot."

"I don't know, Alta. Maybe it's because I was out in the rain or something." Ginger sighed. "Maybe I *will* take off work today. Don't know what I'll do though."

Just then she heard the bellow of a bull. Hmm. Maybe there *was* something she could get done today. She hadn't tried out that new bull yet. She chewed thoughtfully on a piece of steak.

"Alright Alta, I'll find something else to do. Maybe put some more training on Ibby."

Alta shook her head as she moved to the counter to fill her plate. "Oh yeah. If there's one thing Ibby needs it's more training. He can practically answer the phone now," she said chuckling.

"Actually I think I already taught him that trick," replied Ginger with a laugh. "But I don't mean trick training. I mean working stock."

"Well, if you ask me, I think he's smart enough as it is. He's a good stock horse and that's all you need around here."

"People and horses should never stop learning," Ginger insisted.

Alta shrugged. "Well, it's your horse."

The two friends sat and talked while they finished their breakfast. When Ginger was done, she told Alta she was going to the barn and quickly headed for Ibby's stall. He nickered to her from his hayrack. She quickly saddled him and took him to the arena to warm up. As she rode him around the arena she tried to remember what happened last night – and got nowhere.

She put Ibby through some reining patterns at a slow jog, then an easy trot, and then took him into an easy canter. The stallion glided over the ground with the grace and elegance of a gazelle.

Liam watched from the branches of a tall tree. A smile spread over his face at the graceful movements of the horse. He was quite an elegant animal. Liam hadn't seen his like in centuries. His eyes went to the rider. She sat on her horse with poise and grace, earning an approving look from the elf-king.

The woman rode a while longer, warming up her horse. *Warming him up for what?* Liam wondered. He had seen reports of the humans playing with their livestock, but the guards had difficulty explaining exactly what the humans were doing and why.

Liam watched as Ginger left the arena and rode her stallion toward the bull pens. He threw a questioning glance at one of the guards in the next tree.

Now where is she going? he wondered. *Perhaps to the bridle paths beyond the pens?* He watched in horror as she stopped at the gate of the largest bull and opened it. *What is she doing?*

He shifted nervously on the tree limb. Surely she didn't mean to ride into the pen with the bull. He watched in disbelief as she calmly latched the gate behind her and turned her horse toward the bull.

Suddenly she cued her horse into a dancing movement while she shouted at the bull to attract his attention. The bull looked up from his hay and saw the horse and rider near the fence. He snorted and lowered his horns, threatening to charge. Ginger immediately jumped her horse at him while continuing to dance and shout.

Liam couldn't believe his eyes. *Is she trying to provoke the bull into charging?* He quickly fitted an arrow into his bow and held it at the ready.

The bull charged slowly, still full from his morning meal. Ginger didn't move.

"Is she insane? Why doesn't she run?" Liam thought frantically as he took aim. Just as he was about to let his arrow go, Ginger and Ibby leapt aside, leaving the bull with nothing but air to attack.

Liam could hear Ginger laughing. "You're going to have to be a lot faster than that old man," she taunted. "You missed us by a mile."

As she turned Ibby and started his dance once more, Liam realized she was deliberately putting herself in harm's way for amusement.

Has she lost her mind? he wondered angrily. He hadn't saved her in the storm last night just so she could die on the horns of some savage beast. As he watched the game of dodge, he grew increasingly agitated. He would never have allowed one of his own people to take such chances. This must stop. Now.

He put his hands to his mouth and mocked the sound of a jaguar. Both the horse and the bull stopped in their tracks, looking for the predator. The bull was concerned about becoming a meal, and Ibby was worried the jaguar would get away before he could stomp it. Nothing Ginger could do would get the distracted bull to charge again.

Muttering under her breath about the dang bull and dang cat, Ginger left the bull's pen and took Ibby back to the barn. Liam watched them go with satisfaction. He would see to it that this nonsense didn't happen again.

Ginger unsaddled Ibby and put him in his stall. There was no need to cool him out, as he wasn't even warm. She felt cheated. The bull had been working really well, too.

She got her shotgun and headed for the brush. Try as she might, she never could flush the darn cat out of the jungle. She let off a few ear splitting blasts with the shotgun to try to either make it run out where she could shoot it or make it run home to momma. Unsuccessful, she returned to the barn and put up the shotgun. She got on the walkie talkie and warned the hands about the cat. They decided to come in and beat the brush for the animal, just to make sure it was gone. There were kids on the island after all.

Liam's sensitive elvish ears rang for a good hour after Ginger went back to the house. He had been in the tree Ginger was standing under when she fired off the shotgun. *What a horrendous noise*, he thought. *How can she stand it?*

Ginger winced as she walked back to the house. There was a slight stinging pain as she stepped down on her ankle. Had she sprained it? It hurt all the way back to the house. Sighing, she resigned herself to the fact that she was going to have to see a doctor. With all the work to do around here, she couldn't afford to let a neglected injury slow her down.

She walked in the house and made a quick call to Dr. Hunter. Then she called Chad in from the pasture and had him get the plane ready. Before long she was on the way to the mainland. When she got there, she was admitted to the doctor immediately. He x-rayed her ankle and returned in a few minutes with good news.

"Well Ginger, I'm happy to say your ankle is fine. The hairline fracture is almost healed. You just have to be a little careful until it's totally healed."

Ginger looked at him open-mouthed. She had never broken her ankle. Figuring the doctor wouldn't believe her, she simply paid the bill and headed back to the island with Chad.

What had happened last night? she wondered. She tried to remember every detail. She recalled the calf and vaguely remembered sending Ibby home. She concentrated harder. Suddenly an image came into her mind – a shadowy image of a tall figure standing in the blinding rain. *In a cape?*

As the plane touched down on the lighted runway, Liam's soldiers were herding Ginger's precious fighting bull far into the forest.

As the week went by, Ginger felt increasingly on edge. She couldn't find her fighting bull, and there was every chance he had already been eaten by some of the bigger cats in the jungle. Her nights hadn't been too pleasant either. She was plagued with the same dream night after night. Dream? It was getting to be a nightmare.

All in all she was getting frazzled. It finally reached the point where she would only fall asleep from sheer exhaustion.

Ginger moaned softly in her sleep. In her dreams she was walking through a beautiful green field. The sun was shining and the song of birds filled the air. The trees were a brilliant green as if they had just sprung into existence. White blooms floated through the air, carried by the breeze. It was an idyllic setting. She sighed contentedly as she looked around. It was all so beautiful and peaceful. So perfect. She laughed for joy.

A sound caught her attention. She turned and saw a figure standing on the other side of the field. Wearing tattered black clothes, he was tall and well built, his raven black hair and black cape blowing in the breeze. But, try as she might, she couldn't see his face. It was a blur with no features, as if something was preventing her from setting eyes on it. Still, somehow she knew he was handsome. She knew it without a doubt. He was devastatingly, irresistibly handsome. And charming. And desirable.

She sighed as she looked at him. She felt she must catch a glimpse of his face. The feeling welled up inside of her like a flood. She shivered and stepped toward him.

"Who are you?" she asked, mesmerized by his power.

He reached out his hand to her and with a choking sob whispered, "Please help me."

Tears of pity immediately rolled down her face and she started to cry.

Standing silently beside her bed, Braen chuckled to himself, enjoying the sound of her misery. He loved that sound; it thrilled him and made his heart thunder in his chest.

She moaned in torment, a feeling of hopelessness sweeping over her. The figure sobbed again, a heart-rending, pitiful sound. She stepped forward.

"Please. Tell me how I can help you." Ginger desperately needed to help. She breathed rapidly as she struggled with her feelings.

The figure hung his head sorrowfully. "You cannot help me. I have been banished here by an evil elven king – left here to die of loneliness. If only I had someone to talk to. It would mean so much. But I cannot, because the king would harm them if they disobeyed his edict. They would be punished horribly." The figure turned away, sobbing.

Ginger took another step closer to him. "I'll help you," she volunteered. "I'm not afraid of some king."

Braen stopped and smiled to himself. Then he turned sadly to Ginger. "If you would only meet me somewhere in the jungle. I just need someone to talk to. Talking to someone in their dreams is not the same as talking to a flesh and blood person. I feel I will die of loneliness." His voice held a plaintive note.

Ginger was overwhelmed with pity. Bawling loudly, Braen turned and walked away. She tried to follow him, but her feet wouldn't move. She began to cry; the sound of his sobs tore her heart to pieces. She awoke to the sound of her own miserable weeping.

Chapter 10

Emily's Journal

Ginger looked around the huge room. "Boy, this attic is big enough to be a ballroom," she murmured as she stepped forward to explore.

"Sure hope this attic floor is structurally sound," worried Chad, stepping into the dusty attic.

Leroy walked boldly onto the floor. "Well, sure. Look at me. It's safe." He stomped one of his boots down on the stone floor. Of course, the last time Leroy had walked boldly somewhere, the tin roof on the hay barn back in Texas collapsed, taking a surprised Leroy with it. He was found soon afterward huddled under a pile of tin and hay. After that incident, he refused to get back up on the roof.

Chad gave him a dubious look and stepped gingerly onto the floor.

"See?" declared Leroy. "What did I tell you? Safe as if you were sittin' in my truck."

Chad didn't find this comforting. He had seen Leroy's truck. "Deathtrap" was the nicest thing he could say about it.

The trio spread out, looking the area over. Over in a corner Ginger opened a huge trunk to reveal some old dresses, possibly from the 1800s or earlier. Chad found some old furniture in another corner. The pieces were elegant, made of velvet and rosewood. Leroy suddenly cried out in surprise. Chad and Ginger jumped and came running.

"What is it?" Ginger asked excitedly. "Did you hurt yourself?"

"Oh no, boss lady. I'm fine. I just found this old trunk with a carved horse head on it," he said proudly.

"Dang it Leroy, don't scare us like that," Chad scolded. "We thought you fell through the floor or something."

Leroy looked at the floor, remembering the hay barn. "Uh, no. I'm fine," he said, feeling a bit embarrassed at the memory. Turning back to the trunk, he ran his hands over the ornately carved cherry wood.

"Sure is pretty, isn't it?" he commented.

Chad squinted. "It's really hard to see in this light."

"Why don't you boys help me get this thing downstairs and we'll see what's in it?" suggested Ginger. The two young men picked up the heavy trunk and carried it to the attic door. Ginger held the door as they maneuvered through the doorway and down the stairs. She led them to the old study, where they had started a fire. The room was also brightened by the recent addition of electricity to the house. "At least now I can see where I'm going," she chuckled.

The young ranch hands set the trunk in the middle of the floor and flopped down on the old settee. Ginger walked around the trunk, looking it over. It was covered with elaborate carvings of dancing figures, horses, and hounds. Bending down for a closer look at the beautiful piece, she discovered someone had sealed the lid with wax, probably to preserve the contents. Intrigued, she began examining the old lock in the front.

"Leroy, hand me your pocket knife."

"But don't you already have a knife?" Leroy asked.

"Yes, but I don't want to chance breaking the blade on my Swiss army knife." She smiled at Leroy's dismayed look. "If I break your blade I'll get you a Swiss army knife of your own to replace it," she reassured him.

"Oh, man," Leroy murmured as he handed her his knife, half hoping the blade would break.

Concealed by thick leaves, Liam watched the scene from his hiding place in the tree outside the window. *Humans are such curious little creatures*, he thought. He was just about to leave when Ginger opened the lock with a snap. Liam gasped as she pulled open the lid and looked inside. There on the inside of the lid, secured by blue ribbons, was Emily's journal!

His heart thumped with the feeling of impending disaster. The original journal, written so long ago by that lovely young woman Emily Remington, contained drawings and notes about his people. He thought he had obtained the only copy – had Emily made another? He grimaced at the prospect of being outsmarted by a human. This wasn't right. He was the King of Nantuor – how could he let himself be outsmarted by his own wife? He shook his head incredulously.

When Liam saw Ginger tuck the journal under her arm and leave for dinner with the others, he decided to get the journal from her before she had a chance to look at it. He waited until after dinner, then surreptitiously followed Ginger as she strolled into the old garden with a cup of coffee and the journal. She sat down on a bench under a huge oak tree. Under the light from the house, she set down her coffee mug on the bench next to her and carefully opened up the ancient journal. Its pages were still crisp, the years in the trunk having preserved it well.

She turned past the first leaf and read the words "Journal of Emily Remington."

Well Emily, let's see what you wrote, said Ginger to herself. Oblivious to the agitated form shifting nervously in the tree above her, she turned the page to find an account of a handsome and charming person named Liam. He was also described as being some kind of lord – Ginger couldn't read the word well, but it looked like "elf." She chuckled and shook her head. An elf. Cute. What an imagination. Reading further, she found mentions of meetings in this very garden, even kisses exchanged. And something about an adventure. She turned another page to reveal a sketch of her garden. She looked around, comparing the picture to its current state. It had certainly grown.

Liam's mouth flew open. He was sure he had confiscated all of Emily's sketches. Apparently not, he fumed.

Ginger looked closely at the figure in the sketch. Tall and handsome, he was regally dressed like some kind of prince. *What is that on his head?* she wondered. She held the picture up to the light, allowing her unknown guest to catch a glimpse of it. They both saw the same thing – the figure had pointed ears.

"What the heck is *that*?" Ginger exclaimed. She took another look. Yep, definitely pointed ears. "What was the woman trying to draw, Mr. Spock?" she muttered. The figure in the tree held his breath as she turned another page to reveal a sketch of the same figure with four younger looking figures who also had pointed ears. *Okay*, Ginger thought, *so this woman did sketches of elves*. She chuckled to herself at the absurdity.

The image of his sons nearly sent Liam into a nervous spasm. He watched closely as Ginger examined the next sketch. It was of Nantuor – the house, grounds, and surrounding mountains. If Ginger recognized any of the landmarks, she could find her way to the house. He looked on in dismay as her eyes lit up in recognition of the lake at the top of the sketch. She looked over the trees toward the mountain lake above Nantuor.

Oh no, thought Liam. He *had* to get that book! He shifted silently down the tree as Ginger continued turning the pages. She saw sketches of his councilors, his gardens, the path out of the valley behind the waterfall, and even a rendition of the exit into the rest of the island. Liam was close to panic – this would betray all his people to the rest of the world.

Thinking quickly, he turned and threw his voice, mocking the sound of Leroy calling Ginger from the direction of the house. Her head swung around, looking intently for the young ranch hand. Seeing nothing, she stood up and stepped toward the path, the journal still in her hand. "Leroy? Did you call me?" There was no response.

Shrugging and sitting back on the bench, she put the journal down and took a sip of coffee. Liam saw his chance – he swiftly and silently stepped to the ground and came up behind her. He mocked Leroy's voice again, this time adding a desperate tone to it. Ginger rose once more and peered toward the house. Liam stepped quickly behind her and reached for the book.

The hair suddenly stood up on the back of Ginger's neck. Someone was behind her. She instinctively spun around with a heel hook and nailed the surprised elf-king in the jaw with her boot. He stepped back in shock, holding his jaw. She stood open-mouthed, staring at the figure in the drawing – and he had the same pointed ears!

Her mind reeled at the impossibility. Then the practical side of her acknowledged that if he was in front of her, he must be real – ears and all. Okay, so he was an elf; and an incredibly handsome one at that. She stood still a moment, mesmerized by his compelling eyes. They were the most incredible shade of gray, like a dark storm cloud. He held her gaze, trying to keep her becharmed while he reached for the journal.

She frowned as if she were trying to remember something. Suddenly her face lit up in recognition – the figure in the rain! Her temper lit like a forest fire, breaking her trance.

"Just what the heck is going on here?" she demanded angrily. Liam opened his mouth to speak, but she didn't give him the chance. "Who are you and what the devil are you doing on my island? And why are your ears pointed?"

Raising his eyebrow, Liam was about to answer when Ginger cut him off again.

"And why do I seem to remember you in the rain? And how did I get a hairline fracture on my ankle when I have never had a broken ankle in my life? And where the heck is my ten-thousand-dollar bull?!"

By this time Ginger's eyes were blazing and she was toe to toe with Liam, shouting in his face. He took a surprised step backward at this unexpected assault. Then he rallied, drawing himself up to his full height and staring down at Ginger, his face a mask of royal indignation.

"Which question would you like for me to answer first, Madam?" he asked coolly. "Why I bothered to heal your ankle in the first place, or why anyone would be so stupid as to try to play tag with a bull?" He knew he was raising his voice, but the king was unaccustomed to being spoken to in this fashion.

"Who are you calling stupid, you moron?" retorted Ginger. "And you can start by telling me what you are doing trespassing on my island."

Liam's flashing eyes turned an even darker gray. "For your information Madam, this is *my* island, and it is *you* who are trespassing." In his anger he unshuttered his power, its force flowing from him in waves and rustling the plants in the garden.

"I don't think so," spat Ginger. "I have the deed to this land and *my* name is on it." She stopped. "How many of you guys are there anyway?" She turned to pick up the journal. Liam, remembering the pictorial map to his home, stepped forward and snatched the book from her hand. Her eyes blazing, Ginger spoke slowly in a deadly quiet voice.

"I'll tell you this once, Mister. Get your hands off my book."

Liam held the book behind his back and looked down on his opponent in triumph. "I'm afraid Madam, that is not possible."

A wicked grin spread across Ginger's face. "Wanna bet?"

Liam barely had time to duck as her tiny fist hurtled toward his face. He frowned. "Madam, there is no need to act the part of a hooligan."

"Who are you calling a hooligan? And *don't* call me Madam!" Ginger angrily took another swing, trying to get Liam off balance so she could retrieve her book. He slid aside and deflected her gently down toward the bench. When she landed she jostled the mug, spilling scalding hot coffee on her hand. She cried out in pain as she jumped back up from the bench. Liam was mortified. He immediately shuttered his power and approached her, his face full of concern.

"Mada . . . My Lady, I am truly sorry. I never meant to . . ." He reached for her burned hand, but she yanked it away from him.

"Oh, get away from me," Ginger grouched as she turned from him. She held her hand up to the light. Liam stood behind her, trying to see the damage. He said gently, "Lady, truly I am sorry. I never meant to hurt you." He reached for her hand again. "If you would please let me see your hand, I can help."

Ginger gave him a hard jab in the ribs with her elbow and moved away. "I can take care of myself. I don't need your help." The pain in her hand was becoming excruciating, causing a sick feeling in her stomach. She gulped in the night air as she sat back down on the bench, holding her hand.

Liam knelt before her, his face softened by her suffering. "Please Lady," he whispered softly, "let me see your hand. I promise I won't hurt you." His soft, luminous eyes caught hers and held them for a moment. She dumbly held out her hand, still frowning.

Liam gently took her hand in his. He examined the burns and then cupped both his strong hands around her tiny one. For a moment her hand was enveloped in a soft golden glow, the power surging from Liam's hands into her injured one. The pain immediately vanished, and the burnt flesh returned to normal. Still holding her eyes, Liam had just begun reaching for the journal when Leroy came striding into the garden, his voice booming.

"Hey boss lady. Want some homemade ice cream?" He walked up to Ginger, who was sitting alone on the bench beside the journal.

"Hey, is this that book you found this afternoon?" asked Leroy, picking it up. Ginger started as if waking up. She looked up at Leroy, then at the journal in his hand.

"What did you say?" she asked softly.

"Is this that book you found up in that old trunk?"

"Uh, yeah. What did you want?" she asked uncertainly.

"Oh. We were having some homemade ice cream and Alta sent me to get you. Come on. The game's about to start." He stood waiting for her response.

"Okay," Ginger replied. She got up and followed Leroy out of the garden. At the gate she glanced back and took one more look around.

Liam watched Ginger disappear into the house. What would she do? Would she tell the other humans? Liam sighed and slipped silently toward the house, staying in the shadows. His sharp elven hearing picked up the sound of merry voices. *This lady must keep a happy household*, he thought, moving closer to the window while using a large rose bush as cover. He stood listening to the cheerful banter in the kitchen. Finally everyone headed into the living room with large bowls of ice cream.

Ginger settled down on the big, horseshoe-shaped couch with everyone else. She read the journal as she finished her ice cream. Having a photographic memory, she only took about five minutes to thumb through the entire thing. She put it down on the coffee table and watched the game.

Liam sat on a tree limb watching through the window. He breathed a sigh of relief, thinking she had only casually thumbed through the journal. *She hasn't had enough time to get a good look at anything*, he thought as he chaffed impatiently. He worried someone else on the couch would look through the journal, but they were all entranced by the battle on the television screen.

He had seen their television before, but these organized battles were something new. No one made use of sword or arrow, yet at times some soldiers were carried off the battlefield and replaced by other troops as many humans cheered them on. The battle made no sense to him. They seemed to be fighting over a piece of leather. He shook his head in bewilderment. Humans! He settled himself down on the limb.

Ginger absently watched the game, mulling over what she had discovered: elves. There were elves on the island. What next, the Easter Bunny? She wondered how long they had been there. And this Liam fella seemed pretty bossy. She recognized him from Emily's journal, which described him as an elf-king. He certainly had enough attitude to be a king, she smirked. She wondered how many elves were on the island. What kind of problems were they going to make for her and her ranch hands? This guy Liam seemed to think he owned the whole island. Well, her name was on the deed, and she wasn't going to give up her land without a fight. No Texan worth their salt would. She made up her mind to pay Liam a little visit as soon as possible.

She got up from the couch, yawning and stretching.

"You're not going to bed already are you?" Leroy asked. "It's not even halftime."

"Yeah, I'm going to turn in early, Leroy. 'Night everybody."

Ginger picked up the journal. Looking around at the others, she decided not to tell them about the elves until she had proof. She smiled as she went upstairs. *You can take the Ranger out of Texas*, she thought, smiling to herself.

She quickly changed and brought the journal into bed. She studied the drawing of Liam and his sons. *Nice looking family*, she thought. *I wonder where the mother is*. Sighing, she shut her eyes and thought about her next move. Tomorrow she would check out Liam's house and then, if it existed, she would take some of the ranch hands there to straighten things out with this . . . elf. Now that she knew who and what he was, she'd be better able to deal with him. Having made her decision, she snuggled down further under the covers.

Liam was delighted to see her retiring earlier than expected. He had climbed up to her room's balcony and, watching through the French doors, had seen her thumb through the journal before closing her eyes. He waited a few minutes then slipped into the room.

Kept awake by her thoughts, Ginger sensed him enter. She opened her eyes into slits, watching him through her hair. *Boy, this guy doesn't give up does he?* she thought, amused at his audacity. *He certainly is pushy enough to be a king*, she mused as he silently stepped to the bed. Liam reached across her and gently took the journal from her grasp, whispering, "I am sorry my lady, but this is necessary." *I'll bet he'd have a heart attack if I jumped up about now*, Ginger thought.

He lifted her hand and kissed it apologetically. Perhaps he could leave her a gift later to make up for confiscating her little treasure.

Ginger could barely suppress a smile as Liam took the journal. When he left the room, Ginger amused herself imagining his surprise when she showed up on his doorstep the next day.

Ginger woke up at 4:30 the next morning to get ready for her trip. She packed some extra clothes, a medical kit, emergency supplies, her laptop, and extra batteries. She put her Kevlar vest on. Then she holstered her Desert Eagle and packed a second one in her ammo bag, along with two backup pistols called Judges. She packed jacketed hollow points for the larger pistols and .410 buckshot for the Judges. She added her Bowie knife to her belt. The razor sharp blade rested in a hand carved leather sheath that she had made herself – *no harm in being prepared.*

After finishing breakfast downstairs with the ranch hands, she told them she was going exploring, possibly for a few days. The foreman tried in vain to talk her out of the trip – but she was armed to the teeth and confident she could handle whatever might come.

She saddled up Ibby and left through the old garden, following the path marked on the map in the journal. Her memory of it was crystal clear. She smiled at the thought of Liam's face when he'd see her again.

Liam was riding ahead of his sons down the path to the road, Emily's journal tucked safely in his saddlebag. This was the same path Emily had taken when she had followed Liam that first time so many years ago. Emily's memory was still sweet in his mind. Liam's smile faded with the sound of hooves on the road ahead accompanied by the voice of a woman singing. *That annoying woman!* thought Liam.

Signaling back to his sons to take cover, Liam moved his horse Tanet into the bushes.

He looked through the leaves and caught sight of Ginger. She was on Ibby, who was ambling down the road at an easy walk. Liam frowned in puzzlement at the song she was singing. It was about a cowboy dying in someplace called Laredo.

He looked over at his sons, who were whispering excitedly among themselves. Owain turned to his father. "Athair, this is the woman we saw the first day we visited the house."

"She has the most unusual eyes, Athair," added Barram. "They are green and brown. Very pretty."

Shushing his sons and signaling them to follow him on their horses, Liam moved Tanet quietly through the forest. After a few moments he stopped and put his hands to his mouth, mimicking the sound of a panther squall. Ginger jerked her head around, quickly pulled out her pistol, and trained it directly at Liam's hiding place. Liam ducked. Ginger waited silently. Hearing nothing more, she holstered her gun and started back down the road.

Liam jerked his head around at a slight sound to his left. His sons were snickering quietly at the sight of their father crouched down in his saddle. He straightened indignantly, fixing them with a regal stare. They stopped laughing and ducked their heads down, trying to hide their smiles of amusement.

Owain looked up at his father's frown. "I'm sorry Athair, but I have never seen you intimidated by a woman before."

"I am not intimidated!" Liam whispered slightly fiercer than he intended. His sons grew quiet. Owain bit his lip and stared at the ground.

"My sons," Liam said gently, full of concern, "I did not intend to snap at you. I apologize for hurting your feelings."

Owain bit his lip harder and continued looking straight at the ground. Liam smiled kindly and reached out, gently turning his son's face toward him. "My son . . ." he started softly. He stopped when he saw tears of laughter in his son's eyes. All four brothers broke into a laughing fit as their father stared at them from his horse.

Surprised and angered, Liam turned Tanet and rode through the forest in the direction Ginger had taken. *Intimidated by a woman indeed!* he thought indignantly. *We will see who intimidates whom!*

With his sons following, he rode quickly and quietly until he came even with Ginger and Ibby. He stopped, shooing his boys to one side. Putting his hands to his mouth, he mocked the sound of a fierce, growling wolf. This time Ginger wheeled Ibby in the direction of the noise, training her gun on Liam's position, her eyes blazing. Ibby caught Liam's scent and started making horse faces at him. Liam's sons tried mightily to stifle their laughter at their father's failed attempt to get this woman off the road.

Hearing the laughter, Ginger looked down and saw Ibby making faces at the bushes. *It's that elf again!* she thought. Laughing herself, she turned Ibby and trotted down the road toward Nantuor. An incensed Liam rode ahead of her and, bursting through the bushes, turned Tanet to block her path.

Liam sat tall and imposing in the saddle, the embodiment of a powerful elven king.

Ginger smiled. "Well, glad to see you finally got your nerve up, Liam," she remarked. "My name's Ginger by the way." She heard suppressed laughter and shushing in the forest. Liam flushed slightly and sat up straighter in the saddle.

Ginger moved her horse closer to his. Liam frowned, his eyebrow raised in annoyance. How did she know his name?

Ginger laughed. "Don't look so shocked. Your name was all over that journal."

Liam's frown deepened. He would have to make her forget what she had read. His eyes turned a dark, storm-cloud gray as he stared at her, attempting to capture her eyes with his own. She grew suspicious and wheeled her horse away. Doing an end run around Liam, she headed down the road with a cheery "Catch me if you can."

Liam gave chase, his sons' laughter ringing in his ears. He would have a word with them later about their lack of respect. But right now he had to head this woman off before she rode up the front steps into his home.

The four young elves laughed merrily as they galloped after this strange woman who didn't seem at all awed by their imposing father. Liam heard their snickering behind him. It only fueled his determination to catch the woman before she became the ruin of his entire settlement.

Urging Tanet faster, he finally came alongside Ginger. As he looked over at her, he noticed her horse was making faces at Tanet. The stallion wasn't even exerting himself. Frustrated, Liam reached for Ibby's reins.

"Oh no, you don't," exclaimed Ginger, leaning forward and telling Ibby, "At-li" – the Cherokee word for run. He dropped even lower to the ground and shot forward like an arrow from a bow. As Liam watched in amazement, Ginger blew past him and disappeared around the curve in the road.

"Blast," muttered the elf-king. He commanded Tanet to run his fastest. As he came around the curve, he saw something that turned his blood cold. Braen was standing in the road, holding his side as if he were hurt. To his horror he saw Ginger slow to a walk alongside him to offer assistance.

"No!" he shouted while giving Tanet his heels. It was too late. As Ginger leaned down to speak to Braen, he stepped forward with a long knife and slashed at her. Just as swiftly, she instinctively pulled out her desert eagle and squeezed off three rounds at Braen's head. They darted to opposite sides of the road, Ginger leaning over to use Ibby as cover. They were both injured – Braen was shot in the shoulder and Ginger had a deep gash in her side.

Leaping from Tanet, Liam snatched Ginger from her saddle. From behind him, Liam heard the sound of bowstrings just before four arrows came flying through the air at Braen.

Ibby charged across the road toward Braen. Braen spun aside, the arrows missing him, and went for his bow. Turning, he found himself facing an angry Arabian stallion. Ibby reared and struck the bow from Braen's grasp with his right front foot. Squealing, he charged Braen, ears pinned to his head and mouth open to tear out a hunk of whatever he could lay his teeth onto. Braen dodged and Ibby reared again, trying to slam his hooves into Braen's head.

Just then another volley of arrows came flying at Braen. Dodging the arrows with superhuman speed and clutching his wounded shoulder he wheeled and disappeared into the underbrush. Ibby moved to pursue him but Ginger called him back through gritted teeth. He instantly returned to her side and caressed her face with his nose.

Liam's sons rode up and dismounted near their father and Ginger. He laid her on the ground to examine her wound. She was conscious but in extreme pain. She looked up into Liam's eyes.

"I'm okay," she gasped. "Who was that guy?"

"Someone I wish that you had never met," Liam told her. She was bleeding heavily. He had to get her to Nantuor where he could treat her properly. He put his hand on her side and sent a burst of healing energy into her wound. It slowed the bleeding enough that Liam felt she could be safely moved.

He smiled reassuringly at Ginger. "Do not worry, my lady. Everything will be alright." His sons crowded around her.

"Yes," said Barram, trying to cheer her with his most dazzling smile. "Our father is an excellent healer. He will have you well in no time."

"Good," grunted Ginger painfully. "Cause when I get back on my feet, I'm gonna find that guy and kick his sorry behind."

The four brothers laughed at her defiant spirit. Liam stopped them with a stern look. Turning to Ginger, he gently wrapped her in his cloak, carefully picked her up, and handed her to Teagan. He then mounted Tanet and carefully took Ginger into his arms and settled her in front of him in the saddle. Ibby crowded close to his injured owner.

Liam looked down at the fierce pair of eyes staring up at him from the folds of his cloak.

"I understand you are upset, my lady, but Braen is no one to be trifled with,"

"Neither am I," said Ginger grimly. "And my name is Ginger."

The boys' laughter died down as their father carried the human lady home.

"What fire she has," whispered Rigalis.

"Oh, yes, she reminds me of Mother," agreed Barram.

"I told you she was interesting," added Owain.

"You did not," said Teagan, smacking the back of his head.

"Children," came their father's quiet voice, "that will be enough. This lady is wounded. There is no need to add to her distress with your bickering."

The brothers fell silent. Then their elvish ears caught the muffled sound of strained laughter coming from the bundle riding in front of their father.

An amused female voice whispered painfully, "Are you always such a barrel of laughs when you go riding?"

Liam looked down sharply at Ginger. She smirked back at him through her pain. Despite himself, he smiled back. *How amazing that she can joke when she is so gravely injured*, he thought. *A truly intriguing woman.*

Liam cautiously had Tanet break into a soft trot. She needed treatment immediately. Ginger grimaced in pain but didn't make a sound.

Liam looked at her solemnly and then captured her eyes with his. His own eyes grew dark gray while hers seemed mesmerized by his intense stare. She blinked slowly a few times before he sent her into a deep healing sleep.

Liam studied her face. She was quite pretty – for a human. He gently touched her cheek once and then bundled her tighter in his cloak. Noticing his sons watching him, he flushed slightly and then turned and assumed a regal air. His sons followed him home, smiling at each other and trying to contain their silent laughter.

At the house, Liam handed Ginger to Teagan, then dismounted and took her back in his arms. Hurrying up the front steps and down the hall, he passed through the study and gently laid Ginger on the bed in the intensive care room. His nurse Aili quickly entered the room and helped get her settled on the bed. Together they cut away her clothes, exposing the vicious slash in her left side.

Aili applied absorbent cloths woven with strands made from a plant containing a blood-clotting agent. As she worked, Liam hurried back into his study to gather his surgery kit and other medical supplies from his medical cabinet. Shutting the door, he sat down under the cabinet at a table that held several small statues, including a jade dragon, a white marble pair of nightingales perched in a tree, a pink marble winged Pegasus, and a pair of kittens made of tiger's eye. Liam picked up the nightingales and returned to the care room with all his supplies. His sons settled down in the study to wait.

Aili laid out the contents of the surgery kit on a table to the right of the bed. Liam set the rest of the supplies down beside the kit. Moving around to the table on Ginger's left, he set the figurine down in a spot of sunlight.

The sunlight danced across the figurine as if delighted by its presence. Liam blew his warm breath onto the statue. For a moment it looked as if the two birds moved on the limb. Then they were still. Smiling, Liam turned and went back to the table full of instruments. Aili came in with a basin of warm water that had a faint medicinal smell to it. Liam washed his hands in this solution and dried them on a clean cloth. Aili did the same.

Liam bent over Ginger and gently touched her mind, waking her quietly from her sleep. She sleepily opened her eyes, looked up at him, and yawned. He laid his hand on her brow, calming her mind completely.

Smiling reassuringly at her, he said, "Lady Ginger, I am going to repair the damage done by Braen's dagger. I will need to keep you awake to be aware of any changes in your condition while I work."

Ginger looked at him with concerned eyes. She tensed at the thought of surgery without an anesthetic. "I have some Tylenol in my saddlebags. It's a painkiller . . ." she started.

Liam simply continued smiling and looking into her eyes. Her fear melted, and she relaxed again. "Do not fear dear lady. There will be no pain. I promise," he told her softly as he stroked a wisp of hair from her face.

He smiled again and looked at the figurine. Ginger looked at it, too. Liam's calm voice whispered quietly in her ear: "The birds are quite lifelike, aren't they? They look as though they will fly off the tree at any moment." She felt his warm breath on her cheek. For a moment it looked as if the birds had moved. But that was ridiculous – they were made of marble.

As she continued observing the figurine's exquisite detail, a light breeze blew into the room. Had the birds moved? The two birds suddenly dove off the limb and began flying around the tree while singing a beautiful song. Ginger felt as if she could almost make out the words.

Entranced, Ginger lost all track of time as she watched the birds dance in mid-air, sometimes chasing each other, at other times flying in perfect harmony. The scene was both calming and fascinating. Occasionally she would be aware of voices in the room, of the touch of someone's hand, but the birds held her undivided attention. Finally, they fluttered back to their tree and perched on a limb. Ginger sighed calmly, completely relaxed, happy and at peace.

She turned her head and looked at Liam. He smiled down into her sleepy eyes.

"The wound is clean and is healing nicely, dear lady. Do not fear. All will be well." His eyes grew darker and more intense. "And now dear heart, it is time for you to rest. You have been through much today and a long nap will do you good."

Ginger frowned sleepily and murmured, "I'm a little too old for naps, Mister."

Liam smiled and lightly placed his hand over her forehead. "Young one, you are never too old for a nap." He sent her into a deep healing sleep. Then tucking the covers around her, he bent over and kissed her forehead. "Sleep a sweet healing sleep little one, with many peaceful happy dreams."

Straightening up, he helped Aili carry the rest of the supplies back to his study. His sons hopped to their feet, gathering around him.

"Athair will she be alright?" asked Rigalis.

"Yes my sons, she will be alright. But she must rest now." Liam looked at his sons' concerned faces. They had waited an hour as Liam worked on Ginger's side.

"I suggest you all go to your rooms and rest as well before you go to your lessons," he told them. "She will not wake until tomorrow morning."

"But Athair," protested Owain, "we wish to stay by her bedside in case she should need anything."

Liam shook his head emphatically. "Absolutely not, my sons. Your presence might disturb the lady." The disappointed look on their faces softened his heart. "Dear ones, I know you are worried about the lady, but she will be alright. Let her rest quietly now and in the morning perhaps you can see her."

He smiled at his anxious sons. They had so much in them that was good about the Light Elves. Their concern for a wounded human, their bravery in defending her from Braen. Had he even mentioned that to them?

"My sons, I am very proud of you. Your actions today prevented the lady from losing her life. Your quick answer to Braen's threat and the way you escorted her safely to Nantuor was very professional. The Royal Guard could not have done better, and I am very proud of each and every one of you."

His sons' faces shone with joy at such high praise. His eyes sparkling, Rigalis gave his father a bear hug. Liam put his arms around his youngest son, a lump forming in his throat. He praised them far too little – he would have to remedy that. In turn, each son received an embrace and a kiss on the cheek from their proud father.

"Go and rest," he ordered. "I will keep you informed if there is any change in the lady's condition."

His sons obediently bowed assent and left the room. Liam turned and looked back at the care room. Ginger should sleep the rest of the day. He went in and checked her pulse one more time. It was slow and steady.

He left the room and returned to his study. His counselors Ranal, Tiernan, and Egan were waiting for him. So was Oriana, the beautiful daughter of an elven lord. She was quite taken with Liam and never missed an opportunity to try to draw him into a romantic setting.

She stepped forward smiling. "My lord, I believe you promised me a walk in your gardens this afternoon."

Liam smiled kindly at her. "I am sorry Lady Oriana, but I am unable to keep my promise today. A serious situation has arisen that requires my absolute attention."

Her smile turned into an ill-concealed pout. "But my lord, you promised. And a king should never break his promises."

"Oriana!" Ranal reprimanded her with unusual sharpness. He knew this elven lady well. She was the spoiled daughter of an elven lord who had died long ago. With no family left to restrain her, she had become a handful for anyone to discipline. She usually got what she wanted no matter what she had to do to get it. *Well not today, and not by showing disrespect to her king*, Ranal thought.

He looked sternly at her until she dropped her eyes. "You will never speak in such a manner to the King again. You will now go to your rooms and leave the King in peace. Is that understood Oriana?"

She looked up at him to protest and was caught by his piercing gaze. She had never realized how quickly those laughing blue eyes could turn to piercing blue intensity. She was aware of a slight breeze fluttering past her as his body began to glow slightly, his anger barely under control. With a thrill of fear in her heart, she replied meekly, "Yes my lord. My apologies. I meant no disrespect."

"You have been left with no correction far too long, Oriana. I intend to remedy that," Ranal said warningly. "Now go to your rooms. I will speak with you later this evening about your disrespect."

She dropped her head and left the room. Characteristically, she went for a walk instead of returning to her suite.

Liam and his counselors looked at Ranal, then Liam poured a small glass of cordial and handed it to him. "Here," he said jokingly. "You need this more than I do."

"Oriana needs to learn more respect. As it is she respects no one. That can lead to trouble for her and everyone around her," noted Ranal, still a bit miffed at the elf-maid's disrespect of his best friend.

His friends looked at him and then burst into soft laughter.

"I feel," said Tiernan gravely, "that she is in for more trouble than she knows if she defies a certain elf-lord again."

"And you accuse *me* of having a temper," scolded Egan good-naturedly.

Ranal chuckled to himself and drank the cordial Liam had given him. Liam turned back to his desk. "And now gentlemen, to business."

General Arth came in just as Liam sat down at his desk.

"My king, there is no sign of Braen. He has left the area and disappeared. I have trackers out trying to locate him." Arth paused. "They have orders to shoot to kill."

"A wise choice considering what we are dealing with," commented Tiernan.

"Especially since he tried to murder a helpless woman," added Egan.

Liam smiled, remembering Ginger's fiery response to Braen's attack. "A woman yes, but not quite as helpless as Braen assumed. She gave him a terrible shoulder wound for his trouble."

"Indeed?" exclaimed General Arth, surprised. "Quite an amazing woman. Most humans would be quite terrified when faced with such an evil being."

"She actually fought back?" asked Ranal, incredulous.

"Oh yes," said Liam. "In fact she said she wanted to go after him when she was back on her feet."

The elves shook their heads in wonderment. Such courage! These humans were such amazing creatures.

Several miles away Braen lay beside a small stream trying to wash the blood from his shoulder. He heard a soft rustle in the lilac trees that hung over the stream on the opposite bank. He looked up sharply to discover a young elf-maid watching him. She was obviously a Light Elf; her face was alight with elven power and beauty. Her golden hair ran past her hips in thick, luxurious waves. It was intermingled with tiny jewels that glittered in the golden sunlight. She was a picture of elven perfection, obviously of noble blood.

"She looks a bit haughty," thought Braen as he contemplated how he would get close enough to slice her open like a melon. Her blood should taste sweet. He smiled at her, willing her to curiously come to him.

"I have not seen you at Nantuor, my lord," she said. "Are you a visitor from the Realm? I didn't know the Rift had been reopened."

"No, it hasn't," answered Braen, filing away that bit of information for later. "I am of one of the noble houses separated from King

Liam's forces during his retreat to the sea. After many years I was able to find my way to my King." In between lies, Braen contemplated where he would make the first cut. "King Liam found me on the beach and nursed me back to health. I was later assigned as a guard outside the valley."

As he stood smiling, Braen reached his right hand under his cloak and gripped the handle of his knife. If he were careful she wouldn't die immediately. He had a lot of pent up anger, and he would like the opportunity to vent it. He would make her beg for death.

She smiled at him and then gasped at the gaping wound in his shoulder.

"Oh, my lord," she exclaimed. "How did you get such a terrible injury? I will get my lord Liam at once. He is a mighty healer."

She started to step away toward the path back to Nantuor. In a flash Braen was on the path in front of her.

"Why do you not treat it yourself?" he asked, his voice raw silk as he looked deeply into her eyes. "If I must be tended, I would prefer your exquisite beauty to the stern features of a king." He laughed and willed her to relax as his hand tightened on his knife.

Her lovely face turned into an unbecoming frown. "Too stern sometimes, my lord," she said, her lips turning into a lovely pout. She was irresistible.

Braen caught the note of discontent in her voice. He smiled to himself. A discontented Light Elf could be useful. He decided to let her live a few moments longer to get some information from her.

He had learned long ago how alluring he was to the maids of the Light Elves. His charm had proved useful when stalking them. They would never suspect they were to be tortured and murdered until it was too late.

He looked into her eyes and gave her his most attractive smile. "What troubles you, my little lamb?" he cooed softly as he took her hand in his and kissed it warmly.

Oriana blushed to her toes, her ear tips turning a lovely pink. She wasn't able to meet Braen's fierce green eyes as she told him of her unsuccessful efforts to charm Liam.

"He does not appreciate you, my dear. He isn't worthy of your beauty." He was suddenly struck by a deviously brilliant idea. Smiling, he continued, "It was Liam that wounded me. He was jealous of a human female that I had spoken to here on Brisal, so he attacked me. I have never seen King Liam in such a rage. He told me if I ever came to Nantuor again he would kill me."

He turned to Oriana, his eyes full of tears. "I have never known that noble elf to act in such an irrational manner. What has come over him?"

"He is infatuated with that human woman," said Oriana contemptuously. "She is not worthy of the attentions of an elven groom, yet he treats her like a visiting princess. He brought her in yesterday and has had no time for anyone else since. And he promised me a walk in the garden this afternoon." She pouted like a small child.

This could prove a very interesting opportunity, thought Braen. *It wouldn't hurt to have an ally in Liam's household.*

He led Oriana to a log beside the stream. "Come precious one, won't you talk to me awhile as you bind my wound? I am forbidden to go to Nantuor or even be mentioned there. But I feel I will die of loneliness out here by myself. I am all alone."

"Will you not help me my lady?" he implored, adding a note to his voice that he knew would deeply affect her. He watched with satisfaction as a tear rolled down Oriana's face. She sat down beside him and bound up his wound.

He spent the rest of the afternoon sitting by the stream and charming her, using his elven powers to influence her mind, ensuring she fell hopelessly in love with him. When she walked back to Nantuor at sunset, Braen had an unwitting agent planted in Liam's household who would tell him every move Liam made.

Chapter 11

The Morning After

Ginger awoke the next morning to the singing of birds. She yawned, opened her eyes, and then widened them in shock. She was lying in an incredible bed made of emerald green wood woven into intricate patterns. The bed, with an exquisite glasslike finish, was covered in living vines of jasmine and tiny, fragrant pink flowers that Ginger couldn't identify. The enchanting fragrance was better than her best perfume.

The soft, comfortable mattress was covered in cool, white linen sheets. The coverlet was of green silk with finely stitched images of birds, trees, flowers, and deer. The figures were so lifelike she could almost see the birds fluttering from their limbs. Now where had she seen that before? She had a faint memory of something like that, but she couldn't quite bring it into focus.

She smiled to herself. At the moment she was surrounded. Rigalis was on her right, having fallen asleep on the floor next to the bed clutching delicate pink flowers in his right hand. Teagan and Owain were asleep on a couch on her left near the large window opposite the bed. Barram was on the other side of the bed, asleep in a chair pushed close to the bed. Apparently she was surrounded.

Ginger took a deep breath, expecting a sharp pain to shoot through her side. There was none. Putting her hand to her side, she discovered her entire ribcage was neatly bandaged. She felt surprisingly good, considering someone had tried to slice and dice her with an eighteen-inch blade. After what she had seen Liam do with her wound, she suspected he had something to do with her feeling so well.

She looked down at Rigalis. He was sleeping soundly, his dark hair lying like a curtain across his face. Without thinking, she reached out and gently swept his locks aside. He opened his eyes and blinked sleepily, then snapped awake upon seeing her smile. Grinning back, he pulled himself up and whispered, "Good morning my lady. How are you feeling?"

"Better than I did," she whispered back.

Remembering the flowers, he shyly handed them to her. "I thought you might like something pretty to look at when you woke up," he said softly. "I'm afraid they might be a little wilted," he added, looking at the slightly sagging bouquet.

"Oh, I'm sure they will be just fine if we put them in some water," Ginger reassured him. Taking the bouquet, she admired the delicate flowers. "It was very thoughtful of you. Thank you very much . . . uh . . . " she looked at him inquiringly, not knowing his name.

"Oh forgive me my lady. I neglected to introduce myself. I am Rigalis." He pointed around the room at the sleeping elves. "That is Barram, and those two on the couch are Teagan and Owain. We are the sons of Liam."

Awakened by the sound of their names, the other three elves crowded around the bed.

"How do you feel my lady?" asked Owain.

"Are you better?" Barram interjected.

"Oh, I'm fine guys," Ginger replied. "Have you been here all night?"

"No," sighed Barram. "We wanted to stay with you, but Athair made us leave. He said we would disturb your rest."

"So we waited until he left and then slipped in to keep you company – in case you needed something during the night," offered Rigalis. "I hope we did not disturb your rest, my lady. Athair would be very angry."

"Are you upset with us, my lady?" asked Owain, "We meant no harm."

"Now why would I be upset with you for being so kind?" she asked. She added softly, "Staying with me was very thoughtful."

The young elves grinned from ear to ear.

"Can we get you something, my lady?" asked Teagan. "Something to eat perhaps? We would be most happy to go fetch you something."

"Oh, I'm fine for right now, fellas. This bouquet could use a drink though," she said, holding up the flowers. As Rigalis reached for the bouquet, Ginger noticed a large scratch on his hand. "Hey, how did you do that?" she asked as he took the flowers and put them in a glass of water on her bedside table.

"Oh, it is nothing, my lady," he said shyly, "I hurt myself on a jagged piece of wood."

"Well, why isn't it bandaged? It would heal a lot faster."

"It is alright, my lady. Truly, I am fine."

"Sit down Rigalis," she ordered with a smile. "And for the record, I would rather be called Ginger."

The elf obeyed. Ginger gently took his hand and examined the scratch. It wasn't deep but it still should have been covered. Spotting her saddlebags in the corner, she asked, "Would one of you guys mind getting my bags for me please?"

Teagan won the ensuing scramble, setting his prize gently on the bed in front of Ginger. Rummaging around in one of the bags, she pulled out a large package of gummy bears and set it aside, then reached back in and withdrew her small medical kit. Ginger laughed softly as she noticed the young elves fixating curiously on the gummy bears. She opened the package and held it out. "Try these. They are pretty good."

Ginger poured a handful of the treat into all four outstretched hands, then set the package down on the bed. Turning back to Rigalis, she opened the kit and took out some band aids and medical wipes. Rigalis, chewing a mouthful of gummy bears, watched in amazement as she gently cleaned the scratch and covered it with a large band aid.

"You don't even have to tie it!" he exclaimed, showing the band aid to his brothers. Noticing cuts and scratches on the rest of them, Ginger pulled out more band aids.

"Doesn't your mother ever take care of this for you?"

They looked at each other awkwardly. "Our mother is no longer alive, my la . . . Ginger," responded Owain.

The young elves' sad faces touched Ginger's heart. *They really need a mother*, she thought. *That Liam fella should start thinking about that*. She smiled at them, holding up a wipe and a brightly colored band aid. "Next?" she called out.

Liam had a busy morning. He still had to meet with the council to decide what to do about Braen. He hadn't even had time to have breakfast with his sons. *Perhaps if I spent more time with my boys, they wouldn't be so prone to mischief*, he thought. *I really must make the time no matter how busy I am. They need someone to take them in hand.*

Frowning, Liam swept through the door to Ginger's room, his arms loaded with medical supplies and a small silver bottle. He stopped in his tracks at the sight that greeted him. His sons were sitting on the bed encircling Ginger. All five of them were eating breakfast and chattering happily, each elf obviously vying for Ginger's attention. Liam noticed that all his sons sported brightly colored band aids on their hands or arms. Liam's eyebrow raised as he approached the bed.

"I thought my orders were clear, my so . . ."

"Well good morning, your Majesty," Ginger interrupted cheerfully. "And how are you today?"

His sons looked up at him, then at each other. "We were not troubling her, Athair," Owain blurted out. "She wanted us to have breakfast with her. She said it would keep her from getting lonely."

"That's right," declared Ginger. "Care to join us?" She took a bite of egg.

Liam smiled at her. "I have already had my breakfast, thank you my lady. I have brought you some herbs to ease the pain from your wound." He held up the silver bottle.

Ginger swallowed a sip of tea. "Thank you very much Liam, but I already took some pain killers from my medical kit. And please call me Ginger."

The young elves looked apprehensively at their father. They had warned Ginger of his stern insistence that his patients follow his orders to the letter.

Liam stared at Ginger and then set down his supplies. Sure enough, he spoke to her in a disapproving tone. "Lady Ginger, it is not wise for you to medicate yourself. Your wound is very severe and it requires care from a practiced healer."

Ginger tried not to roll her eyes. "For heaven sakes Liam, it's not like I'm going to OD on Tylenol." Liam glared at her silently, provoking her to sigh in surrender. "Okay, okay, I'll follow doctor's orders from now on. Better?" she asked smiling.

"Much, thank you. And now," he said, looking at his sons, "shouldn't you be getting to your studies?"

"They need a good breakfast to be able to study Liam, and they haven't finished eating yet," Ginger noted. She looked at the boys and told them, "You guys finish your breakfast so you can go study." Despite their father's admonition, they immediately began devouring their food.

Liam smiled to himself. *How strange.*

Liam's sons quickly finished their meal and left to study, each gallantly kissing Ginger's hand on the way out. Liam hadn't seen their eyes shine like that in years.

Ginger turned to Liam. "Those are nice boys. You should be proud of them."

"I am" Liam replied as he stepped to her bed to examine her side. He sat down in a chair and started to unwrap her bandages.

"You should tell them so," she said as he unfastened the bandages.

Liam looked up, slightly irritated. "Madam, I appreciate your concern, but I think I know how to raise my own children."

Ginger wasn't impressed. "Then why don't you tell them how proud you are of them? Kids need to hear that from a parent. It means a lot to 'em."

"I am well aware of the psychology of raising children, thank you Madam," replied Liam curtly as he looked over the knife wound. It was healing nicely. A few more treatments and it would disappear.

"Then why were you so grouchy on the road last night?" asked Ginger, looking him in the eye. "And don't call me Madam."

"Madam!" Liam started sharply. Then he stopped himself. This was a human lady who had no previous contact with elves. She didn't know any better. He must be patient.

He started again, gently this time. "Lady, I think I know what is best for my own children."

"Then why are they so starved for attention? Don't you ever just sit down and talk to those boys? They need a father to listen to them. And while we're on the subject, it wouldn't hurt you to find a mother for them either. Every last one of those boys had an untreated scratch or cut on them . . ."

"Madam, please," Liam interrupted irritably. He stopped himself again. Why was he letting this woman aggravate him? She was under his care, and he had to keep calm. He started once again, calmly. "Lady, I am a very capable father I assure you. There is no need to worry about my sons. Now if you will allow me . . ." Turning back to her wound, he placed his hand gently over the gash and sent a burst of healing energy deep into it. He held his hand to the wound for several moments, then lifted it, satisfied with his efforts.

"They still need a mother," Ginger muttered.

Liam ground his teeth and placed his hand back on the wound. This time he sent a massive burst of healing energy through her body, draining his own strength. Ginger was getting on his nerves, and the sooner she was healed and out of Nantuor the better. He sat back and looked at her. She stared back silently, as if appraising him. The look unnerved him and he glanced away. Noticing Ginger idly rubbing her fingers over her wrist, he reached for her arm.

"Does your wrist trouble you Lady?" he asked with concern.

She looked up. "Oh, no. I've worn an old charm bracelet for years, and I'm not used to it not being there. I lost it coming up the path to your house." She bowed her head and looked wistfully at her wrist. "It belonged to my grandmother."

Liam caught the sad note in her voice. He looked at her, noticing something his sons had pointed out the previous day: her eyes were brown and green with flecks of gold. *How unusual. And how beautiful.* They brought to Liam's mind the peacefulness of the forest, with its browns and greens. Looking into her eyes, he felt as if he were staring at a still pool of water, watching the reflections of the trees and the golden sunlight.

Realizing he'd been staring deeply into Ginger's eyes, Liam looked away. Ginger raised an eyebrow, an inquiring look on her lovely face. Liam glanced back down at her side and quickly finished rewrapping the fresh bandages.

He gathered up his supplies, cleared his throat, and told his charge, "You should be well enough to leave by tomorrow, Lady Ginger." He felt he should immediately leave the room before something happened, though he wasn't sure what exactly he feared.

He sighed and stood up, preparing to make a quick exit.

"Liam, thank you for patching me up," interjected Ginger. "I know I am not the most cooperative patient in the world." She held out her hand. Liam looked at it, feeling as if something important was about to happen.

She took his hand in her tiny one and looked up at him with her lovely forest eyes, the warmth of her hand warming his heart. His glance moved from her mesmerizing eyes to her soft lips. She gave his hand a friendly squeeze, causing Liam's heart to skip a beat and sending a shiver up his spine.

What is happening? wondered Liam. *I can't be attracted to this woman. This annoying, opinionated, fiery, disobedient . . . graceful, soft, warm . . .* He closed his eyes and chastised himself. *What am I thinking? This is a patient and a human!*

He took a deep breath, assuming the dignified air of a high elven healer. "You are quite welcome my lady. I am glad to see that you are healing so beautifully . . . er, nicely." Flustered, he felt his mouth turn dry and was strangely unable to continue speaking. So he pulled his hand quickly from Ginger's and abruptly left the room. He would forget about this woman. He was Liam Midir, King of Nantuor. He was in charge of his surroundings and certainly his own feelings. He would brook no obstacle to his rule of this island, be it personal or otherwise. He was in command.

Ranal sat in the tree enjoying the morning breeze. A pain passed through his heart as he thought about similar mornings he'd shared with Eve. His wife had been dead for two thousand years, and he still missed her. He sometimes would come here to the forest, where he'd shared so much time with her. He remembered how he would carry her to a perch at the top of a tall tree, and they would look out over the vast forest together, sometimes talking, other times simply clinging to each other and enjoying the solitude. Tired of being lonely, Ranal had recently contemplated looking for companionship again.

The sound of soft footfalls below brought him out of his reverie. Looking down, he saw Liam walking along the forest floor, moving slowly and scanning the ground as if searching for something. Ranal, ever curious as to Liam's movements, quietly climbed down the tree. Keeping to the bushes, he passed his king and then waited for him in a concealed spot in a curve along the forest path

Liam was searching the ground so intently that he almost ran into Ranal. He looked up with a start into Ranal's smiling face and then, looking slightly embarrassed, dodged his gaze as if caught doing something wrong.

"What are you looking for?" Ranal asked, sweeping his eyes over the ground.

"Nothing," Liam muttered, frowning at his friend's unexpected appearance. He stepped around Ranal and continued his search.

"I just thought with all the talk of late of finding a wife, perhaps you had taken it into your head to look for one," Ranal smirked.

Liam looked up sharply at his friend. Was he trying to be amusing?

"Very funny," Liam remarked before turning his attention back to the ground.

He wasn't amused. In fact, Liam felt like an idiot, out here in the forest looking for some trinket for that woman, with her forest eyes, those soft, exquisite . . . Liam scolded himself. What was he doing out here anyway? He would probably never find that blasted bracelet and even if he did . . .

Suddenly Liam spotted the bracelet and pounced on it like a cat on a mouse.

Ranal watched this performance with a puzzled look.

Ignoring his smirking companion, Liam quickly stuffed the bracelet into his shirt, turning his shoulder to Ranal to hide his discovery. Ranal's sharp eyes caught the bracelet anyway.

Ranal gave Liam an appraising look, a triumphant smile cracking his lips. "You're fond of her, aren't you?"

"I don't know what you are talking about," Liam growled. "We should be getting back. It's almost time for the council meeting." He ignored Ranal's chuckle and led the way back down the path to Nantuor.

Liam stopped at the door, wondering at his own reticence. Why was he so hesitant? He was acting like a young elfling with his first crush. This was ridiculous. It was only a bracelet that he happened to find on the forest path and wanted to return to its rightful owner.

Squaring his broad shoulders, he opened the door and stepped into the room. Ginger was sitting up in bed, stroking a visiting cat. She looked up and smiled. Liam immediately forgot the greeting he had practiced. His mouth went dry again, and he couldn't speak for a moment. He silently moved to her bedside and sat down in the chair. Liam looked at her, or rather, looked into her eyes.

She smiled again. "Hi Liam, what brings you to my neck of the woods?"

Suddenly remembering his remarks, he cleared his throat and began, "I was walking in the forest . . . and happened to find your bracelet. . . . I wasn't looking for it mind you. . . . I just happened to find it . . . and I thought I should bring it back to you." He breathed a sigh of relief. *There – that wasn't so hard. It was only a bracelet after all. A trinket. Of her grandmother's. Such trifles mean a lot to humans.*

He looked up at Ginger and handed her the bracelet. He'd been anxious to deliver it to her – after carefully cleaning it. That was simply the polite thing to do.

Ginger's eyes lit up and she gave him a dazzling smile as she took the bracelet with a little cry of joy. Liam smiled in spite of himself.

She set about trying to fasten it to her wrist. Liam gently took it from her and put it on her with nervous fingers. Her hand brushed his as he finished, and he felt his pulse quicken and his breath grow short. Groaning inwardly, he realized he was falling in love with this woman, and in accord with the nature of his kind, he would stay in love with her all the days of his life. He sat back trembling, not knowing what to say.

Ginger's eyes were on her bracelet. It meant a lot to her. She impulsively reached out and kissed Liam on the cheek. He shut his eyes against the storm of emotion that suddenly raged in his heart. He watched as a delighted Ginger sat looking once again at her bracelet.

"Thank you so much, Liam. I thought this was lost forever." Realizing his odd silence, she looked up at him.

He was still in his chair, his eyes drawn into hers, as he looked at the one who had completely captured his heart. He had come undone – and he didn't care.

Chapter 12

Captive Heart

Liam sat in his study immersed in thought, the pile of documents that demanded his attention lying untouched on his desk before him.

So many things had happened in just a few days: Braen suddenly appearing on his island and seriously wounding his youngest son; Ginger discovering Emily's journal and setting out to find Nantuor; and Braen viciously attacking her on the road.

And then there was what happened yesterday. His heart and mind were still in a state of utter confusion. He counted all the reasons why he shouldn't be involved in courtship. He was the ten-thousand-year-old King of Nantuor, not some lovesick elfling fretting through his first crush; he was the Commander of the Elven Hosts – with four sons; and with a kingdom to rule, he didn't have time for romance.

But somehow all the reasons didn't seem to matter when he thought of Ginger. How could he lose his heart so quickly? He had courted his first wife Aife for ten years before he decided to wed. And she had been the loveliest elf-maid in all the Elven Realm.

But then there was Emily, his second wife. She had been quite a lovely human, and he had lost his heart quickly to her. Perhaps his great love for humanity had something to do with it.

He recalled his father's benediction five thousand years ago upon sending him out of the Elven Realm to become King of the Light

Elves: "Go out into the world my son and protect what the One has given us the honor to protect. And may your affection for mankind only increase with the years."

He sighed deeply. "Well Father, you certainly got your wish," he murmured as he glanced at the door to Ginger's room.

"Talking to ourselves are we?" purred Ranal's silken voice from behind him. "That doesn't bode well for the House of Midir."

Ranal broke into soft laughter at Liam's sour look. "I am sorry my friend. But you have seemed a bit preoccupied these past few days. May I attribute it to a certain lovely young human?"

Still laughing, Ranal stepped back a few paces as Liam arose and stepped toward him.

"Ranal, I am in no mood for your jokes today. If you persist, you may attribute your ejection from my office to your odd sense of humor."

Liam returned to his desk and the parchments scattered there. He sat down and tried to finish writing his report to the High Council.

This only fueled Ranal's amusement. "A bit huffy today, are we?" he smirked as he sat on a corner of Liam's desk. He bent his head over Liam and watched him write. Liam opted to ignore him. After a moment, Ranal gently cleared his throat. "Ahem. My lord, I think 'endanger' is spelled . . . "

Liam looked up irritably. "Ranal, will you please stop hovering over me like a carrion crow? I am trying to finish this report."

Ranal leaned back, looking like his feelings had been hurt. Liam stared at him. "Ranal is there something you want to talk about? I am extremely busy." He motioned toward the papers on his desk.

"Well," Ranal drawled slowly, "I was just wondering when you were planning on finishing Ginger's treatment and sending her home." A devious glint came to his eye as he looked at his impatient friend. "Of course, a longer stay would certainly be more conducive to romance. Perhaps you should . . ."

This brought Liam back to his feet. "Ranal, don't I have enough on my mind right now? Braen is endangering my kingdom, not to mention all of humanity. I certainly don't have time for frivolous romance."

"Of course not my liege," answered Ranal. He flashed that same maddening smile that had caused so many Dark Elves to lose their cool during battle and end up on the business end of his sword.

His grin infuriated Liam further. He sized up Ranal with a grim stare as he wondered why, of all the elves in Nantuor, it was this one who had come to "help" with his personal problems.

"Alright Ranal," he said with forced calmness. "When would you like for me to send her home?"

"Oh, I was just thinking of your happiness, my liege. Heaven knows how stressed you have been lately. I think a nice romance would do you a world of good."

A sullen smile froze on Liam's face. Ranal's words hit close to home.

"Ranal, there is going to be no romance," he said evenly. "I have a kingdom to look after. This is not the time for pleasure-seeking. I will heal her immediately and then send her home."

Liam stepped to Ginger's door and knocked lightly. Invited in, he entered and shut the door behind him. From outside the room, Ranal heard a moment of quiet conversation and then saw a blinding white light glow under the door. A moment later Liam stepped out of the room and quietly shut the door. Weak from his effort, he moved slowly to a side table containing several decanters of fine wine.

Liam attempted to pour himself some wine with his shaking hands. Ranal gently steered him to the couch and then poured the wine for him, smiling sympathetically at his friend as he handed him the glass. Liam took a sip of wine and then leaned back, weary from using so much healing power at once.

He certainly is fighting this romance tooth and nail, Ranal thought. He felt a twinge of pity at his old friend's plight, recalling how Liam had barely spoken during dinner the previous night; he had quickly eaten and then left see to Ginger. Even clever Oriana couldn't keep him at the table. Ranal had also noticed he had absconded with the finest looking dessert on the serving tables. The small golden vase containing one of the best roses from his garden was absent from his place setting as well.

"Liam," he said softly, "why don't you just calm down and admit to yourself that you are in love? There is nothing wrong with that."

Liam sighed tiredly. "Ranal, how can I seek my own happiness when so much evil is threatening my people right now?"

"Perhaps that is when you *should* seek happiness, my lord," replied Ranal kindly. "Cannot two bear a burden more easily than one? Perhaps the One has sent her here for just that purpose. She may not be able to fight the Dark Elves herself, but perhaps her kindness and love could give *you* the strength to fight. Cannot the encouragement of a loving heart be a better tonic than the most potent herbs?"

Liam opened his eyes and looked at his friend. "You are not going to leave this alone, are you?"

"No," responded Ranal. "I care too much for the welfare and happiness of my best friend." His bright blue eyes held that twinkle of mischief that had repeatedly led both of them into trouble as young elflings.

Liam sighed in defeat. "Alright, I love her. Are you happy now, Ranal?"

"Ecstatic my friend," laughed Ranal.

Liam looked toward the papers on his desk. "May I please get back to work now? I have three reports and two farm accounts to finish before supper."

"Oh no, you don't," declared Ranal. "You have weakened yourself by speed-healing Ginger." He stood his full height before his king. "Go to your quarters at once and take a nap," he ordered. "And finish your wine. I want you fully rested before supper. Tiernan, Egan, and I will finish the reports."

Liam started to protest but was hauled off the couch. "Must I sling you over one shoulder and carry you like a stag taken in the hunt?" demanded Ranal. Liam gave his friend a humorless stare, but Ranal's impudent smirk soon had him laughing as he was gently dragged from his study to his suite.

That afternoon Liam took Ginger riding, accompanied by several elves including Ranal and Oriana. As the group rode through some trees, Oriana nudged her horse into Ibby, causing him to slam Ginger's foot against a tree. Liam wheeled around at her cry of pain.

"What happened, Ginger?" he asked as he dismounted. He pulled Ginger from her horse, setting her gently on the grass.

Before Ginger could reply Oriana spoke up. "My horse spooked and caused her horse to run her against a tree, my lord." Ranal didn't find her explanation convincing.

Liam examined Ginger's ankle. "I am going to take you back to the house for healing and some rest."

"Liam," Ginger protested, "I don't need any rest. I'm fine."

"Nevertheless," he said, "we are going back to the house."

"I'll come with you," offered Oriana.

"Oh no," said Ranal. "You will stay here with me. We will return at our own pace." Seeing he would brook no argument, Oriana pouted but remained with him.

Liam gently put Ginger on his horse and climbed on behind her, holding her gently in front of him. He turned and rode off toward the Royal House with Ibby following closely.

At the house, Liam held his hand over Ginger's ankle, releasing healing power into the injured joint. A soft glow shown under his hand and then faded as the healing was completed.

"You are probably getting sick of healing me," Ginger laughed gently as she pulled her boot back on. "Maybe I had better be getting back."

She saw the concern in Liam's eyes. "Well, you said I was alright. And I've been gone five days. I really need to get back."

She paused. "You don't want Leroy to come looking for me do you? If he finds me here, your face will be plastered all over the National Inquisitor before you can say scat."

She laughed at Liam's disturbed look. It was quickly replaced with a regal one.

"I think not, my Lady. He would soon find himself with either a severe case of amnesia or swimming in a pond as a pollywog for a week."

Ginger burst out laughing.

"What is so funny, my Lady?" Liam asked. "I was serious."

"I know. Don't worry, Liam. I won't let anyone find this place. I wouldn't want Leroy to suffer post-pollywog stress syndrome."

"What?" Liam asked perplexed.

"Never mind," she replied, still laughing softly. "I'll start back in the morning. How about that walk in the garden you promised me?"

Liam perked up and offered his arm in courtly fashion. They stepped out onto the terrace and into the vast garden's moonlit perfume.

A pair of elvish eyes watched jealously as Liam carefully guided her through the elegant garden, showing her the loveliest of flowers or pulling down a branch full of fragrant blossoms for her to enjoy. *He is mine. You will never have him*, the she-elf thought as she watched her rival being favored with Liam's most elegant compliments. His smoky voice was raw silk as he spoke gently to her. Oriana's heart seethed with hatred as she watched Liam give Ginger attentions that should have been hers – would have been hers – if not for Ginger's unexpected arrival.

The next morning Ginger rode out with Liam. Oriana's face was impassive as she watched her king ride away, laughing and talking with her rival. *Do not come here again human wench*, she thought. *Next time you will die.*

Oriana slipped out of her suite and walked quickly to the stables. After having the groom saddle her horse, she rode out of Nantuor on the pretense of going for a ride. She went to her meeting place with Braen and waited. An hour later she felt Braen's presence as he slipped up behind her. He pulled her to him and kissed her deeply, willing her to respond. She sighed and relaxed against his shoulder, her head beneath his chin.

"How lovely you look today, my treasure," he purred softly as he caressed her face.

"How was your day?"

"Not good," she pouted. "Liam is involved in some ridiculous infatuation with a human wench."

Braen's eyes glowed with triumph. A weakness! He smiled down at Oriana and kissed her tenderly on the head. How useful she had become. He would have to reward her for this. "Tell me more, my love"

Liam watched Ginger's changing expressions as she rode beside him. She had never seen this part of the island. Long ago Liam had his gardeners decorate the landscape on either side of the road with flowering plants and trees. There were also naturally growing fruit trees and vines, making the path look like a fairy road in an ancient tale. Elegant birds of paradise flitted from tree to tree while peacocks strutted regally alongside the road. Songbirds filled the air with lovely tunes, and petals from flowering trees floated across the road like multicolored snow, making a flowered path for Ginger to ride upon.

I feel like a princess in a fairy tale, Ginger thought idly as she rode along on Ibby.

Little did she know that Liam had called all these beautiful creatures to tarry alongside the road for her amusement and had stirred up just enough breeze to cause the gentle shower of flower petals that covered her path.

She laughed out loud when a white peacock blocked their path, his long tail spread like a tremendous, delicate, white lace fan. Liam first pretended to be stern with him, then plucked a peach from a nearby tree and threw it to the side of the road. The peacock dashed for the treat, and Liam and Ginger continued down the road, laughing at the easy ransom.

As they rode, Liam told her of his many adventures on the island. Ginger heard enchanting stories of giant drakes and hunting parties and friends dancing among the trees during the spring festivals. Liam told a particularly entertaining tale from his childhood about a dare from his brother that resulted in them burning down his mother's prized rose garden.

At that moment, a snow white doe and fawn stepped out onto the road. Seeing Ginger's eyes light up at the beauty of the pair, Liam called to them in Celtic and beckoned them closer so Ginger could pet them. She dismounted carefully, trying not to alarm the animals.

"Do not worry, Lady Ginger," said Liam. "They will not run. I have told them that I am not hunting today."

"Alright," responded Ginger under her breath. She had never seen white deer before. They were beautiful, their snow white hides soft as silk, their huge dark eyes shining with curiosity at the elf-king and his companion.

"These deer belong to the Royal Household of Midir," explained Liam. "They are from the Elven Realm and are exceedingly rare."

"They've got Ol' Trouble beat all to heck," remarked Ginger as she lovingly stroked the doe's sleek neck. It was soft as rabbit fur and held a strange sheen that caught the sunlight softly. *It almost looks like it's glowing*, she thought.

Liam noticed her looking at the doe's coat. "They have a soft glow in the moonlight," he noted.

"Must be heck during the hunting season," she chuckled softly.

"None may hunt them but the Royal House or their guests," said Liam. "Perhaps you would like to go hunting one of these nights, my lady?"

"No," said Ginger, thoroughly enchanted. "I could never shoot one of these guys. They're too beautiful. I'll just stick with Texas Whitetail."

As if understanding the conversation, the fawn gently butted her small head against Ginger's leg, begging to be petted. Ginger smiled and reached down to stroke her little face. "She's so soft," murmured Ginger. "Like a little white rabbit."

"Careful lady," warned Liam softly, favoring her with a gentle smile. He reached down and began stroking the fawn, his lips close to Ginger's ear. "Don't fall prey to the enchantment of the white deer. They have been known to put humans to sleep for several days. We used to take them to humans who were grieving or were worried and could not rest. They would sooth them gently into a sweet, restful sleep with many sweet dreams."

"Boy, you bottle that and you could make a million," joked Ginger as she looked up at Liam.

She found herself caught by his gaze; his gray eyes seemed to draw her to him. Their lips were inches apart. Liam was startled at first, but then, looking into her enchanting eyes, he felt tempted to steal a kiss. He slowly moved a little closer. Ginger stood still, mesmerized by his compelling gray eyes.

Suddenly she felt Ibby bumping her in the back. Her concentration broken, she straightened up, turned, and mounted her horse.

"Guess we better get a move on or we're not going to get back before midnight," she said, ducking her head slightly in embarrassment. What was she thinking? Did she really think he was trying to kiss her? Was she crazy? He was an elven king. And what if she had kissed him first? He probably would have turned her into a parakeet. She shook her head at her own foolishness.

Disappointed, Liam sighed in defeat. But his mood quickly improved when he looked up and received one of Ginger's smiles. *Ah*, he thought, *if you only knew how far I would go for those smiles. What deeds I would do just to gain one of them.*

He smiled back at her and remounted his horse. They started off down the road again, chatting happily. He looked back and his sharp elven eyes spied the troop that accompanied them unseen through the forest. He was no fool, and he would not allow Ginger to come under Braen's attack again – even if he had to have the whole of Nantuor's army escort her home.

His determined look gave way to confusion when he heard Ranal's triumphant laugh in the forest behind them. Only Liam's ears caught the sound of his friend, who was amused by the missed opportunity he'd just witnessed between Liam and Ginger.

Liam cast a royal frown in Ranal's direction, then turned and continued his conversation with Ginger. Behind him in the forest, Ranal and General Arth exchanged amused grins.

It was just after sunset when they arrived at the old rose garden beside Ginger's ranch house. Liam waved to his guards, who moved a discreet distance into the forest to wait for their king. Dismounting and opening the gate to the garden, he grabbed Ibby's reins and gallantly helped Ginger down.

"Thank you, Liam," she said, turning around. She suddenly stopped, having drawn uncomfortably close to him again. Liam caught his breath as he looked at her face in the moonlight. He was enchanted and couldn't stop staring into her eyes.

Finally Ginger broke the long silence. "Well, I guess it's time for me to go in," she said nervously.

"Yes," whispered Liam, still mesmerized by her eyes. He felt himself drifting closer to her as his gaze fell to her soft lips. He slowly leaned forward, having finally steeled his nerve to give her a kiss.

Just then Jake came bounding into the garden. He jumped up on Liam, nearly knocking him down.

"Jake, bad dog," scolded Ginger softly. "I've told you a hundred times not to jump on people."

She took the Great Dane by the collar and pulled him off Liam. The elven king muttered something in Celtic to Jake that sounded like a threat. Jake answered with a threatening growl.

"Sorry about that, Liam," Ginger said. "I'd better take him inside before he starts raising the roof and we have half the ranch coming to see what the ruckus is about."

Liam gave Jake another disapproving look and then took Ginger's hand. "Very well, lady. Sleep well. And may your dreams tonight be as enchanting as your beauty."

He bent and kissed her hand slowly until Ginger felt a slow blush climbing up her cheeks. Finally Jake broke up the moment with a loud bark, nearly jerking Ginger off her feet as he headed back through the gate to the house.

"Good night, Liam," she murmured softly, turning and allowing Jake to pull her through the gate.

Liam watched her until she was out of sight. Liam knelt and kissed the stones where Ginger had been standing. "If I could call the moon and the stars down from the sky," he whispered, "I would wrap them in the blue velvet mantle of the night and give them to you, my sweet beloved." Hearing a slight sound behind him, he turned to find General Arth and Ranal smirking at him.

"I thought you two might have some idea of courtesy and discretion," he said, stiffly eyeing their smug faces.

"And I thought you might have a better battle plan, my lord," responded Arth. "That was two missed opportunities for a kiss by my count."

Ranal bent over in a fit of laughter. Liam raised a royal eyebrow in annoyance.

"I don't recall asking my counsel to keep count – or anyone else," he said sternly, eyeing Ranal. His friend finally caught his breath and straightened up long enough to snicker, "Someone should. You are much too entranced with the lady to keep proper count."

Liam made a disgusted noise at his annoying friends and wheeled to mount his horse. He rode stiffly back down the road to Nantuor, his laughing companions in tow trading their own battle plans, much to his irritation.

Chapter 13

The Charmer

Alta awoke with a start, having heard her name whispered in the wind. She quietly got up from her bed and put on her robe and slippers. She moved as if in a dream, not fully realizing what she was doing. Why couldn't she come fully awake? She heard it again. The words were difficult to make out, but she knew the pleading, tearful voice was urging her to come outside and help him.

Without understanding her own actions, she moved down the staircase and out the door. She crossed the yard, entered the jungle, and walked toward the first patch of forest. Her movements were followed curiously by unseen observers.

Alta moved through the dense forest toward the sound of the cries. As she brushed past a small fir tree a thicket came into view. A male elf sat there sobbing quietly, his hands covering his face. Her heart filling with pity, she moved toward the thicket.

Suddenly an iron hand clamped over her mouth. A strong arm encircled her waist and pulled her behind a large clump of fir trees. "Quiet little one," whispered a male voice.

Finally beginning to wake up, Alta saw she was surrounded by several elves. She looked back toward the thicket. The weeping elf had risen to his feet and stepped toward the clump of trees that concealed her. After listening intently, a sudden change came over his features. As he gave off a low growl, his beautiful face became distorted with rage and his eyes burned with hatred. The hair began to rise up on the back of Alta's neck. Her heart pounded and she shuddered, though she didn't know why.

The elf holding her put his other arm protectively around her shoulders and gave her a reassuring squeeze. "Don't be frightened little one," he intoned in a melodious voice. "I will not let him harm you." She relaxed and waited.

Suddenly, with a flash of motion, the Dark Elf turned and ran. Three elves standing beside Alta quickly gave chase. A bloodcurdling scream rang out, then the forest grew deathly quiet. The elves soon rejoined Alta, who was still being firmly held by a fourth elf.

"Are you alright, dear one?" asked Teagan as he released Alta and turned her to face him.

Alta gulped and stared. "What . . .?" she started.

Teagan gently put a finger to her lips and smiled kindly. "Please don't be frightened, dear one. We will not harm you. We are good elves."

Alta wasn't sure what to think. "But that other elf I saw . . ."

Barram stepped forward and looked down into her frightened eyes. "You need never fear him again. He will not trouble you, dear heart." His bright blue eyes seemed to fill Alta's vision, making her suddenly feel warm and sleepy.

Barram caught her in his strong arms as she slumped over and fell asleep. "Sleep a blessed sleep, dear one. When you awake you will remember nothing of your terrible fright." He kissed her gently on her forehead and started toward the house. His brothers followed, wiping the blood off their swords, a look of grim satisfaction on their faces.

After supper Ginger headed toward her study to finish up some paperwork. Halfway there she stopped in her tracks, feeling a strange, growing urge to go outside. Her heart thumped in her chest and her breath become short. She found herself slowly moving to the front door and out onto the porch. Moving as if in a dream, she walked down the steps and into the yard.

Ginger stood just inside the glow of the porch light looking longingly into the darkness. She could hear a voice calling her. The yearning to go to him, whomever it was, welled up inside her like a flood, drowning out the voice inside that screamed at her to run into the safety of the house.

She heard a soft sigh in the darkness. Her pulse racing, she looked urgently into the darkness, trying to catch a glimpse of him. *There* – she spotted the tip of his black boot under the tree at the edge of the yard. The rest of him was swallowed up in darkness. She looked harder, desperate for a mere glimpse of his face. A shadow in the darkness shifted a little closer to the light, allowing Ginger to see a pair of piercing green eyes shining in the moonlight.

Still in a daze, she swallowed thickly and took a tentative step toward him.

"Hey boss lady, what cha' lookin' at?"

Ginger jumped and spun around to face Chad. Her swift movement startled the young ranch hand.

"Sorry Ginger. Didn't mean to sneak up on you."

Ginger's fever immediately broke, replaced by a sickly cold feeling all over. She started trembling violently. Nearly in tears but not understanding why, she hurried into the house and went straight up to her bedroom.

Chad turned and walked back into the house. Suddenly a shrill scream rang out like the enraged cry of a bird of prey that had just missed its kill.

In the jungle just outside the ranch, Liam's guards looked at each other, knowing there were Dark Elves nearby. Captain Brennus nodded to his first guard unit. Without a word they jumped silently to the ground and disappeared into the jungle in search of their prey. Brennus then sent two guards from his second unit to Nantuor to report the incident to Liam.

Upon hearing the news, the elven king immediately left Nantuor and rode to the ranch with Egan and Ranal. As Brennus briefed him at the scene, Liam felt a growing sense of uneasiness. A human was in danger – he felt it. Ginger's face came into his mind.

"Captain Brennus, I feel the Lady Ginger is in peril. Take your men and search the surrounding area. Egan and Ranal will oversee the search. I will go and see to the lady." He quickly made his way to the ranch house and let himself in the French doors that opened into Ginger's bedroom.

She was asleep. Her bed was drenched in sweat and her nose was bleeding. She moaned as if in agony.

Liam knelt by the bed. He took some tissues from the side table and gently wiped the blood from her face. She moaned again and a tear ran down her cheek. Lightly brushing it away, Liam quietly reached into her mind, trying to calm her. What he found sent icy chills up his spine. His heart pounded with anxiety.

Braen!

Liam reached out with his mind, entering her dream. He found himself standing in a beautiful field full of greenery and flowers, heady perfume wafting gently in the breeze. Far across the field he saw Braen holding Ginger in his arms. Liam felt the presence of his nemesis as the Dark Elf prepared to rip her mind to pieces. Liam began running, anger rising in his heart as he heard Braen speaking softly to Ginger, his lying lips close to hers.

"Precious one, please help me," Braen sobbed. "I do not have the strength to free myself from his evil grasp. If you could only help me, I know I could break free of this evil king. If you could let me draw my strength from you . . . just a little strength." He looked at her and wept hopelessly.

Braen's mesmerizing eyes commanded Ginger to obey. She slowly nodded her head in assent. Braen's face glowed in triumph. If Liam thought what he did to his first wife was horrendous, wait until Liam saw what he would do to this human wench. Braen violently entered her mind, causing as much pain as possible. Ginger flinched as the pain cut through her mind like a saber.

"Oh, Lady Ginger, what have I done?" Braen purred. Ginger, still caught by his eyes, only saw concern shining from them. "Truly I never meant to hurt you," Braen lied softly, satisfaction burning in his jade eyes. "I will not buy my freedom through your pain, sweet lady. I must stop." He moved as if to pull away from her. She couldn't let him go.

Her heart pounded wildly as her body recoiled at her close proximity to the evil creature. But she was so entranced by Braen that she never noticed. "I'm fine Braen. Please don't give up. You have to break free. Keep trying."

Braen felt a surge of exhilaration as he gathered his strength for one final slash at her mind. This would end her once and for all. He would bask in her screams before she died.

Braen was suddenly aware of another presence behind them. He smiled to himself – *Liam*. This would make Ginger's death all the more enjoyable. He knew Ginger was too entranced to listen to Liam now. He could do as he pleased.

Liam took an angry step toward him. Feigning terror, Braen broke away from Ginger. She moved back toward him, desperate to be near him. He gave Liam another phony look of horror and fear.

With anger flaming from his eyes, Liam stepped quickly to Ginger's side, jerked her away from Braen, and moved her behind him. Braen fell to his knees as if to beg for mercy, all the while ripping savagely at Ginger's mind. Ginger gasped in pain. Liam angrily forced Braen away from her, mentally expelling him from Ginger's mind with a tidal wave of anger. At the same time he sent an urgent order to Captain Brennus to deploy his troops and find Braen's hiding place.

Braen reeled backward into the dirt, hitting the jungle floor with stunning momentum. He had forgotten how ferocious Liam's mental powers were. With an angry snarl, he picked himself up and looked out from the jungle at the house, his green eyes catching the moonlight like a cat's. It wouldn't end here. He still hadn't made his kill and he wouldn't allow Liam to cheat him out of the pleasure of presiding over Ginger's death. Suddenly he was aware of more movement around him –Liam's guards were closing in. He stepped into the shadows and disappeared from view. After the guards passed by his hiding place, he sullenly and quietly left the area.

As Braen's form disappeared from Ginger's dream, Liam turned to her. He smiled kindly and held out his hand as she stood shaken and uncertain. "Come, dear lady. Let me lead you from this terrible place." Shivering, Ginger took his hand, her mind still in shock from the savage attack. Liam led her gently from the field and into the real world.

Ginger jumped awake and looked at Liam, terrified. She started to cry, shaking violently from the shock of Braen's assault. Liam gently took her in his arms, kissed her forehead, and whispered, "All is well my Lady, all is well." He cradled her closer in his strong arms and softly spoke into her ear, "Sleep a blessed healing sleep, little heart."

He kissed her lips, perhaps a little longer than necessary, sending her into a deep, healing sleep. He held her cuddled up to his chest for a moment as he sent a fervent prayer to the One for her protection. He gently tucked her back into bed and took up guard nearby. He would not let Braen have another chance at her. He stood watch over her dreams all night, then quietly slipped out her window just before dawn.

The next morning, Ginger woke up determined to go after Braen. With her Desert Eagle on her hip, she prepared to leave. But as she turned from gathering extra clips she nearly bumped into Liam, whose guards had alerted him to her actions. The elf-king stopped her.

"Ginger, this is ridiculous. You can't just go after Braen by yourself. He is far too dangerous." He fixed her with a regal stare. "As king, I expressly forbid it."

Ginger immediately stepped toe to toe with him and stared right back.

"Listen buster, when you use words like *forbid* to me, you better smile." She turned and grabbed the rest of her gear. "I haven't seen the day I need a man's permission to go take care of my own business."

She turned to find her path to the door blocked. Liam stood immoveable.

"Liam," she warned, "I'll say this just once. Get out of my way! Now! That is a direct order."

Liam looked down at her, his eyes blazing. "Ginger, you are not going anywhere."

"Okay." She stared at him a moment, her face unreadable. Then without any warning she crouched down and swept Liam's legs out from under him. He hit the floor with a thud. "I'm really sorry, Liam," Ginger said as she stepped over him. "But I don't take orders from men." She walked quickly to the door. Suddenly there was a whirring sound and a knife pinned her sleeve to the doorway. She tried to pull it out but it was in too deep.

"Dang your hide, Liam!" she yelled as she pulled at the knife. Continually impressed by her spirit, Liam chuckled softly. Now fire blazed in *her* eyes.

"You know Liam, sometimes you elves are just a little too pretty and prissy for your own good," she said as she continued to tug at the knife. "And someday I'm going to kick your butt."

Liam's hand grabbed her elbow and the other hand gripped her chin, bringing her face up to his. He caught her with his eyes.

"Maybe so," he said, "but not today." With that, he sent her to sleep. She woke up at noon to find Liam's troops had formed an impenetrable barrier around the ranch.

Chapter 14

Deceiver

Brennus took one more look around to ensure everyone was at his post and well concealed. Satisfied, he turned his horse and started for Nantuor. Halfway there a rainstorm blew in from the sea and soaked him to the bone. He decided to take shelter under a large oak tree near the road. His grateful mount stepped underneath the drooping branches of the tree – and that is the last thing he remembered before he lost consciousness.

He awoke in utter darkness, his head aching from a savage blow. He was lying on his back on a hard surface. He tried to move and discovered he was firmly tied down to something.

He felt a presence in the dark, one of deadly evil. His skin crawled as he realized it was a Dark Elf. Brennus shivered, feeling the evil being step closer to him. He turned his head and looked into the darkness. Near him there seemed to be an especially dense darkness that swallowed up everything – it was like looking into a bottomless pit. As this darkness stepped closer, he heard a soft snicker and then felt a hand grab the hair on the back of his head and jerk his head around.

The darkness was inches from his face now, as if he were being held over a dark pit. He swallowed nervously and waited.

A voice hissed in his ear, "Not so threatening now, are you? Where's your bow now, mighty warrior?"

The voice sent a thrill of terror down his spine.

Braen!

Brennus closed his eyes, listening for any familiar sounds that could help him identify where he was. A hard slap broke his concentration. The torches hissed to life and spread their flickering light throughout what seemed to be a small cave. He found himself looking straight into the jade colored eyes of the most evil being he had ever seen. As Braen glared into his eyes, Brennus could feel the cold hatred emanating from him; hatred of light, hatred of all living things. Brennus shivered again in spite of his efforts to remain calm.

"I still owe you for shooting that arrow at me," Braen whispered. "One evil turn deserves another. And I have plenty of time."

Brennus felt the cold metal of a knife laid lightly across his face. He took a deep breath and waited for the pain.

Hours later he lay in a pool of sweat and blood, his body quivering with shock. Braen had broken at least three of his ribs and crushed his left hand. His face and body covered in knife cuts at sensitive nerve points, Brennus squirmed in agony. Braen had also rubbed foul smelling poison into the cuts, which added to Brennus' sickening torment. Braen stepped close to him again as he tried to hold back a sob of pain.

"Sweet," Braen hissed as he licked blood from his blade.

"I know you are wondering why I am doing all this," Braen began. "I wanted to leave Liam a little reminder, just to let him know I'm still around. Besides, hiding out can be so boring. One needs a little diversion every now and then. I am sure Liam will not have any trouble deciphering my signature on your face."

"You need no excuses for what you do except your insatiable lust for blood and the suffering of others," Brennus whispered through his pain. "You are a despicable being."

He was rewarded with a savage blow to his mangled face. Despite his best efforts, a cry of pain escaped his lips.

"So, you are not the invincible warrior you appear to be," Braen cooed. "And your brother was an even bigger weakling than you are. He screamed like a coward just before the end."

Braen's words sent a cold stab of anger through Brennus. Evan's fair face flashed through his mind. He turned his head and looked at Braen for a moment and then spit a mouthful of blood in the Dark

Elf's face. He could see Braen's features contort with anger in the flickering torchlight. Braen took a torch from the wall and stood over Brennus.

"You are just like the rest of them," he growled. "More trouble than you are worth. Let us see how the elf-maids will like you now." He reached out and stabbed the burning torch into Brennus' face. Brennus' screams echoed through the cave before he finally passed out.

He awoke in pitch black night. He was laying in the road near the entrance to the hidden ravine leading to Nantuor. He sobbed as the pain of his torture sent his mind reeling with shock. Suddenly a pair of soft hands stroked his head.

"Calm yourself my darl . . . my lord," a voice whispered in his ear. "You are safe. I am going to take you home." He felt someone tenderly kiss his hair.

His vision scarred by the poison, Brennus looked through his bleary eyes to see who it was. He could just make out the face of a she-elf with long dark hair. She helped him up with soft, gentle hands and got him on her horse. She mounted behind him and sent her horse into a gentle walk, trying not to jostle the wounded elf. As they rode along she sang a song of comfort to Brennus, one he hadn't heard since he was a child. It soothed his grief and pain and sent him into a light sleep.

He awoke in Liam's special care room. Liam was on his left and the she-elf was on his right, gently holding his hand. He was covered with a soft, warm blanket. His face and body had been salved with a sweet-smelling ointment that dulled the pain and lifted his beaten spirit. His left hand had been carefully bandaged as had his ribs. His vision had cleared a little, allowing him to see the faces of the two elves close to him, though the room beyond them was a blur. The she-elf smiled sweetly at him and gave his right hand a gentle squeeze.

"How are you feeling, my lord?" she asked softly, her eyes shining as she looked at him. Brennus smiled faintly at her and her face lit up, a faint blush coming to her cheeks.

"I am a little better, my lady" he said weakly.

"Please call me Lynet, my lord," she responded shyly. She had dark green eyes, long dark brown hair, a sweet face, and a gentle smile.

"Lynet," Brennus whispered. "A beautiful name for a beautiful lady. Truly fitting." The tips of Lynet's delicately pointed ears turned a charming shade of pink. Brennus smiled at her again before turning to his king.

"Thank you my lord. How did you find me?"

"It was Lynet that found you on the road and brought you here," Liam replied. "If not for her, you probably would have bled to death before morning."

Brennus looked over at the she-elf. "You have my most sincere thanks, my lady. I owe you my life."

Lynet ducked her head. "You owe me nothing, my lord. It was a privilege to help you."

Brennus frowned sleepily, trying to remember something. "Lynet . . . Lynet. Are you the same Lynet who sang so sweetly last week at dinner?"

Lynet bowed her head shyly and whispered, "Yes, my lord."

Brennus was finding it hard to keep his eyes open. "You have a beautiful voice Mistress Lynet, like the voice of a nightingale. It thrills the heart and comforts the soul. A beautiful voice . . . you are beautiful."

Brennus pulled her hand shakily to his mouth and kissed it gently. "I will never forget my lady . . . Lady Lynet . . . what you have done for me. It will always be in my heart."

Lynet stood abruptly. "I . . . I will get you something to eat, my lord," she stammered and quickly left. Liam watched Brennus follow her with his eyes. He yawned once more and then drifted off to sleep.

Later that evening Liam sat with Brennus as he ate his supper. When he finished Liam pulled a chair to his bedside and looked at him. Brennus knew Liam had something important to tell him.

"Brennus," Liam started. "I wanted to discuss the extent of your injuries with you."

Brennus took a deep breath and looked at his king. "I know that my injuries are grave, my king. And I know Braen's poison will create many scars."

Liam looked into his eyes with compassion. "There will be scarring Brennus. But it will not be forever. I can work on the scars a little at a time. It will take time – probably around a year – but they will all be gone."

He took Brennus' hands reassuringly and continued. "Do not fear, dear friend. The rest of your injuries will all heal as well. Your hand will be normal within two months and your eyesight will recover within a month. You will need someone to help you get around until you are fully yourself. Lynet volunteered to act as your nurse, and I told her she may do it with your approval."

His lips quivering, Brennus did not appear reassured. Liam put his hand on Brennus' shoulder and spoke softly. "Do not fear, dear friend. As I said, the scars are not permanent. I know a year is a long time to suffer, but you have my word, as your friend and your king, they will not remain. All will be well."

The young elf struggled to control his emotions. Liam continued murmuring words of comfort until he finally calmed down. Knowing that sleep would be the best healer for now, Liam smiled at him and then kissed him on the brow, sending him to sleep. Taking his pulse one more time, Liam was relieved to find it steady and slow. The elven king picked up the tray with the dinner dishes and turned to leave the room.

He caught sight of Lynet standing in the doorway, her arms loaded with a pillow and blankets. She was trembling, her eyes filled with tears.

"My king, is there nothing that can be done for Lord Brennus? He has suffered so much already. Can you not heal his scars sooner?"

Liam set down the tray and stepped toward her. Taking the load from her arms, he led her to a chair and eased her into it. He set the bedding on another chair and knelt before her. Lynet's lips were trembling as a tear rolled down her cheek. His eyes filling with pity, Liam gently wiped the tear from her face.

"Little one, I am healing his wounds as quickly as I can. Healing raw flesh can be done quickly. Healing the scar tissue is going to take time, but when I am finished Brennus' skin will be as flawless as ever." Liam reached up and tipped up Lynet's trembling chin with his fingertips.

"Brennus is going to need all the kindness and patience we can muster now. He will feel anger and shame at the scars on his face.

He will resent being treated differently by some of his friends. They will not mean to treat him so, but it will happen. Elves are not perfect. Only the One may make that claim.

"He will also be upset by his dependency on us, which may cause him to lash out without meaning to. He will need all our love and patience until he is himself again. Are you prepared to help him through this, knowing that there will be times when you will have to endure much for his sake – perhaps even endure his rejection and yet still have to continue to help him?"

Liam looked into her eyes. She looked steadily back and lifted her chin. "I would endure anything to see Brennus whole again, my lord."

"You love him very much, don't you Lynet?" Liam asked softly.

She looked at Brennus as he slept peacefully. She flushed slightly and looked back at Liam. "More than I love my own life, my king."

Taking a deep breath, she continued. "How long have you known?"

Liam smiled sympathetically. "It beams from your face like sunlight, little one. I saw your first blush when you met him at the encampment just before we left for the ships. I have watched it develop into love over the years. What I do not understand is why you have not told him. Do you think that he will not return your affection?"

Lynet looked down at her hands.

"My lord, you have seen the beautiful she-elves that surround him every day. I am just a simple singer. I am not from a high family or from a family of great accomplishments. How can I possibly compete with them? What can I offer such a renowned elf-lord?"

Liam lifted her face gently with his hand and stroked away another tear.

"You can offer him the joy and security of a loving, caring heart. That is worth more than all the noble blood and accomplishments in my kingdom."

Lynet smiled gratefully through her tears.

Chapter 15

The Rival

Ginger yawned as she walked down the hall to her room. *What a day!* She went into the shower and let the hot water cascade over her tired muscles. *Not as nice as the hot tubs of Nantuor*, she thought, *but not bad after a long day working cattle*. After slipping into her pajamas and robe, she went into the bedroom.

Liam stepped through the French doors with a handful of jasmine blossoms. He smiled as she approached.

"Good evening, Lady Ginger. Your guards tell me you have had quite a busy day today. I will not keep you from your rest. I only wanted to give you these flowers and to ask your favor."

Smiling, she accepted the flowers along with a soft kiss of greeting on her hand.

"Favor for what, Liam?" she asked, enjoying the jasmine's sweet perfume.

"We will be celebrating Spring Festival a week from now," Liam explained. "It is a celebration of the One's love for us and ours for Him. There will be a hunting party, an archery competition, and many other interesting events across the valley."

He stepped closer to her. "I was hoping you would join our festivities, my lady."

He looked down at her hopefully.

"Sure," she replied. "It sounds like fun. I'll have to find some excuse to get away from the house." She thought for a moment. "I guess I can tell Doc that I need to get away from the ranch for a while to think, and I'm going to camp out for a week."

"That would be agreeable as long as you are not forced to tell a lie. The festival is a celebration of the One, and I would not want you to start it by breaking one of His commandments."

"Well, I do need time to work out some things that I have been wrestling with lately, and as long as I sleep outside part of the time I won't be telling a lie."

Liam kissed her hand. "Thank you my . . . dear lady. It would have been dreary indeed without you there. Yours will be the most elegant tent on the grounds."

He leaned down to kiss her hand again. Just then a night bird began calling urgently from one of the trees near the house.

"Duty calls," he sighed and quickly kissed her hand.

Turning to go, he looked toward the yard. "One day that 'bird' is going to interrupt one too many times," he muttered with a frown as he disappeared over the railing to go find Captain Kendhal.

The sentry outside Ginger's window slipped a little farther back into the darkness. With Liam's remark still ringing in his ears the sentry decided that tomorrow morning he would speak to Kendhal about getting reassigned back at Nantuor. This house duty was getting perilous.

A week later Liam met Ginger at the edge of the jungle just out of sight of the house. She followed him to the road and quickly found herself surrounded by a large group of elves who had moved noiselessly onto the road. They were armed to the teeth. She caught sight of a bird's shadow moving along the ground. She looked up in time to see several huge eagles and their armed riders glide silently overhead as they kept watch on their companions on the ground.

"All this just to go to visit for a week?" Ginger asked Liam.

"I have no intention of risking your well-being on another encounter with Braen," Liam said firmly as he moved alongside Ginger. "Shall we go?" he asked.

He signaled for the troop to move out. Ginger soon lost track of time as she chatted with Liam and his troops on the way to Nantuor.

When they reached the courtyard Liam quickly helped Ginger down and escorted her to her room to prepare for the party. Oriana followed Liam and tried to detain him, but he hurriedly made for his room to get ready himself. Oriana had not seen him so excited in centuries. She grimaced and left for her own room to put on her finest gown. *We will see who outshines whom,* she thought bitterly.

A short time later Liam found himself pacing impatiently back and forth in front of Ginger's door. *Will she ever be ready?* he wondered. *Everyone is waiting!*

Ranal smiled at his king. He noticed Liam had put on his finest clothes and his most elegant crown, one usually reserved for state occasions. He wore a robe of soft gray satin interwoven with silver leaves intertwined into intricate patterns. Around his neck was a silver chain that held an elegant ruby pendant. He hadn't worn the pendant in several thousand years – it signified he was an eligible bachelor.

Ranal figured Liam would surely capture Ginger's attention. Indeed, he expected all the eligible elf-maids in Nantuor to be fawning over his king all evening.

"I would relax if I were you, Liam," Ranal said. "It probably won't be the last time you have to wait on her."

Liam stopped pacing and turned on him sharply. Ranal put up both hands defensively and sat back down on the couch.

Finally Ginger's door swung open. She stepped out and looked up at Liam, feeling slightly anxious. She had never worn such an elegant dress. Its emerald green color shimmered in the waning sunlight. Her feet were adorned with sandals decorated with mother of pearl. On her head was a wreath of jasmine mixed with a multitude of other flowers. Her hair shone in the fading sunlight, the highlights sparkling like fire.

Liam froze and stared at her. She looked like an enchanting elf-maid. He stood speechless, his heart in his throat.

Ranal, ever the lady's man, gave her an appraising look and smiled his approval. He got to his feet.

"Your beauty rivals that of the moon and stars, Lady Ginger," he said as he gave her an elegant bow. Liam still hadn't found his tongue so Ranal nudged his ribs. Liam blinked and came to himself.

"You look quite lovely, Lady Ginger," he whispered, trying to catch his breath. He caught the scent of her jasmine perfume and his heart started to slowly pound.

Ginger smiled at the two elves. "Thank you gentlemen, you look pretty nice yourselves."

Ginger's eyes were on Liam's as he offered his arm in courtly fashion. She placed her hand on his sleeve, and the elven king led her through the corridors and out to the terrace where many elves in fine clothes were gathered. Liam's sons nodded admiringly at Ginger's elegant attire. She smiled back, and the four young elves followed their father and Ginger out onto the terrace.

Lanterns hung in branches and the full moon shone overhead, shedding a softening glow on everything. There were tables, covered in white linen, that sparkled with gold, silver, and crystal. They were loaded with hors d'oeuvres: fruit and cheese, smoked fish, and small grilled meats on golden bejeweled skewers. There was even a large tray stacked high with honey smoked quail, an elf favorite. Indeed, Ginger noticed there was a lot of honey around – the elves seemed to have quite a taste for it. She even saw several elegant silver basins filled with mead, a wine made from honey.

She felt self-conscious as she surveyed the crowd of elven nobles and sensed their otherworldliness. She was unnerved by the immense power emanating from them, which made her feel like a small child among angels. The feeling was almost overwhelming, but Ginger was determined to overcome it. After all, she was a Christian too, and the ground at the foot of the cross was perfectly level.

Oh for heaven sakes Ginger, she told herself, *find your spinal column and calm down. These are the good guys.*

She was startled to glimpse one golden haired she-elf staring at her angrily. *Well, what put a cockle burr on her coattail?* Ginger wondered before losing her in the moving crowd.

Oriana, schooled in millennia of courtly behavior, was trying not to betray her disgust. *Liam was escorting that human woman! How dare he! How could he lower himself?* She grabbed a piece of cheese and stuffed it inelegantly in her mouth.

"He'll be bored with her soon enough," she thought with a huff. *"She is merely human. He is an elf, and a king as well. But he's staring into her eyes like a lovesick elfling. What* does *he see in her?*

She sipped at a glass of wine. *Perhaps she is just a diversion: a pet, or a toy. He could not actually want her, could he?*

Liam, beaming like the sun, carefully squired Ginger through the group, introducing her to all and sundry while she valiantly attempted to remember names and faces. Eventually they circled back to Oriana.

"Lady Oriana, this is my . . . this is Lady Ginger. You remember her from the hunt." Liam bowed slightly to the tall she-elf dressed in white, a silver string of diamonds and pearls woven through her golden hair.

Ginger recalled her angry stare as the she-elf looked her rival up and down. "Of course, Lady . . . Ginger?" She bowed slightly in return.

The two females glared at each other in silence. Sensing the tension, Liam's sons fidgeted nervously. Finally Ginger smiled at Oriana, wondering what was on her mind.

Oriana took Ginger by the arm and said gaily, "If you do not mind Liam my dear, I shall just take her and introduce her to some of the ladies present."

Liam tilted his head curiously at Oriana. She was usually rather distant with strangers – perhaps she was intrigued because Ginger was so unusual.

"I would appreciate that, Oriana. Thank you." Liam took Ginger's hand and pressed a warm kiss to the inside of her right wrist, his eyes never leaving hers. Ginger felt a thrill course through her. It was a moment before she realized Liam had strolled away, his sons in tow.

Missing none of this, Oriana felt her blood begin to boil. She looked at Ginger's gown and sniffed in disdain. *My, my, my, the human is trying to shine here,"* she thought jealously. *"Looks dull as swamp water to me . . . like wrapping silk around an old hen. And those highlights in her hair, makes her look as if her head's on fire!*

She reached out with a bejeweled hand and pinched an edge of fabric on Ginger's right sleeve. "How . . . *nice* you look Lady . . . ah, Ginger was it?"

Having maneuvered Ginger to a group of her friends, the she-elf pulled back a moment and looked the human up and down. "Ginger . . . such an unusual name. Named for a spice, were you?" Oriana smiled at her friends.

"Actually, I was named for my grandmother," retorted Ginger. "She spent a lot of time during World War I taking care of frightened aristocrats who decided to cut and run when the fighting started." Ginger took in the aristocratic air of her antagonist. She could almost hear Oriana sniff in disgust. "Well, if you are talking about humans, that is understandable. They are often weak and in need of protection."

"That's what you're here for, isn't it?" Ginger asked smiling.

Oriana smirked and nodded regally.

"You're not doing a very good job, are you?" Ginger asked sharply, looking her straight in the eye. "I didn't notice you leaping to the rescue when I got sliced and diced by Braen."

"I am a member of a high elven family," Oriana responded contemptuously. "I don't participate in brawls between humans and other lower species. And dear Liam is the healer amongst us. Lucky for you."

Now it was Ginger's turn to look Oriana up and down. "You're a bit taken with yourself aren't cha' sweetie?"

Oriana bristled, her eyes blazing. Ginger steadied herself, waiting for her next move.

Just then Liam came back and took Ginger silently by the hand. Bowing to the circle of she-elves, he said quietly, "Ladies. Thank you for entertaining Lady Ginger while I was seeing to some arrangements." He looked down at his companion. "Come, dinner is being served."

Chapter 16

Trouble

Liam carefully escorted Ginger to the Great Hall for the feast. It was a huge room with elegant arches opening out onto the terraces. The long table shone with gold and silver accented by precious gems. Bowls of flowers were everywhere, and candlelight sparkled about the room. Each chair was twined with a garland of flowers. Ginger noticed with a smile that her chair was twined with sweet-smelling ginger blossoms. It sat at Liam's right hand, a seat Oriana usually managed to secure. Liam's sons sat across from Ginger. Oriana and her friends had been moved several chairs down the table to Liam's left.

Everyone stood while Liam said the prayer of thanks for the meal. Then he moved gracefully to Ginger's side to seat her in her chair, his hand placing a lingering caress on her arm. Oriana was seething.

Liam insisted on serving Ginger, choosing the finest dishes from many trays offered them. As they dined he cajoled her into speaking of her time as a Texas Ranger. She described several difficult drug busts, and then when Liam begged her to tell more, she spoke of her time working on the border. Halfway into her story an aide stepped lightly to Liam's side and motioned that he was needed. Reluctantly leaving Ginger with a tender kiss to her dainty hand, he stepped away and huddled with his counselors.

Oriana glanced at Ginger and then spoke disdainfully in a low voice. "She thinks to capture the heart of a king when she speaks like a country bumpkin. How poetic she sounds . . . like the braying of a lovesick donkey."

Flushed with embarrassment, Liam's sons looked at one another. How could Lady Oriana so blatantly insult a guest? Perhaps Lady Ginger's human ears did not hear.

Ginger smiled at Oriana, but it wasn't a friendly one. In Texas it was the kind that usually came before a fight. *Apparently*, Ginger thought, *this little heifer underestimated the quality of human hearing – or maybe she just didn't care. Well, maybe I could* make *her care.* Looking at Oriana, she spoke in an almost soundless whisper.

"You know Oriana, you strike me as being a bit too pretty and prissy for your own good. Care to step outside later and have a little heart to heart?"

Owain choked on his juice and burst out coughing. His brothers pounded him on the back while trying to conceal their laughter.

Oriana's eyes registered her shock. How dare this human speak to her in such a way! But her retort was stilled on her lips by Liam's return.

"Are you alright Owain?" he asked his son.

"Yes, Athair, I am fine." Owain smiled. "It was simply a matter of . . . how was it you put it, Lady Ginger? Letting one's mouth overload one's equipment?" His brothers snickered at the comment.

Liam sat down and insisted on hearing the end to Ginger's story. When she finished Liam took her hand. "My lady, rarely have I heard of so much adventure in so short a time. You are truly unique, in spirit as well as in beauty." He looked deeply into her eyes and then kissed her hand in salute.

Ginger blushed as she smiled at Liam's compliment.

The rest of the dinner progressed with Ginger receiving most of Liam's attention and Liam's councilors asking numerous questions about the world outside their island. Ginger gave them a short world history lesson of the past century.

"I felt back then as if something were terribly wrong," said Tiernan when he learned of the two world wars.

"We all did," added Liam. "We prayed constantly for several decades before the feeling lifted. It cheers me to know that the evil troubling your people during those times was defeated."

"And then there was 9-11," said Ginger. She told of that horrible day and the war that followed.

Liam was silent for a moment. "Lady, is this war still going on?"

"Whether it is an official war or not, it still goes on," Ginger said, " until the danger is wiped out."

"This will also be in our prayers until it is resolved," said Liam.

"And what of your own history, Lady Ginger?" asked Ranal. "I would be interested to know what country gendered such an entrancing woman."

Liam grimaced at his friend. Ranal smirked back.

"Who were your ancestors, little one?" asked Tiernan. "Where did they come from?"

"Yes," said Egan. "Perhaps we would know some of them."

Ginger proudly told them about her ancestors and their courageous stand at the Alamo. The elves listened in awe.

"What a brave group of comrades," commented Liam solemnly.

"Would that we could have been there to help them," said Barram, his young archer's heart burning with passion. His brothers clamored their agreement, the fire spreading around the table.

"What noble warriors," said another archer. "There should be a memorial for them," piped up another.

"There is," said Ginger softly, family pride burning in her eyes. "They won't ever be forgotten."

"We should have a memorial for them here," suggested someone.

Oriana was aghast. A memorial to petty human squabbling when none existed for her own noble line? What an insult to her family's heritage!

"Athair, what about the hill in the archery fields?" suggested Teagan. "It would be a fitting place for such a tribute." His brothers heartily agreed.

So it was decided to put a memorial to the heroes of the Alamo on the archery fields of Nantuor. Ginger couldn't seem to stop smiling after that. Liam was entranced.

After dinner most of the elves returned to the terrace to enjoy the night. Oriana slipped away to a corner far from Ginger. She secured a seat with an unobstructed but discrete view of Liam and his new companion. An alert Ranal missed none of this.

Ginger stood at the exquisitely carved railing overlooking the valley of Nantuor, its beauty lit by a radiant full moon. The perfume of roses and jasmine was in the air. The soft moonlight shone down on Liam's gardens like a gentle shower of silver light. It sparkled on the waterfalls around the valley, turning them to liquid silver and shining on her hair with a soft glow. Fiacra's watchful children wheeled overhead.

Liam stood behind Ginger, his heart caught in his throat. She was so beautiful in the moonlight, like an elven princess standing in the courts of old. If he was going to enter courtship, now was the time. He stepped forward, a million thoughts and emotions warring with him at once. It had been so long since he had courted a maid. Taking a deep breath, he started his suit.

Ginger felt Liam approaching her, his presence raising the hair on the back of her neck. He slowly began to unshutter his power to allow Ginger to become accustomed to his true elfish nature.

She shivered slightly as Liam took her hand and laid it on his sleeve. Her heart pounded at being so near him in his unshielded state, giving her difficulty in catching her breath. Liam shuttered his power a bit and allowed her to readjust to a more comfortable level. She started to relax as Liam sent a gentle command to her body to calm itself.

Keeping his warm hand over hers, he led her from the terrace.

"There is something I want to show you, Lady Ginger," he said softly in her ear.

His warm breath sending a shiver up her spine, Liam led her down into his private garden. A soft mist swirled at their feet as they moved down the moonlit path. He walked her slowly through the moonlit garden until he was sure they were alone. He stopped and looked at Ginger. A feeling of immense power radiated from him. Ginger could not look away from his eyes, which seemed lit from within by some strange power.

"You are the most lovely flower in my garden," he whispered as he kissed her hand tenderly. "The most exquisite blooms in the Elven Realm pale before your beauty."

Flustered, Ginger took a step back. She could feel her cheeks flush as she turned to look at some roses. What was wrong with her? Liam wasn't being threatening; and she never acted this shy around men.

Liam followed her, his eyes tender with emotion. "Lady Ginger . . ." he started softly.

Ginger swallowed nervously. "These are really beautiful flowers, Liam. I've never seen anything like them." She stepped away until the rose bushes blocked her retreat. She was anxious, unsure if she liked this feeling of not being in charge. Why did Liam have to be so unnerving when she was least ready for it?

She felt him come up behind her. The air seemed to be charged with electricity. She trembled as he put his hands on her shoulders and gently turned her around. "Precious one, please let me have your attention for just one moment."

She looked up at Liam. His face was intense with emotion as he looked deeply into her eyes. A slight breeze seemed to flow past him as he gently unshuttered more of his power. His eyes turned a darker, storm cloud gray. He looked down at her for a moment and then spoke.

"Do you like it here?" he asked gently.

Ginger stood uncertain for a moment. Why would he ask that? "I . . . I think it is a beautiful home, Liam. Anyone would like it here."

He stepped closer until their faces were inches apart. She felt an immense power surging before her, like she was standing on the brink of a raging river. "Would you like to stay a little longer?" he whispered.

"I . . . I . . ." she stammered. She stopped and tried again. "I have to get back. I . . ." Her voice trailed off as his presence overwhelmed her. She couldn't think of anything to say.

Liam moved closer and took her gently in his arms. He reached down and gently kissed her lips with his own. Ginger's heart pounded as Liam whispered, "You could stay here a while longer, could you not Ginger?"

Pulling her closer, he enveloped her in his strong arms and kissed her gently. Ginger's head spun. His kiss wiped out the world around her; she felt like she was being swept along on a raging current. When he released her, she was shivering. She stepped back out of his embrace feeling dizzy, uncertain of what to do next. Then she did something she hadn't done since she was a kid. She ran away and didn't stop until she was in her room.

Liam started to follow her but was deterred by a firm hand on his arm. He turned and looked into Oriana's eyes.

"Let her go, my Lord," she said with a demure smile. "She is hardly worth your attentions." Her hand caressed Liam's arm.

"It is I who shall decide what her worth is, Oriana," Liam said with a frown. He pulled himself from her grasp and ran through the garden after Ginger.

Oriana stood for a moment in silent indignation. *How could he choose that . . . human . . . over me? I am the daughter of an elven Lord*. Her heart boiled with hatred as she listened to Liam's footsteps fade into the night.

Liam arrived at the royal quarters and ran down the hall until he reached Ginger's room. The door was shut tight. Pausing to gather his thoughts, he finally stepped to the door and put his lips close to the wood.

"Ginger?" he said softly. There was no response. "Please answer me," he pleaded softly.

After another moment of silence he heard her approach the door.

"I'm getting ready to go to sleep, Liam," she said falteringly. "Can we talk in the morning?" As she drew close to the door, she felt his unshuttered power flowing through the wood.

Liam smiled to himself. "I did not mean to frighten you with my ardor. I am sorry."

He heard an indignant huff through the door. "I was *not* frightened. You just startled me, that's all. I'm tired anyway, and I'm going to sleep." Ginger frowned at Liam through the door. Just why did he think he could frighten her?

Liam leaned his head against the door, wanting to be closer to her. "Let me in for a moment so I can talk to you," he implored. He could will her to open the door, but no honorable Light Elf would do such a thing.

Ginger tensed and glanced at the lock. Yep, it was locked. "I'm going to sleep Liam. Good night."

"Just open the door then. Just for a moment. Please," he said in a plaintive lover's voice.

He stood in silence a few moments. Then the doorknob slowly turned and Ginger opened it a crack. "What?" she asked suspiciously.

Liam smiled down at her, catching her with his eyes. Ginger found she couldn't take her eyes from his, nor could she move. She felt a calming warmth flood over her, a feeling that there was no reason to be afraid. She opened the door wider.

Holding her gaze, he reached down and took hold of her hand. He feathered her wrist with kisses. "I just wanted to tell you goodnight," he said softly as he kissed her lips.

Her heartbeat quickened once again at the elf-king's kiss. She felt as if she were being swept away by the power surging from him.

Releasing her, he smiled and told her goodnight. Then he turned and strode down the hall. He felt a bit guilty at using such ancient trickery to steal a goodnight kiss, but all's fair in love and war. He smiled happily as he walked back to the terrace.

Ginger stood at the door puzzled. How did he do that? She hadn't been able to move. And she never let a man kiss her without her permission! Huffing indignantly, she shut the door, climbed into bed, and drifted off to sleep to the sound of elven music.

Oriana stood fuming in the shadow of a nearby pillar. She dug her nails into her palms until blood flowed. Liam would pay for this insult. He would pay dearly.

The next morning Ginger awoke to the sound of the valley in song. The elves' angelic voices blended with the eagles' deeper tones to create an anthem that seemed to rise up to heaven itself. She couldn't understand the words, but the melody brought up memories of home and love and joy. The longer she stayed in the company of the elves, the more she felt at peace, it seemed.

The sound of voices in the hall caught her attention. Several elven maids came in to help her bathe and get dressed. As they waited on her like a queen, she felt a growing sense of anticipation – there was something special about this morning. She remembered Liam telling her that today was the . . . what had he called it? The Day of Praise?

Several she-elves brought in a gown and several small trunks. They talked excitedly as they opened the trunks and laid the clothes out on the bed. Ginger stared at the gown in awe. It looked to be made of spun gold, as fine as spider's web yet it shone like silk. The matching tiara and jewelry were just as fine and otherworldly. Her attendants giggled as they helped her into the gown and shaped her hair around the tiara. When they were done she looked into a large mirror. She saw a queen looking back at her.

An escort soon came to guide her to the main terraces where Liam was waiting. She heard him catch his breath when she stepped into view. Looking every inch a king, he was dressed even more elegantly than the previous night, his golden crown glittering with jewels and a bright ruby pendant hanging from his neck. He bowed over her hand with a formality befitting a state occasion. She wished she had listened more carefully last night at dinner instead of simply being overwhelmed by Liam's elfish charm.

A hush fell over the terrace as Liam said the prayer of thanks over the meal. The blessing touched her heart with its simplicity and sincerity. Liam then turned to help her into her chair. She was seated to Liam's right with his sons across from her and to her right. She smiled faintly; once again she seemed surrounded by the Midir clan.

Ginger glanced around at the tables. Elegantly set in lace and silk, they were loaded with food. Each was covered with jewel-encrusted golden dishes, serving plates, and utensils.

Liam loaded her plate high with delicacies from each dish while his sons vied for her attention. Each seemed to have a hunting story that outdid the previous one in bravado and adventure. Ginger smiled as she listened to each tale and enthusiastically asked questions. Finally Liam broke in.

"My children, have any of you told Lady Ginger of the significance of this day?"

All four princes spoke at once. Smiling, Liam held up his hand for silence and told Ginger, "Please relax and enjoy your meal. I will tell you."

As she ate breakfast Liam explained The Day of Praise. This was the day that the One's generosity was celebrated. Every elf displayed his finest possessions – not for show, but to display them before the One as His own possessions that had been generously lent to the elves. The display was considered a joyous surrender of all they owned at His feet.

Breakfast was filled with laughter and song as the elves celebrated their love for the One. Ginger was enchanted by their angelic voices. Liam's voice was especially moving, the great love he held for his Creator flowing in his song like a rushing river.

When the song ended, Ginger's eyes were filled with tears. She had never heard anything so beautiful. Liam reached over and gently brushed the tears away. His touch was gentle, and his eyes were tender and loving. Then, as if by an unheard command, everyone rose, took each other's hands, and bowed their heads. Ginger quickly followed suit. She felt immense power flowing from the elven group as they prayed to the One. The words were strange and melodic, more like a song.

Ginger felt the love of God settle over her like a blessing. All her tension drained from her body, and every care faded away at His presence. She didn't feel overwhelmed as with the elves – it was more like being held in her father's arms. She felt safe and protected and unconditionally loved. She sighed in relief and started a prayer of her own. The elves ended their prayer just as Ginger did, the entire group in perfect unity.

The elves left the tables laughing and talking, some breaking off into small groups, singing softly as they walked the grounds.

Liam took Ginger's hand and led her gently toward his private garden, which was even more breathtaking in the sunlight. It was lush and green, bursting with beautiful flowers. It seemed that just by growing in this valley the plants were more colorful and robust than any she had ever seen. The trees were filled with climbing roses and jasmine, their trailers hanging down like elegant ribbons. The air was filled with their exquisite perfume. Flower petals floated around her, spreading their perfume along the path. Exotic birds of paradise flitted from tree to tree as peacocks strutted below them. A small herd of white deer grazed nearby.

Liam felt the time was right to again present his suit to Ginger. He gently led her down the path deep into the garden.

As they stopped walking Ginger recognized the same spot where Liam had taken her the night of the party. She tensed up, wondering what was on his mind. But instead of approaching her for a kiss, Liam took her by the elbow and led her to a large bed of rose bushes at the far end of the path. He began to point out roses of unusual color and shape, remarking on their rarity and beauty. As he did so he sent out a soothing thought to Ginger's mind, calming her fears.

Without realizing it, Ginger began to relax. Satisfied, Liam began his suit.

"The roses look quite beautiful this morning, do they not Lady Ginger?" he asked, looking casually over the colorful display before them.

"Yes they do," replied Ginger. A silver and lavender bloom caught her eye. She smiled and stepped closer to the rosebush. "I have never seen a rose that color before."

"Yes," said Liam. "It is a beautiful, rare blossom." He stepped closer behind her, his breath warm on her hair. "Much like yourself, sweet lady," he whispered in her ear.

Ginger froze, unsure how to react. She felt anxious as she sensed Liam unshutter his power again. The hair rose up on the back of her neck.

As Liam gently kissed her hair, she trembled and turned around. Taking a deep breath, she started to speak.

"Liam, I appreciate your attention but . . ." she started nervously. Liam caressed her face gently with his fingertips, sending a shiver down her spine as he looked deeply into her eyes. She began again. "But we hardly know each other and . . ."

Liam gently kissed her lips. "I know you well enough, sweet Ginger. My heart is so lonely whenever we are apart. I would like to ask you . . ."

Suddenly an alarm bell sounded. Liam looked at Ginger dejectedly. “I have to go,” he said with a quick sigh. He began to walk away but then, with a determined look, he hurriedly pulled off his ruby pendent and put it around Ginger’s neck. Worn by unmarried male elves, the charm is placed around the neck of the one they love when they propose marriage. Liam used it to mark Ginger as being taken until he had a chance to propose.

Ginger was confused. “I’ll explain later,” Liam told her. “Please, please wait for me here. I will be back as soon as I can.” With that, he rushed from the garden.

Ginger sat down on a nearby stone bench and looked at the pendant curiously. The stone and silver shone as if they had just been created that morning. The ruby glittered in the sun, shining as though lit from within. The silver’s elegant filigree was exquisite. Ginger had never seen such workmanship.

Suddenly Ginger heard a gasp. She looked up and saw Oriana staring at her in shock. She knew what the pendant signified. *He can’t give it to . . . her!* she thought fiercely. *It should be mine!*

“Thief!” she spat at Ginger.

“Now just a minute sister . . .” Ginger started angrily.

“Ladies! Please!”

It was Ranal. Having seen Oriana follow Liam and Ginger into the garden, he’d kept her in his sights. He figured that Oriana, as the spoiled daughter of a high elven lord, as someone who hated humans, and as a she-elf insanely jealous of Liam’s attentions, might not take the current situation well.

“She stole Liam’s pendant!” snarled Oriana defensively.

“I did not!” protested Ginger. “He gave it to me!”

“Impossible!” yelled Oriana indignantly.

“Oriana! Please go,” said Ranal sharply. The authority in his voice commanded her obedience, but not before she shot Ginger a look that would have felled an ox.

Ranal turned and looked at the pendant in Ginger’s hands, realization hitting him hard. He looked at Ginger’s confused face with some pity. *Young one,* he thought, *you might as well lower your battle standard and surrender. I have yet to see Liam lose a battle once he has committed himself.*

Still fingering the pendant, Ginger gave him a puzzled look. "What?"

Ranal's radiant smile lit up his face. "Can I get you something cool to drink, Lady Ginger?"

"No, I'm fine, thank you. Liam told me to wait here for him."

"Then I will leave you to wait, dear Lady." He turned to go, murmuring to himself, "And may the One have mercy on you when once my lord king begins his campaign."

Ranal caught up with Liam as he was headed back to the garden, having been informed that the alert was a false alarm. In fact, it was Oriana who had the alarm sounded, claiming she had seen a Dark Elf lurking by the entry to Nantuor's valley. It was her way of trying to get Liam away from Ginger in the garden.

Smiling dryly at his king, Ranal remarked, "My lord, it is not for me to say, but doesn't one usually inform one's intended before he marks her as his own?"

"Very funny Ranal. There was not time. I merely wanted to ensure my suit would not be superseded before I had a chance to propose."

"And what elf in his right mind would try to move in on the chosen of Liam Midir?" Ranal asked, a mischievous twinkle in his eye.

"Nevertheless . . ." Liam started. He was stopped by his friend's good natured laughter.

"Liam, everyone in Nantuor knows your intentions toward the Lady Ginger, except perhaps Lady Ginger." He smirked at his king. "And when do you intend to inform the lady of your intentions?"

"Just as soon as all of creation will stop trying to restrain me from doing so," said Liam, slightly exasperated. "Now, if you will excuse me dear friend, I have an appointment with my destiny."

"I wonder," mused Ranal, "if lady destiny will be as compliant as the rest of creation?"

Liam escaped to the garden and looked for Ginger. She was sitting on a stone bench under a branch loaded with pink shell flowers. She was looking at his pendant as she held it in her hands. He stood for a moment, enchanted by the beautiful picture she made. Finally Ginger looked up and smiled.

"Okay Liam, I waited. What did you want to talk to me about?" she asked, the sunlight catching the green in her eyes.

Liam stood for a moment, his heart racing. The sun reflecting off the ruby pendant caught his eye and brought him back to himself. He stepped to the bench and knelt in the grass before Ginger. Looking up at her, he considered the many things he might say to restart his suit. She smiled at him as he played absentmindedly with the end of her sash.

"Liam, what's going on? You really are acting very strange." She waited for an answer.

"Lady Ginger. . . You are aware, I hope, of my feelings for you. I . . ." He swallowed and started again. "I have deep feelings for you, my Lady. I am in love with you."

Uh oh, thought Ginger, looking for a place to run. Her heart was racing. She hadn't let herself get close to anyone in a long time – not since she lost Felix and Harry. She wasn't going to get hurt like that again. Not even for an elven king.

Noticing her tense up, Liam gently took her hands in his own. "I know you have been hurt in the past by the loss of those you love. But you have nothing to fear. I offer you love, security, and stability. I will not promise that I will never die. Even elves can be killed. What I do promise is that I will love you with all my heart, all my strength. You will be my heartbeat, my light. I will love you always. And I will wrap you up in my love and hold you close to my heart for as long as the One allows us to be together in this world and in the world to come." He gently pulled her close to him. "I want to be your husband," he whispered as he looked into her eyes. "Will you have me?"

His strong arms and compelling eyes calmed her confused thoughts and soothed her fears. She looked at him, considering his words. The love in his eyes was unmistakable. Finally she made her decision.

"Yes Liam," she said softly. "I'll marry you. And I hope you know what you are getting into."

Any further words were silenced as Liam swept Ginger up and kissed her, drawing their heartbeats together. Ginger felt him gently stir in her mind. The pair connected, their thoughts whirling together like two graceful birds flying in unison. She melted into his embrace, and the world receded from her awareness.

Over the week of the Spring Festival, Liam continued to court Ginger, doing little things to gain her favor. He frequently spoke of his feelings for her while slightly unshuttering his power to help her grow accustomed to his true self. He did not want her to feel overwhelmed when he was near. He was hoping to instill more intimate feelings.

The Festival began with an archery competition. Ginger was impressed with the elves' skills and even tried her hand at it at Liam's insistence. She did pretty well, managing to hit the target dead center several times. She smiled as the rest of the archers cheered and threw flowers at her feet.

Liam was impressed. Oriana was not – riding behind Liam and Ginger, she pouted all the way back to the house.

That afternoon at Nantuor, Ginger went out with Liam's hunting party. They were having a wonderful time in the fresh air and sunshine. Oriana grew more jealous at each of Liam's compliments to Ginger. Finally she could stand no more. As Oriana had done previously, this time appearing to dodge a thorn bush with her horse, she nudged another she-elf's horse into Ibby until Ginger's leg got smashed against a tree.

Liam quickly took Ginger back to Nantuor for treatment. Oriana moved to follow them but Ranal insisted she stay with the group.

"The loss of one lovely lady is tragic enough," Ranal said as he showed Oriana his most charming smile. "The loss of a second would be unbearable."

Ranal had his suspicions about what had happened, but since Oriana's horse had blocked his view of the accident, he couldn't prove anything. All he could do was to resolve to watch Oriana even closer. He moved his horse alongside hers, blocking her way to the path as he favored her hand with a tender salute.

Oriana smiled back. She was flattered that she had finally caught the attention of the most handsome elf in Nantuor – except for King Liam of course.

How sad, she thought, *that he isn't king*. She hated to waste her time on anything less than the royal house. *Perhaps he will be a worthy diversion until Liam gets back, hopefully without that simpering human hanging on his coattail.*

She took in Ranal's handsome features. *Well, I certainly have his undivided attention*. She didn't know how right she was.

Back at Nantuor, Ginger's leg had been healed and she was laughing and smiling with Liam.

"Maybe I'd better get back to the house before something else happens, like an earthquake," Ginger laughed gently as she pulled her boot back on.

Liam's smile lit up his face. "Surely you wouldn't mind being rescued by an admiring king, would you?"

Ginger laughed and finished pulling her boot on. Sometimes she had no answer to Liam's comebacks. She could only smile and shake her head.

Early the next morning Oriana rode to her meeting place with Braen and waited.

Braen stepped out of the bushes and came up behind Oriana. He moved noiselessly to her and put his hands playfully over her eyes as he subtly took control of her mind. Oriana started and then laughed. She turned to him with a beautiful smile.

She is hopelessly in love with me, Braen noted with a slight smirk. *That will make her so much easier to control.*

"Good morning my love," he purred, his voice raw silk. Oriana was enchanted.

"Good morning Braen, my love," she responded warmly. She looked at him expectantly, wondering why he had been so insistent that she meet him this morning. What could be so urgent that she should miss the day's celebration on the terraces? To her utter surprise, he slipped a diamond pendant out of his pocket.

"Oriana my darling, my love for you has grown so much that it is impossible to live in this world without you," Braen said in a silken tone. He gave it just the right amount of inflection to stir her elven maid's heart. "Will you marry me? I will surely die of loneliness for you if you refuse." He spoke the last phrase with such a pitiful tone that a tear ran down Oriana's lovely face.

"How can I refuse such a sincere proposal?" Oriana asked, smiling through her tears. "Yes Braen, I will be your wife." All thoughts of Liam disappeared from her mind.

Braen took her in his arms and held her close, all the while getting a firmer grip on her mind as he kissed her lips. He motioned to Morfran to come out of the bushes. His companion obeyed and assumed his place beside Braen.

Oriana drew back, startled. Braen sent a command for her to be at ease.

"Oriana my darling, this is Morfran. He is my friend and shepherd. It is he who helps me stay close to the One where I belong," he lied. Oriana smiled at Morfran, and he returned his most winning smile.

Braen stroked Oriana's cheek as he looked deep into her eyes, willing her to obey him. "Oriana, Morfran can marry us this instant if you would but say the word. I am so lonely for you, my darling. Please, please say yes and ease my wounded heart."

"Of course my darling. I will marry you whenever you wish." Her beautiful face was wet with tears. Braen's eyes glowed with triumph.

Braen nodded to Morfran to begin the marriage ceremony. When it was done, Braen kissed Oriana tenderly on the head. How useful she had become. "Now, come spend the afternoon with your loving husband."

He spent the rest of the day corrupting Oriana's heart and mind, sending subtle mental suggestions for a plan that would send her down the same dark path on which he prowled. She would now grow hateful and vengeful, her mind bending to Braen's will. Given time she would become as evil as he.

When she rode away that evening she was carrying Braen's child.

On the last day of the Spring Festival Oriana attended a gathering in Liam's home. Lynet came in carrying a serving tray full of glasses. She stopped when she saw Brennus surrounded by several elf-maids in their finery. Oriana noticed Lynet looking at Brennus, an evil thought coming to her mind. This would be a perfect time to put Braen's plan into action. She smiled and stepped toward Lynet.

"You are in love with him, are you not?" she whispered in Lynet's ear.

Lynet jumped at the sound of her voice. She turned to look at Oriana, dismayed by her easy discovery. Oriana looked back at Lynet with disdain, then glanced slyly at Brennus.

"Please, don't," Lynet whispered pleadingly.

"How could you presume to love someone when you are not even their equal?" Oriana asked, her voice rising a little. Several nearby she-elves turned and looked at Lynet.

"*Please*," begged Lynet, her lips trembling and her eyes glistening with tears.

"You are no more than a servant, and Brennus is an elven lord. And you dare to love him?" she demanded loudly. "You are pathetic."

Bursting into tears, Lynet dropped the tray and ran from the gathering toward the main garden. Brennus began following her, then stopped near Oriana.

"You have the manners of a beast, Madam," he told her coldly. For a moment she thought he would hit her.

"But," she started.

"The only thing that is pathetic is the disregard with which you hold true love – perhaps because you have none of your own."

He swept roughly past her and found Lynet sobbing quietly beneath the great oak where they had spent many days talking and reading. She didn't hear Brennus approach until he knelt beside her and wiped the tears from her face.

"Why did you not tell me?" he asked her softly.

"What do I have that I could offer you as a wife?" she asked miserably.

Brennus' eyes filled with tears. "What could you offer me?" he repeated. "You have been nothing but love and kindness since I have known you. When no one else could bear to look at me you did, even with my scars . . ."

"There are no scars," she whispered. "I see only you."

Without a word Brennus took his pendant off and slipped it around Lynet's neck. He held her to him and stopped her sobs with tender kisses.

They didn't even raise their heads as shocked cries rang out from Liam's guests. Oriana was on her back on the floor holding her hand to her bloody nose and Ginger was standing above her flexing her right hand. Oriana cried pitifully, hoping for some sympathy. Liam hurried in and stepped between them.

"What happened here?" he asked Ginger.

Ginger glanced up from her throbbing hand. "She made Lynet cry so I introduced my fist to her face." She looked down at Oriana with a satisfied smile. "Anytime you want some more, sister, just let me know – because there's plenty more where that came from."

Shocked laughter escaped from several onlookers.

Liam looked down at Ginger's fiery eyes "Ginger, I realize you may have been upset, but I don't think violence is the way to settle matters like this."

"Oh stick it in your pointed ear, Liam," she said in exasperation. "She had it coming. And frankly, I'm getting tired of you turning a blind eye to Oriana's vindictiveness. I thought a king was supposed to be fair. Maybe you should marry Oriana, since you've done nothing but make excuses for her since I met her." With that, Ginger pushed past him and stalked straight to her room where she cried for an hour.

Liam watched her leave, his mouth wide open. Oriana tried to hide a smug smile behind her crocodile tears. *Braen's plan is working perfectly,* she thought. *By morning the wretched human will be gone.*

When Liam appeared at Ginger's door that night, she refused to speak to him, despite his sincere pleas.

She awoke in the dim hours before dawn at a sound near her door. Sitting up and looking toward the door, she saw a dimly lit piece of paper that had been shoved under the door. She got the note and came back to bed to read it. The short missive suggested that she go back to her ranch while Liam reconsidered his proposal. It had the royal seal at the bottom. Unknown to Ginger, it had Oriana's fingerprints all over it.

The next morning Ginger didn't come down to the terrace for breakfast. Liam finally knocked on her door for several minutes. Hearing no response, he opened the door. All of Ginger's belongings were gone except the ruby pendant he'd given her, which was lying on the bed.

Liam sighed. He couldn't let her go home, not like this. He didn't understand why she was so angry, but he knew he couldn't lose her to a childish argument. He turned to go to the stables.

Several miles from Nantuor, Ginger woke up in utter darkness. She was laying on a cold, rough surface, tied securely by her hands and feet. The last thing she remembered was riding underneath a tree. A flash of worry went through her mind – she hoped Ibby was alright.

She could feel a presence in the darkness, one that sent a chill down her spine. She didn't know what it was, but something evil was standing near her.

Chapter 17

Tortured

Her left leg throbbing with pain, Ginger took a deep breath to calm herself. She must have been hurt when she fell from her horse. She could hear nothing in the darkness, and the evil presence – whatever it was – wasn't moving. "Jesus, help me get out of this," she quietly prayed. "But if this is it, we both know where I stand. I'm ready to go. Just help me get through this please."

Suddenly the torches flickered into flame, illuminating the inside of the cave. She felt the evil step closer. A hand roughly grabbed her hair and jerked her head around. Her face was inches from Braen's, his green eyes boring into hers. Recognizing him from her dreams, Ginger flushed with anger. She had lost a lot of sleep because of this . . . elf. Someone was going to get his butt kicked – if she could get loose.

"You're very pretty, human. I can understand why Liam would find you so . . . diverting." Braen smiled and licked his lips. "I'm sure your skin tastes like honey. Most human flesh does."

Ginger watched him slowly walk down her right side, tapping his fingernails down her leg. He turned and roughly jerked her boot off, examining her foot.

"Very pretty, very delicate. I'm sure there are many bones that could easily be broken with hardly any effort at all."

He stopped and looked at her. Ginger remained silent but glared back defiantly. Then he leaned down and licked her leg, running his tongue from ankle to thigh. She shivered but stayed calm. Having been captured and interrogated by Columbian drug lords, she knew this game well – and he wasn't going to win.

Braen smiled at her discomfort. Then he ran his fingernails lightly on the skin on her leg. In spite of herself, she jerked away. He chuckled.

"Don't worry, I have no interest in you that way. I wouldn't lower myself by giving my attentions to a human." He leaned in closer. "Are you afraid?" he whispered, looking down at her, his eyes catching the torchlight like a cat's.

Ginger stared stubbornly at him. No way was she giving an inch if she could help it.

Suddenly Braen's arm was a blur, and she heard a knife being imbedded in the table next to her left cheek. Grabbing her by the hair on the back of her head, he pressed her cheek against the huge blade. He jerked her head back toward him, close enough that she could feel his breath on her face. She shuddered again.

"Answer me," he ordered in a deadly calm voice.

Knowing she was about to be tortured, Ginger wasn't going to give this creature the satisfaction of cowering before him. Staring straight into Braen's green eyes, she answered him.

"You'd be the last one I'd tell, you freak of nature."

"You are not the first one I've played this game with, human wench, and you won't be the last," he hissed. "I have done this for thousands of years, with countless humans."

He smiled at Ginger's look of surprise. "You really don't have any idea how old I am, do you?"

He could see Ginger's stubborn eyes glaring back at him in the torchlight.

"I was there when they crucified your so-called Redeemer," he spat triumphantly. "I laughed when He drew His last breath."

"I'll bet you weren't laughing three days later, were you?" Ginger shot back.

His eyes aflame in anger, Braen squeezed her throat. With his other hand he slapped her hard across the face. Ginger gasped for air, spots dancing before her eyes.

Braen released her just before she passed out. He walked around the table again, stopping and staring at her legs. Then a smile played on his lips.

"Oh, I made a mistake," he said softly. "You hurt your *left* leg, didn't you?" Before she could react, he jerked off her other boot and pants leg in one savage movement. Despite her best efforts, she gasped with pain.

Braen ran his nails slowly down her left leg to her ankle. He wrapped his hand around it and looked innocently at Ginger.

"Isn't this the ankle you hurt? Does it bother you, dear heart? Injuries like that can be so painful, can't they?"

He squeezed her ankle and was rewarded with a grunt of pain. He frowned. She should have screamed. He smiled menacingly at her.

"You are not playing the game, dear heart. I hurt you, and you cry out. If you play well enough, I let you rest for a while. If not . . . then we have to play until you learn the rules."

Ginger looked at him and screwed up her face in a defiant smile. "I always had a problem with that when I was a kid. It seems I didn't play well with others." She paused. "We both know you're not going to stop until you get tired or bored. And I'm not going to give you the pleasure of cooperating with you or soothing your ego. I don't socialize with livestock. So get on with it."

His jaw clinched in rage, Braen squeezed her ankle harder. There was a loud crack as the bone broke, then silence. Ginger had fainted.

Liam pulled Tanet to a stop. He looked desperately around at the surrounding countryside. He'd been over this piece of road three times already. There was no sign of Ginger anywhere. His heart raced with anxiety. Where was she? He felt a burst of panic at the answer – if she wasn't at the ranch, and she wasn't at Nantuor, and she wasn't on the road in between, there was only one possible explanation: Braen.

He closed his eyes in horror and tried to order his thoughts. If Braen had her . . . . He couldn't finish the thought. With his heart in his throat he wheeled Tanet back toward the search party. He had to get more troops – Ginger's life may depend on it. A tear stung his eyes and he prayed for her safety as he galloped to catch up to the rest of the search party.

Meanwhile, Brennus and his elves were moving cautiously through the forest looking at every inch of ground for a clue as to Ginger's whereabouts. The forest was thick here; the only break in the greenery was the entrance to a small cave back down the trail. Numerous other caves were hidden by the dense greenery. It was a perfect place to hide, a fact discovered by the remaining small drakes on the island.

There was something disturbing about this area. Brennus was uneasy, a feeling he had whenever a Dark Elf was about. Even the birds had either left the area or seemed to be hiding. Every elf in the search party was on edge.

Brennus looked over at Lieutenant Niall. He was walking in front of his horse, carefully examining the ground for tracks. As he stepped forward there was a sudden rustling in a nearby bush. Brennus motioned him to stop. Brennus and two other elves dismounted and approached the bush. At their captain's signal the two elves swept back the bush's branches to reveal its occupant.

Brennus' face lit up with a smile. Crouched at the base of the bush was a large lizard. It cringed and gave a frightened croak as Brennus gently picked it up. He could see that its right hind leg was broken and part of its tail was missing. It struggled in his grasp, desperate to get away.

He held the terrified animal and stroked its head.

"There now, old fellow," he said softly. "No one is going to hurt you. We are Light Elves."

The lizard nipped one of Brennus' fingers. Brennus held it firmly and began to sing a song of comfort. Slowly the lizard ceased struggling and looked up at Brennus. He smiled down at it and spoke soothingly.

"Now see? I told you I was a Light Elf. No one is going to hurt you. What is your name? How did you get your leg broken old one?"

The lizard relaxed in his grip. "My name is Eli. The dark one hurt me. He seemed to enjoy it."

Brennus tensed. "The dark one?"

"Yes," answered the lizard. "You know him. He hurt you too. I saw them carry you out of that cave and take you toward the road some days ago." The lizard looked back down the trail at the cave.

The elves turned grim eyes on the cave entrance, half hidden in the shrubbery. Brennus turned back to the old lizard.

"This is important," Brennus said. "Did you see the dark ones with a human woman?"

"Yes. They took her to the same place they carried you from. I don't hold much hope for her safety."

Brennus sighed deeply and sent a quick prayer of thanks to the One for allowing them to find Ginger. He immediately had his troops encircle the area, with stern orders not to be discovered or to allow Braen to leave with Ginger. Then, carefully holding the injured lizard, he mounted his horse.

"Where are we going?" Eli asked him.

"To King Liam. You must tell him all you know of the dark ones and the human woman."

"I will be happy to," chuckled the old lizard. "I understand King Liam has little love for the dark ones."

"Indeed, he does not," replied Brennus.

"In that case," said Eli, "it will be a story that will give more joy to the teller than to the listener."

Brennus smiled. Wheeling his horse, he rode swiftly for Nantuor.

When they arrived at Nantuor, Brennus went directly to Liam's study, where he knew his king was making plans to expand the search. After Eli told him what he'd seen of the Dark Elves, Liam immediately dispatched Brennus to have General Arth prepare his troops for battle.

While Liam was setting his broken leg, Eli spoke at length about his mistreatment at the hands of the Dark Elves. Listening patiently, Liam finished with the leg and moved on to his damaged tail. When he finished, he placed a large soft pillow in front of the fire and gently set the lizard down to rest.

"This is much better than crouching under a bush, my lord. Thank you," said Eli, cocking an eye at Liam.

"It is I who thank you, Master Lizard. You have found my love. You will have my gratitude always."

"Ah," said Eli softly, "your love for humans remains, even after the hunts."

At Liam's startled look, the old lizard chortled deep in his throat. "Elves and Man are not the only ones who enjoy a good piece of gossip."

Just then Aili came in with a saucer of warm milk. "I want you to drink this, Eli. It will help you rest."

Eli tasted the milk and looked up at Liam. "It has a bit too much poppy in it for my taste, my lord. But I suppose you know best. You are the healer, not I. Nice splinting job though."

Liam was about to comment on Eli's medical expertise when General Arth and his counselors entered the study.

Arth went straight to the map on Liam's desk. As they looked over the area Eli had indicated, he spoke up from his cushion by the fire.

"My Lords, there are far too many openings for your elves to cover them all. I have lived in that area for years and I find new ones every few days."

Arth and Liam bent over the map, studying the surrounding area. His counselors on the other side of the table waited for their verdict.

"Eli is right, my king," declared Arth. "There are too many openings to effectively cover them all. The entire area is riddled with caves."

"And the scouts say they only have thirty troops?" asked Liam.

"And thirty grey warriors," noted Tiernan. "That makes sixty. We can have one hundred troops at the caves, but we also need to leave one hundred here to guard the families of Nantuor."

"I agree," said Egan.

Ranal nodded. "It is wisdom, old friend."

"I know," said Liam. "I just want Ginger back safe and sound." His friends could see the worry in his eyes.

"So do we, my lord," said General Arth. "We know what she means to you."

Liam smiled faintly as he continued to study the map. "Nevertheless, we must use caution. Leaving half our army here is wise. It would be much like the Dark Elves to use my love as a diversion to draw my forces away, leaving Nantuor defenseless."

He stared at the spot on the map that Brennus had marked as Ginger's location. Finally he straightened and looked at his counselors.

"This is what we will do. Ranal, Tiernan, and Brennus will remain behind with half the troops in case of attack. General Arth, Egan, and I will seize control of this area before we attack. We cannot let them know we are there. They will leave the area immediately if they suspect our presence. If they do that I . . . *we* may never see Ginger again."

His eyes were black with intensity. "We cannot let that happen."

"Do not worry my King," proclaimed Arth. "They will not know we are there until they feel the bite of our blades."

Immediately after resolving that the Light Elves would go to war, Liam put his sons in a secure room in the family quarters. It had one entrance and was easily defended from intruders. When his sons objected that they wanted to join the battle, Liam overruled them with a soft reply.

"You are my precious children. Braen would make you his first targets above all else."

Ranal waited by the secluded garden path leading to the main path that rose up to the lake above the valley. Before long, he heard Oriana's soft footsteps. He stepped out onto the path and blocked her way.

"I'm sorry Lady Oriana, but no one is allowed to leave Nantuor right now. It's much too precarious."

Oriana smiled sweetly. She had to get past him to warn Braen of the impending attack. "But my lord, I only wish to sit by the lake and enjoy the sunset."

Ranal gently took her arm and motioned to the two guards he had brought with him.

"I am sorry my lady. No one means *no one*."

The two guards escorted Oriana back down the path. He had already posted guards at her quarters to ensure she didn't leave. He was still suspicious of her, and he could not afford to be careless with the safety of Liam's children. Besides, he told himself, he had spent just as much time as Tiernan helping raise them. He could not love them more if they were his own.

With grim determination, he started down the path to go report to Liam.

Chapter 18

The Wait

Arth stood in the courtyard of the stable awaiting his king's orders. Liam took one more look at Nantuor and then signaled his troops to move out. The riders passed swiftly through the path under the waterfall and down the ravine to Athdar. Their elven horses barely made a sound as they crossed the ford and melted silently into the forest.

They arrived at Camdan several hours later and left their horses safely hidden in the dense trees. Gathering their weapons, they proceeded to Acamar, where they silently spread out to surround the entrances to Braen's cave. Everyone had been ordered to keep silent this close to Braen's hiding place. Fearing that Braen's troops might pick up on mental commands, they operated by hand signals alone.

Lieutenant Niall watched five Dark Elves pass underneath the tree where he hid. Two were looking around nervously as they neared the cave's entrance. *Seems like they feel something's amiss*, thought Niall. Crouched on the tree limb like a cat ready to spring, he awaited the order to attack.

Nearby, Brennus slid back into the shadows as a wary Dark Elf stopped and looked around. He took a tentative step toward Brennus, but was distracted by a screeching bird that suddenly flew from an adjacent tree into the surrounding forest. Brennus recognized the bird – it lived in Liam's private gardens. He and Lynet had often fed it small treats as they walked together there. As the Dark Elf wandered off, Brennus hoped he'd remember to thank the bird for the diversion.

Liam sat in the shadows listening intently. He could catch the barest whisper of Braen's voice. It held a note of anger and frustration. But try as he might, he caught nothing of Ginger's voice. She was either whispering or not talking at all. Braen's voice rose in anger. There was a note of desperation in his words. "Stop it! Stop praying! Stop it now!"

Liam heard a hard slap, then silence. Finally, he heard the lilting sound of Ginger's laughter. Had she gone mad from the torture? Liam's heart pounded with anxiety as he sent a desperate prayer to the One. "Please, please help her hold to her sanity. Please my Lord." He bowed his head and then jerked it back up at the sound of Ginger speaking.

"If it bothers you so much, why don't I just sing?" she asked defiantly. "How about a rousing chorus of How Great Thou Art, huh? What's the matter Braen? Does it remind you of what you're going to face when you finally shuffle off this mortal coil? Or should I say when Liam *kicks* you off?"

"Shut up!" Braen shouted shrilly. "Shut up human wench! If you don't shut up I'll kill you."

"Do that and Liam will finish you for sure." Ginger's voice was calm, even in her pain. "Right now," she added, "I'm the only thing standing between you and a short trip to hell, and you know it."

Braen knocked Ginger unconscious. Liam bowed his head at the sound, barely able to contain his rage. He had to wait for all his troops to get in place before he moved against Braen. He sighed deeply as he felt Egan's steadying hand on his shoulder.

His face a twisted mask of anger, Braen looked down at Ginger. He had almost killed her with that last blow. He couldn't afford to lose his temper now. She was far too useful to him. He would make her pay for her insolence though. He carefully calculated her next torture. Not wanting to inflict too much physical damage, he decided to torment her in her dreams. He approached her unconscious form as he reached into her mind, setting up a ferocious nightmare.

Ginger found herself walking down a forest path. She felt a spark of anxiety as the light faded and the forest was wrapped in darkness.

She moved slowly, barely able to see the path. Suddenly she felt something brush past her face. Startled, she turned. There in front of her was a hooded, cloaked figure, hunched over as if in pain. She felt a wave of pity and stepped toward the figure. It moaned and moved down the path. Unable to control herself, she followed it down the trail.

Finally she found herself running frantically, trying to catch up to the mysterious figure. She rounded a bend and realized it had vanished. She stood in the middle of the path, unsure what to do next.

A tingle crawled up her spine as she realized something was behind her – something terrible. She took a deep breath and turned around. Gasping, she found herself face to face with a huge dragon, his green scales glittering in the pale moonlight. His malice-filled eyes glared at her like two glowing rubies. His breath was a hot sickening stench as he snorted threateningly.

His jaws gaped open as he lunged at Ginger. She screamed and ran back down the path. The dragon followed, his steps shaking the forest. Suddenly he whipped his tail around in front of her, knocking her to the ground. He stood over her, baring his teeth in her face, then raised his head far above her and inhaled deeply. In an instant, Ginger was hit with a scalding hot blast of green fire. She felt her hair burning off her head like dry grass. Her blood boiled in her veins and her skin cooked under the intense flames. She tried to take a breath to scream, but the heat scalded her lungs and rendered her voiceless.

Ginger tried again and again to scream but could do no more than moan. Tears flooded out of her eyes and sizzled down her cheeks. The ground underneath her began to smoke from the heat. The fire continued burning her, but her body was not consumed. She prayed to God to stop the unbearable pain.

Braen stood by the table as Ginger moaned in her sleep. She was stronger than he had anticipated, but she'd soon be begging him for mercy. He smiled to himself and allowed her to wake with a violent start. He would let her rest for a short while and then start again.

Outside Liam sensed Ginger's horror. He fought the urge to enter her mind to help, since it would instantly tip off his presence to Braen. No, he had to wait for his troops to be ready. He could not let

Braen escape this time. Liam shuddered at Ginger's suffering as a tear coursed down his cheek.

Back at Nantuor, Tiernan and Ranal had kept a majority of their troops near the house while dispatching others to every vulnerable place in the valley. Every inhabitant in the area was on the alert. Fiacra and his clan hovered in the air, watching for any sign of Braen's troops. Every dog in Nantuor was prowling the valley hunting for Dark Elves. Every bird was flitting from tree to tree or floating on the breeze above the valley floor, watching for intruders. Every house cat crouched above the doorway to its home, waiting to pounce on invaders.

In Liam's quarters, Eli lay on a pillow by the fireplace calmly observing the room's occupants. Tiernan and Ranal also watched as Barram and Rigalis fidgeted, both brothers chafing at their confinement.

Teagan and Owain stood watch on the terrace with the guards. Teagan could tell his brothers were restless – not restless enough to become reckless, he hoped. Owain smiled at his older brother.

"You can't watch everything, Teagan. They will have to fight for themselves when the time comes."

Teagan's jaw firmed. "You are my brothers. I am responsible for you all."

"It isn't easy being the eldest, is it Teagan?" asked Owain softly.

Teagan turned and smiled. "I would not change it if I could. I am honored to be your protector."

"If it comes to it, I will always be at your back," replied Owain. "And theirs."

They both gazed amusedly at their two younger brothers. Even now they managed to find something to bicker about – Barram wouldn't let Rigalis out of his sight, much to Rigalis' annoyance.

"I am not some helpless little elfling, Barram. I can defend myself," Rigalis snapped.

"That is not the point Rigalis," retorted Barram.

"Well, what is then?" demanded Rigalis angrily.

Barram's fierce eyes softened as he looked at his younger brother. "The point is that you are my brother and I love you. I could not live with myself if you were to come to harm."

Rigalis dropped his head. Barram clapped him on the shoulder and turned back to watch the terrace.

Tiernan turned and spoke softly in Ranal's ear. "I pity the unfortunate fool who tries to harm any of these boys."

"I do too," said Ranal, nodding in agreement as he watched the boys guard each other. "Midir blood runs strong in this family. They are very much like their grandfather. Did you know he once killed a green drake by himself? And he was just a stripling then."

"Indeed?" responded Tiernan. "I had heard stories about Liam's father being a great warrior. But a green drake? They are as big as a whale!"

Ranal chuckled. "My father was captain of the Royal Guard at the time. He said he had never seen anything like it. The entire palace was in an uproar wondering where their young prince was. Just then, he came in covered in blood bearing a large dragon's tooth. Most amazing."

The two fell into conversation about the old days as they kept an eye on the youngsters.

Oriana paced her room like an angry she-cat. How would she warn her husband about this horrendous impending attack? She stopped walking and looked toward the terrace. The two guards stationed there stared back. She smiled at them and turned away. Stepping to her dressing table, she sat and brushed her hair, trying to think. Nothing came to mind. She was trapped. There were guards at the door and on the terrace. There was no way to get out of Nantuor. She hoped that the One would keep her beloved husband safe until all this confusion was sorted out. Surely after Liam saw how kind and gentle Braen was, he would pardon him for whatever little transgression he had committed.

She huffed to herself and sat fretting over Braen. How could anyone think Braen was evil? He was kind and gentle to her. True, he had asked her to keep an eye on Liam for him, but that was only because Liam unjustifiably hated him. Surely if he would just talk to Braen he would see how wrong he was. But her poor husband was so afraid of the elf-king that he would never consent to meet with him. She frowned in frustration and continued contemplating a way to get word to Braen.

Chapter 19

The Chase

Captain Brennus acknowledged the hand signal from Lieutenant Niall and relayed it to Captain Gildas. Gildas looked to Captain Kendhal's position and motioned to him. Kendhal sent a signal to Captain Trahern and General Arth. Arth moved silently to his king's side and signed to Liam that everyone was in position.

Good, Liam signed back. *Prepare to move on my signal.*

Arth nodded and settled down to wait as a Dark Elf slid past their hiding place in the dark. The enemy soldier fretted with an unruly rope as he walked toward the cave's entrance. *Soon*, Arth mused, *a tangled rope will be the least of your worries.*

Inside the cave, Ginger was covered in sweat as she started dreaming again. She found herself walking through a beautiful field. She moaned "No" as she approached Braen from behind. He turned suddenly, long claws protruding from his fingers. He smiled sweetly at her and clawed at her face. The pain burned as he dug deep into her face, wrenching a scream of agony from her lips. She woke up screaming – again.

Outside, Liam heard her screams. His fists were balled in frustration and grief. He looked over at Egan.

Soon, Egan signaled. *Wait. Soon.*

Taking a deep breath, Liam tried to calm his storm of emotions. His eyes were cold with anger as he watched the cave entrance. This time there would be no mercy. This time Braen would die.

Braen laughed and came over to the table. Leaning over Ginger, he cooed "Oh" softly in her ear and stroked her face. "Did you have a bad dream, dear heart?" Suddenly he grabbed a handful of hair and jerked her head around to face him.

"Well, you haven't seen anything yet," he hissed. He slammed her head back down on the table and stalked a few paces away. She wasn't breaking, and it was beginning to annoy him.

He looked up as a Dark Elf fearfully approached. After they exchanged whispers, Braen grew enraged and grabbed his subordinate by the throat. "Make sure he doesn't find his way in here!" He threw the Dark Elf away from him, and the frightened creature scrambled to leave the room.

Braen stood with his back to Ginger, his chest heaving with rage. How had Liam found his hiding place? No one could have told him – except . . . Braen ground his teeth in frustration. That lizard! He would twist him in two when he found him.

Just then he heard Liam's troops begin their attack on the barrier in front of the cave. He would have to move fast. He stopped and looked at Ginger with an evil smile. He would survive so long as he held her hostage.

He walked back to the table, leaned down, and looked Ginger in the eye. "So, your boyfriend found you. I'll put his head on a pike when I take over Nantuor."

He stroked her face as she tensed, angrily glaring into his eyes. He put his hands on her leg and head, and she became covered in a red flickering light. She immediately felt her wounds healing; even the crushed ankle stopped throbbing. The light faded and Braen grabbed a handful of her hair, yanking her head to face him. Leaning down in front of her face, he whispered, "I have healed your body so you will not hinder me during my escape. If you slow me down I will show you your own entrails before you die. Do you understand?"

Braen ran the tip of his dagger lightly across her cheek. She shut her eyes and shuddered. *Good*, he thought, *she is afraid of me. That will make her easier to handle*. He cut her ropes and jerked her off the table and onto her feet. Just as Liam's troops broke through the barrier, Braen dragged his captive out a side entrance and disappeared into the night.

The Light Elves hit with savage intensity, sweeping the Dark Elves and gray warriors before them. Liam's eyes blazed with fury as he led his troops through the cavern, cutting down any evil thing that moved. At last he came to the chamber where Ginger had been tortured. Finding the table empty, he shouted with rage. His counselors and troops rushed into the room. Liam gazed helplessly at the table, then turned to search for the exit Braen had used. He found it quickly and dashed through it, followed by his eager troops. Their king's beloved was in the hands of a monster! They would not rest until she was safe.

Egan glanced at his king as they raced down the passage and emerged outside. Liam looked like a hungry wolf chasing its prey – in this case, a prey that had depredated on his family for thousands of years, and now had tortured Liam's love. One thing was for sure – Egan did not envy Braen when Liam Midir found him.

Braen raced through the forest, dragging Ginger with him. She deliberately ran slowly, tripping and falling repeatedly. *Stupid, stupid human*, thought Braen. *If I did not need her for a human shield, I would have ripped her heart from her chest.*

Braen heard distant shouts from the cave's side exit. Liam had found his trail. He ran faster, Ginger's feet barely touching the ground as he dragged her along. Arriving at a wide, deep stream, he jumped in with Ginger and made for the other side. Ginger struggled to keep her head above water. Her flailing annoyed Braen, but he didn't have time to punish her clumsiness now. Amid her thrashing, he failed to notice her throw a button in the mud beside the embankment. Liam would recognize it – it was from a shirt he had told her he liked.

Emerging with Ginger from the river, Braen broke into a run. He dragged her through the forest at breakneck speed for a full hour. Finally he stopped when Ginger developed chest pains that left her gasping for air. He threw her to the ground and squatted beside her, listening intently. He sat for several minutes but heard no sound of pursuit. He turned sharply upon hearing Ginger's soft laughter, slapping her hard across the face.

"What are you laughing at, human wench?" he demanded, his green eyes blazing.

"You. You're scared to death of Liam, aren't you?" Ginger wheezed, still trying to catch her breath.

Braen's eyes narrowed to slits as he grabbed Ginger by the throat and brought her face close to his. "You are the one who should be scared to death, wench. Or haven't I convinced you of my hatred for your kind?"

"Oh, I believe you Braen. But guys like you have always been around. They just go by different names. Hitler, Stalin, Saddam Hussein . . . . Your kind are all monsters, but you're nothing new. And just like the others, you'll go down."

Braen's face twisted in rage. How dare this worm of a human speak to him like this? He took out his knife and reached up to put out one of her eyes. Just before his knifepoint touched her, Braen felt a shiver go up his spine. Someone was behind him. Ginger looked at him and smiled.

Braen leaped to his feet, dragging his hostage with him. He spun around with her in front of him, his knife to her throat. There stood Liam, his eyes blazing with an elven light that Braen hadn't seen in several thousand years.

Fear stirred in Braen's heart. He could feel Liam's fury. It even affected the trees, their branches swaying frantically as if in a high wind.

Without uttering a word, Liam looked at Ginger's bruised and bloodied face. His eyes shifted to Braen, and Braen saw death staring back at him.

Hearing Liam's troops approaching, Braen quickly thought of a possible way out. With a lightning fast movement, he slammed his knife deep into Ginger's chest and threw her at Liam, then disappeared into the forest. He heard Liam's anguished cry as he ran away.

Liam held Ginger to him, frozen in shock and grief. Then he came to himself. Gathering all his strength, he sent a massive wave of healing energy through Ginger's body, immediately stopping most of the bleeding. With the poison from Braen's knife slowing the healing process, Liam doubled his efforts. But his strength quickly waned, and his councilors intervened to make him stop.

"You cannot help her if you kill yourself, old friend," Egan told him softly.

Liam hastily pulled a bandage from his healer's kit and tried to stop the bright red blood seeping from Ginger's chest. Raising his head, he made his decision. He sent out an urgent mental summons to Fiacra. He prayed silently as he waited for the short time it took the great eagle to reach him. Liam picked up Ginger and turned to his counselors.

"I could not stop all the bleeding. I am taking Ginger to Nantuor." He looked at Egan. "Take your troops back to Nantuor and surround the house and grounds. When General Arth catches up have him do the same."

He gently handed Ginger to Egan and climbed on Fiacra's back. Egan returned Ginger to him and stepped back. Fiacra rose in the air and flew swiftly toward Nantuor. As Fiacra flew, Liam prayed fervently to the One for Ginger's life. He loved her. If she were to die now . . . He started the thought over again. If she left him now, she would leave a void that he could not fill.

Fiacra sped quickly to Nantuor, landing lightly in front of Liam's medical facilities. Liam dismounted and hurried inside with Ginger.

He swept through the doors of his study preceded by several scurrying elves. They moved swiftly to clear the way for their king and his patient. He gently lay Ginger down in the surgery and quickly cut away her bloody clothing. Aili came in followed by several attendants with large basins of hot, scented water. Aili and Liam washed and dried their hands and began to work on Ginger.

Aili applied absorbent bandages to the wound. The bandage fibers were made from a plant with a blood clotting agent. They worked quickly to slow the flow of blood.

As Aili was caring for Ginger, Liam rifled through the medicine cabinet in the surgery. Finding a bottle of the same blood clotting agent, he poured it into the wound as he sang a prayer song of healing. For a moment everything was still, then the flow of blood stopped. The wound closed from the inside out, leaving soft pink skin where the horrible gash had been.

Ginger sighed and opened her eyes, finding herself looking straight into Liam's concerned gaze.

Liam sent an inquiring thought through her mind and body. The answer was encouraging: the damaged flesh had been repaired.

Moreover, her eyes were clear, and her temperature and pulse were normal. He smiled at her sleepy yawn and then gently kissed her forehead.

"How are you feeling my little dove?" he asked softly as he lovingly stroked her face.

"Sleepy," she replied, yawning again.

"Well then, perhaps you'd better sleep," Liam chuckled softly.

"But I just woke up," Ginger protested.

"I know precious one," Liam replied. "But you have lost a lot of blood and you must rest to recover your strength." His fingers gently caressed her face as he brushed a wisp of hair away from her forehead.

"What happened with Braen?" she asked.

"Braen is no longer your worry, my love. He will be dealt with." Liam's voice had a ring of finality that didn't escape Ginger even in her grogginess.

"Sleep a blessed sleep my beloved," he whispered. He leaned over and kissed her on the forehead. She sighed softly and fell quietly into a deep, restful sleep.

Liam gently picked her up and took her to the private suites, where his impatient sons waited. They quickly helped him settle Ginger comfortably in his suite as Eli watched from his cushion by the fireplace.

"This is where I want you to remain, my sons," he told them firmly. "She must be kept safe."

"We will not let her come to harm, Athair," Teagan told his father. His brothers stood behind him with the same determined look in their eyes. No one would cross this threshold who did not belong here.

Liam smiled at his sons. "In the past I have called you children. After this day you are children no more, but warriors." His eyes shone with pride. "Keep her safe, my sons. And remember: the Dark Elves are creatures of darkness. Trust no shadow." He pointed to Ginger. "She is a renewing light in a house that has long needed one."

"We will keep her safe, Athair. Don't worry," Teagan said. He turned and motioned to his brothers. They took up defensive positions around the bed.

Liam stood looking down at Ginger for a moment. His ears had not missed the sound of battle in the valley as he had worked to save her life. Now he heard it drawing nearer. He heard Arth shouting orders to his troops as they fought at the bridge to the house.

Liam swiftly crossed his bedroom and stepped into the small room that held his battle gear. He dressed in mere moments and left to join the fray.

A rustling sound caught the boys' attention. They looked down to see Old Eli trying to climb onto the bed with Ginger. "My lords," he wheezed. "Let me not be useless. Let me guard the king's lady. I owe him much."

"As you wish, old one," said Rigalis as he gently picked up the lizard and placed him on the foot of Ginger's bed. The creature settled down onto the soft covers, his eyes never leaving the terrace entrance.

In the valley below the sound of the battle intensified.

Braen had built up an army of three hundred gray warriors, using the larger island animals as hosts to hatch them out. His Dark Elf troops, however, had dwindled – he had lost five of them when he shot Rigalis, and another five at the caves. And ten had been dispatched to swim across the river and go after Liam's sons in the king's family quarters, leaving ten Dark Elves to command thirty gray warriors each during the attack on Nantuor.

His attack was getting bogged down at the bridge, where General Arth and his troops stopped most of the invaders. Liam arrived on the battlefield and immediately willed a barrier over the river. At the sight of Liam, five Dark Elves deserted and ran into the brush. Another five, swimming across the river in pursuit of Liam's sons, were trapped by the barrier. Liam increased the river's current and had it drag them to the bottom. He rolled huge boulders over them, crushing and killing all five.

Liam took up position in the huge oak tree by the river, from where he could see the entire battlefield and direct his troops' movements. He noticed a disturbance in the Royal Stables. The horses chased a Dark Elf out of the barn and into the trees, right into the jaws of a waiting drake that the horses had lured into the area.

Liam surveyed the rest of the scene. Fiacra and his clan were flying back and forth, dropping trees and boulders on the Dark Elves and their gray warriors. The Light Elves' archers and swordsmen were fighting ferociously. Casualties among Braen's troops were mounting.

A few Dark Elves broke through the battle and made for Liam's tree. Capt. Gildas and his elves took them out before they reached it. His archers eliminated most of the Dark Elves that tried to make it across the bridge. The ones that got past them were faced with Kendhal and his swordsmen.

Liam killed the two Dark Elves that managed to reach his tree. By that time they were pretty battered.

Liam finished the two ragged Dark Elves quickly and then looked up at Gildas and his archers.

"Gildas, your archers barely left me any Dark Elves at all."

Gildas chuckled and shook his golden head. "Did I not leave you a taste, my liege?"

"Just barely," muttered Liam.

"Ah Gildas, you were always a greedy child, and I see you haven't changed your habits," a laughing voice rang out from behind Liam.

It was Kendhal, Liam's chief swordsman. He was surrounded by his fellow swordsmen. Gildas' face darkened into a mock frown.

"Nay, it was merely efficiency that ended the battle so quickly. We could not wait forever for your swordsmen to get close enough to find their targets with your little metal sticks."

Kendhal's eyes widened in mock anger. "Little metal sticks indeed! These are the finest swords in all elfdom, wielded by the finest swordsmen in Nantuor. I trained them myself."

"Ah," responded Gildas with a mischievous glint in his eye. "That explains a lot."

"And we could not wait forever for your weak-eyed archers to finally find their targets," Kendhall exclaimed. "Victory could not wait on nearsighted elves who depend on little wooden sticks to defeat their foes."

Liam smiled as he listened to the friendly banter. It reminded him of his younger days, when these elves had been his playmates and friends. The boastful exchanges had not changed in the succeeding millennia.

"My friends," he interjected, "may I remind you that a few Dark Elves are still at large?"

"Not for long, sire," replied Kendhal. He nodded to his troops and left for the mopping up operation. Gildas and his troops quickly caught up.

"Have you no respect for your betters?" he scolded Kendhal. "You should have waited for us."

"Why?" purred Kendhal. "If you seek protection go back to the house."

Liam shook his head as the voices faded down the valley. Although the banter was a habit from childhood, it served a fighting purpose – it misled enemies into believing the elves weren't paying attention. For numerous opponents, that was the last mistake they ever made.

Teagan frowned. Something was wrong. The sunshine that had danced across the terrace only moments before seemed dimmed. A gloom hung over the elegant garden.

Old Eli's voice croaked warningly from the foot of Ginger's bed. "Beware, young prince. Beware!" A bird chirped a warning from the trees and then darted out of the garden.

Teagan listened intently. He heard nothing but he was tense, feeling evil was nearby. He stood on the terrace searching the shadows. There! Had something moved? His piercing gaze focused on a faint shadow under a tree. His father's words came to mind: "Trust no shadow."

He sent out a mental alert to his brothers in the room. They instantly began watching the shadow, but it didn't move. Rigalis' angry voice interrupted the silence.

"I'm tired of waiting. Why can't we go down to the bridge with Athair?"

"You know why, Rigalis," answered Barram sternly. "Lady Ginger must be kept safe.

"But Teagan and Owain can guard her. Athair himself said we are warriors. I want to go fight," complained Rigalis. Without another word he swept out of the room. Barram quickly followed, trying to coax him back.

"I'll go get them," said Owain darkly. "And the One help them when I do."

Teagan sighed in disgust and turned back to the terrace. The shadow was gone. Wondering where it moved to, he left the terrace to go investigate, leaving Ginger alone in the room.

Shortly after his departure, a shadow near the terrace door motioned to some nearby bushes, and all five Dark Elves entered the room. They approached the bed and stood smirking down at Ginger's sleeping form.

Eli raised himself up.

"Nay. Keep away," he croaked angrily. "Leave her alone." He hissed at the intruders, his mouth wide open to bite any who came closer.

The Dark Elves ignored him. Their leader Morfran looked down at Ginger's peaceful face.

"So this is what the great Liam Midir would risk his kingdom for," he spat contemptuously. He looked at his fellow assassins. "Let us finish off this human wench and then move on to Liam's whelps."

"It is *you* who are finished," said a deadly voice behind them. The Dark Elves turned to find themselves surrounded by Liam's sons. Their eyes were burning with the same elfish light their father had shown so many years ago in the Great Battle.

Morfran cursed inwardly. They had walked into a trap, set by four children no less. The Dark Elves shifted uneasily at the waves of power surging toward them from the brothers. The plants outside swayed and rustled. One of the Dark Elves reached for Ginger but his hand was repelled by an invisible barrier. He pulled it back with a hiss of pain.

"In fact," continued Teagan, his eyes filled with cold anger, "I'd say you're extinct." Teagan's sword came up and took off a Dark Elf's head. The other four lunged at the Light Elves with howls of rage.

Teagan stepped easily aside, sweeping his sword down beside him with the grace of a cat. Another head rolled across the carpet. He swiftly turned to defend his siblings.

Owain stepped aside and let his attacker pass, kicking him in the backside as he did. Hissing furiously, the Dark Elf turned to lunge at him again but ended up impaling himself on Owain's blade. Owain shoved the body off his blade with a disgusted grunt and turned to see how his brothers fared.

Rigalis was playing with his opponent, tormenting him with sharp swats and several insults that Owain was unaware he knew. Panting and outraged, the Dark Elf finally thrust his sword at Rigalis, who easily put his blade through the monster's heart.

Similarly, Barram was dancing about the room, taunting his opponent. The Dark Elf's blade repeatedly flew straight and true at his opponent, but when it reached its destination, Barram simply wasn't there. His laughter rang through the room, just as it had so many times at the practice field. His brothers were glad not to be on the receiving end of his taunts for once. Finally noticing that his brothers were unoccupied, he neatly stepped forward and stood still in front of the Dark Elf, presenting an easy target. He smiled at the intruder.

"Oh, surely he's not going to fall for tha . . ." started Teagan with a frown.

The Dark Elf shouted in victory and lunged at Barram, who easily dodged his blade and put his own through his enemy's heart. The Dark Elf slid to the floor, a look of surprise etched on his face.

"I guess he did," remarked Owain with a shrug. He recalled numerous times he himself had fallen for Barram's favorite maneuver.

The four brothers removed the bodies from the room and returned to their guard positions, their faces burning with satisfaction and determination. They were indeed elven warriors. The trees outside swayed with delight at the feeling of power and victory they exuded.

Just then Liam burst into the room. Having sensed something was wrong at the family quarters, he'd raced up the hill and entered the Royal House. When he came through the door to his quarters, he encountered four elven swords pointed directly at his throat. He skidded to a quick stop as his heart skipped a beat. The fierce light in his sons' eyes shone with the same intensity as their grandfather's. He remembered well the immense power behind that look.

"Well, either kill me or put them away," he remarked, motioning toward the drawn swords.

His sons sheepishly lowered their weapons and allowed him to enter the room.

"I see my love has been well protected," he commented as he moved toward Ginger.

Reaching for her before his sons could warn him, Liam was flung clear across the room and out onto the terrace. He hit the stones and slid into the grass.

"I meant to warn you Athair," said an embarrassed Teagan as the boys quickly moved to help their stunned father to his feet. "After the Dark Elves attacked the first time we got together and created an even stronger barrier around Lady Ginger."

"We wanted to make sure no one would even think of touching her," chimed in Rigalis.

Liam stood for a moment trying to get his bearings. Seeing his head was still in a whirl, his sons sent a wave of healing energy into him. Finally his head cleared and he looked around the terrace. He could feel the waves of energy coming from the bedroom and noticed the branches on the trees swaying. He looked at his sons.

"I doubt that even old Draco would dare to cross that threshold," he said ruefully, brushing dirt from his backside.

His sons laughed proudly and led him back into the room to Ginger's bedside.

"Well, my sons, you created this barrier," he said with a proud smile. "So you must be the ones to remove it."

"Remove it?" gulped Teagan. He turned to his brothers. "Did Tiernan ever tell us how to remove barriers?" he asked, a note of desperation in his voice. Liam looked down at Ginger in despair. It was too much for Teagan, who burst out laughing.

"I'm sorry Athair. I could not resist," he said, his laughter mingling with that of his brothers. Turning toward the barrier, they dismissed it easily and watched it melt away.

Liam breathed a sigh of relief. His sons were going to make a formidable team, one that might even rival their grandfather.

He turned as Lieutenant Niall entered the room, his face full of concern. “My lord, we have hunted down all the Dark Elves except for one. Braen is missing.”

“Renew the barrier and stay with her,” Liam ordered his sons.

He left the room to join the search for his old nemesis.

Chapter 20

The Bitter End

Under the direction of Liam and General Arth, elven troops searched the forest surrounding the valley but found no sign of Braen. The elves in fact passed his hiding place several times. He had pushed himself into the crevice of an old tree trunk, the darkness swallowing him up into nothingness.

With the lengthening shadows heralding the coming of sunset, Liam feared Braen would remain hidden a while longer, then slip away in the dark of night. He didn't have much time to draw out his crafty enemy.

On Liam's orders, Arth signaled the trumpeters to summon the troops back. They gathered quickly, mounted their horses, and prepared to leave. As Liam's Fianna approached their commander, Arth mounted his horse and waited for his king.

"Go back to Nantuor, Arth," Liam told his general. "I will join you later."

"But Braen is still at large, my lord," Arth answered, his eyes filled with worry.

"I know," said Liam "but he will not emerge until he feels safe. If you leave with everyone else, I will have a better opportunity to find him."

"Be careful my lord," Arth replied. "Braen is deadly."

"Which is why I need to deal with him immediately. We cannot allow him to be loosed upon this world. They would never be prepared for such a monster."

He smiled reassuringly at his old friend. "Don't worry Arth. I can handle him. Go back to Nantuor and make sure all is secure. I will join you later."

He handed Arth the reins of his horse. Reluctantly, Arth turned to go. He rode away murmuring a prayer of safety for his king.

After the last rider disappeared into the forest, Braen breathed a sigh of relief. At that faint sound, Liam's head snapped around instantly in Braen's direction. He stood motionless, trying to gauge Braen's location, his eyes burning with intensity. Braen caught sight of the elven king and froze, his heart beating wildly.

Liam stepped forward, listening intently. His sharp elven eyes scanned the forest for any movement, even that of a single leaf. His eyes focused on the shadows. He knew his foe could disappear into the shade of a tree or any other darkness. Liam's entire being was bent on finding Braen. He could feel the Dark Elf's evil presence nearby. He knew Braen was waiting for a chance to escape – so he gave it to him.

Seeing his nemesis turn his head up and away from his hiding place, Braen slithered quickly from the tree and bolted into the forest. His heart skipped a beat when he heard Liam's light footsteps closing in behind him. He doubled his pace and ran down a side trail that led to the thickest part of the forest.

Running at top speed, Liam never took his eyes off his quarry. He watched Braen's form disappear as he darted under the shade of trees, then pop back out into sunlight. Braen took him through several twists and turns in the woods but could not lose him.

Braen ran down a narrow forest path, jerking down several smaller trees across the trail behind him. Liam leapt lightly over the trees and continued his pursuit. Reaching a hilltop, Braen spotted a huge boulder resting beside the trail. He shoved it down the hill, then turned and continued his retreat. The boulder came crashing down toward Liam, who angrily sent it to the side of the trail with a shattering wave of elven light. Its smashed remains scattered in smoldering pieces in the tall grass beside the trail.

Braen spied a black leopard lazing on the broad limb of a large oak tree. Running up the tree trunk, he jumped lightly over the surprised cat and sent out a mental command for it to attack his pursuer. When the cat hesitated, Braen sent a burning hot wave of pain through its mind. Snarling with fear and rage, the animal jumped at Liam as he ran up the tree trunk. Liam instantly sent it to sleep in mid-air, and it landed harmlessly in the thick bushes below. The elven king followed Braen back to the ground and continued the hunt.

He heard Braen up ahead furiously splashing through a stream. The Dark Elf made his way across the water and clawed his way onto the embankment. Stumbling upon a young doe at the top, Braen slashed her with his knife and threw her back toward the stream, knowing Liam would not let her bleed to death. He ran to the other side of the glen and disappeared into the forest.

Liam crossed the stream and reached the embankment. Seeing the doe and hearing its pained cries, he briefly touched her back, sending a massive surge of healing energy into her body that closed the gaping wound in her side. He dashed up the embankment and ran down the forest path to the river.

Liam approached the swiftly flowing river, his eyes scanning for Braen. He stopped in his tracks when his eye caught a dark shadow on the opposite bank. The shadow hesitated for a moment and bolted into the forest. Liam jumped into the river and swam to the other side, losing precious time as he fought the strong current. He then made his way up the bank and vanished into the forest.

Braen waited at the edge of a clearing deeper in the forest. He crouched behind a tree and listened but heard nothing. He got to his feet and took a few tentative steps into the clearing. As he reached the center he felt the hair rise up on the back of his neck. Someone was behind him. He whirled around, his sword at the ready.

Liam stood before him, power surging from him in great waves. The trees in the clearing shuddered, their leaves rustling at his anger. His eyes blazed with rage as he gripped his sword, sunlight glancing off its razor-sharp edge. There would be no exile this time.

Moving swiftly, Braen tried to put his sword through Liam's midsection. Liam leapt lightly aside and swung at Braen's head. Braen rolled out of the way and came up on his feet, slashing at Liam. Liam blocked his blow and delivered one of his own. Braen deflected it and jumped quickly out of the way.

As he fought, an evil thought came to Braen's mind and a faint smile formed on his lips "You never did find out who killed your wife and daughter, did you Liam?" his voice hissed like a snake.

The question surprised Liam, though he never slowed his attack. "What difference does it make now, Braen? That was over two thousand years ago." He blocked another blow from Braen and countered with his own. Braen leaped backward to avoid it.

"It might make a world of difference to you, elf king," Braen answered as he swung his blade at Liam's neck. "I headed the party that found them that day. I made your wife scream nicely before I killed her. Her blood tasted sweet." Braen smiled at the brief look of shock that flashed across his enemy's face.

Liam continued his attack, looking for a weak spot in Braen's defense.

"And your daughter, and her husband, what a fool," continued Braen as he struck at Liam's sword hand. "He was the first to die." Liam smoothly blocked Braen's stroke and continued his assault.

"He actually tried to keep me busy so your wife and daughter could run away," Braen laughed, relishing the memory. "They were all surrounded before they knew it. Your daughter begged for the life of her unborn child. His blood was the sweetest of all."

Liam's eyes flashed, and the trees around the two warriors swayed with his anger. A huge limb crashed to the forest floor. The ground around them shuddered as the wind blew with a fury. Thunder rumbled in the sky, then gave way to a deafening explosion as a lightning bolt came down and hit the ground at the edge of the clearing.

Braen realized he had provoked the reaction he wanted, but Liam still was not distracted enough to kill. He tried again.

"You are a fool Liam, risking your life just to save a human wench. There are plenty more where she came from." He swung at Liam in another missed attempt to knock the sword from his hand.

"You are wrong Braen," Liam uttered coldly as he blocked Braen's blows and drove him back into the center of the clearing. "There are none like her."

"And you are about to die for her," Braen growled savagely.

"No," replied Liam. "You are."

Braen's handsome face distorted with rage. He lunged at Liam's head.

"Killing me won't keep her nightmares away, will it?" Braen said fiercely, his jade eyes aflame. "She will have them forever. They will probably take her sanity; unless of course you wipe her memory of anything to do with elves."

He noticed a spark of dismay in Liam's eyes. "Oh, I'm sorry, that will mean she will have to forget you too, won't it?"

He stepped forward, slashing at Liam's throat. Liam countered easily as the fight grew faster and more intense, each opponent looking for an opening to deliver a death blow.

"How sad," Braen continued, his voice an evil, gloating whisper, "to lose the only love you have had in over two thousand years. How lonely for you; and what a difficult choice – between her sanity and your happiness."

Finally Braen saw what he was looking for – a split second of distraction on Liam's face. In a flash Braen's knife was out. With lightning speed it flew from his hand and plunged deep into Liam's right thigh. Liam grimaced in pain as Braen darted out of the clearing and into the surrounding forest.

Liam pulled out the knife. He felt the poison from the blade burn deep into his flesh, sending a dark cloud of depression into his mind. He spent several precious minutes partially healing his leg, then followed Braen into the darkening forest. His leg still throbbing, he shuddered and moved into the trees.

Braen quickly made for the path to the bottom of the cliffs. If he could reach the path before Liam caught him, he could escape. Then he could go back to Cluse for more troops.

The relentless chase went on all night. His limbs trembling with exhaustion, Braen felt like his lungs were on fire, while Liam reeled with sickness and dizziness caused by the poison seeping through his wound.

Near dawn, Liam followed Braen's trail into the south part of the island near the caves. The elven king limped wearily down the forest path searching for signs of his quarry. Sitting to catch his breath, Braen watched Liam's approach from a hiding place in the trees.

Sadness shadowed Liam's face as the poison continued to cloud his mind with depression. He thought of Ginger's suffering at Braen's hands, and his own helplessness outside Braen's hideaway. He could still feel Ginger's horror as Braen forced her to relive nightmare after nightmare.

Braen's voice startled Liam out of his sad reverie. It dripped with malice as he whispered from his dark hiding place, throwing his voice to disguise his location.

"You never knew, did you?"

"Knew what?" asked Liam wearily, his eyes searching the dark. He trembled with fever as the poison worked its way into his vital organs.

"That you didn't capture all the Dark Elves," Braen hissed.

Liam's face grew pale as he absorbed the icy shock. Dark Elves loose in this unprepared society? The humans would never survive.

"You never knew because you never bothered to look, never bothered to find out if any Dark Elves had remained hidden to carry out my orders." Braen's accusing voice grew hard and cold. "That's why any deaths among your people are your own doing, Liam."

He paused to let the words sink in and then continued, his voice cracking like a whip.

"Did you ever stop to ask yourself why your beloved humans turned on you? Why the very people you vowed to cherish and protect with your lives began to hunt you down like rabid dogs?"

Liam felt the stab of betrayal like a blade through his heart. In two thousand years the Light Elves had never learned why their human brethren had suddenly turned their wrath on them. It was a wound carried by every Light Elf.

Smiling, Braen continued. "Humans are so easily seduced, so easy to corrupt. They will even murder their own children simply under the influence of a few whispered words while they sleep." His voice was a silken whisper, like a serpent's hiss burrowing its way into Liam's mind.

Liam held his sword unsteadily, his sweat-soaked body shaking from the poison. He fought to keep his fevered thoughts clear as Braen's words pierced his mind like worms burrowing into an open wound. This could not be true.

Braen reveled at the pain in Liam's eyes. "That's right elf-King, I arranged the seduction of the first human, and the next, and the next. Did you really think I would submit to your exile on a dead mountain while you enjoyed life among the humans? Just think about all those brave young soldiers, all those lovely young elf-maids, ripped to pieces because you couldn't be bothered to do your job."

Braen's voice hammered Liam, relentlessly ripping away his defenses and exposing his greatest fear – that he would fail to protect those he had sworn to defend.

"And you call yourself a king," continued Braen contemptuously. "But you are a butcher. You murdered your own people and your beloved humans with your own carelessness."

"I cannot have been the cause of all this," Liam whispered, his voice trembling with shock and pain.

Braen reveled in his agony. "And all those innocent little human children, all murdered, all soaked in their own blood because of you! And that's your greatest fear isn't it – the fear of failure? Does it bother you to know that it was *your* fault – that all the bloodshed was over *you* because *you* couldn't leave well enough alone; couldn't leave us to live as we pleased on this earth? You had to start interfering and now all those lost lives are on *your* head."

Braen's eyes gleamed in triumph. "How does it feel to know your entire life has been soaked in the blood of innocent humans whose only crime was knowing *you*?"

Liam's fevered mind tried desperately to reject Braen's words, but they stabbed deep into his conscience.

"You were butchering them, Braen," Liam finally exclaimed. "I had to do something. The war between us was inevitable."

"Did you really think your friendship with the humans would last forever?" Braen retorted venomously. "You wallowed in filth every time you came in contact with them. You might as well have wallowed with the beasts of the field."

"You are wrong," Liam declared, his voice shaking. "It is a privilege to know such a noble race."

Braen laughed. "Remember Liam, when comrades died in senseless accidents; when loved ones disappeared and their bodies were found hacked to pieces; when those two little war orphans who you thought you hid so cleverly were found twitching like impaled rabbits. Think of all that and just remember, I warned you not to interfere." His evil whisper cut through Liam's soul like a white hot blade.

"Now you will have my wrath to deal with until the day that you die," Braen crowed. "For the rest of your long life, wherever you look, wherever you go – we will be there, ripping to pieces everyone and everything that you love."

A sob broke from Liam's parched throat as he thought of his four sons suffering at Braen's command.

"And then finally, when you can no longer stand the agony of living in this world, you will beg me to kill you. You will die as a maimed animal that must finally be put out of its misery. That is the price you will pay for your beloved humanity."

Just then, out of the depths of darkness and despair, Liam suddenly felt a warmth flood over him like a blazing ray of sunshine. It soothed the savage wounds in his psyche and instantly eradicated his searing depression. As Liam stood in that warmth he heard the strong, loving voice of the One.

"You answer only to Me and I love you."

Liam felt his battered soul rise and soar with hope. His mind cleared and he began to get his bearings in the darkness. "Thank you, Mighty Father," he whispered. From somewhere in the darkness he heard Braen utter a faint growl. Once again he heard the One's reassuring voice.

"Fear not, help is coming."

With the sun just beginning to rise, Liam raised his sword and stepped into the fading darkness. He heard a faint sound as Braen leapt out at him from behind. Liam swung around to face his nemesis, barely stopping Braen's blade before it reached his throat.

Braen countered by delivering a savage kick to Liam's bloody right thigh. Gasping with pain, Liam fell to his knees. Braen kicked the sword from Liam's grasp and slammed his sword hilt into Liam's head, knocking him into the dirt.

Liam's mind reeled. With the poison darkening his vision, he struggled to make out Braen's form. He fought to remain conscious as Braen stood over him and raised his sword for the final blow.

Suddenly there was a loud crack, and a blinding light appeared behind Braen. As Liam's consciousness slipped away, he saw his father Brig step through the Rift, sword in hand, his own troop of Fianna at his heels.

Brig's eyes smoldered when he saw Braen standing over his bloodied son. Braen felt the High King's immense power prickle up his spine like electricity. Terror stole his breath away as adrenaline shot through his body like a lightning bolt.

Braen immediately bolted across the clearing, barely keeping his head as Brig's blade sliced the air just behind him. Brig's Fianna then came bursting through the Rift in an angry wave, their enraged faces fixed on the Dark Elf who had attacked their Sovereign's son. They were followed by elven soldiers who joined the pursuit of Braen into the forest.

Brig moved quickly to his son, barking orders for a stretcher and a bottle of water. Seeing the poison oozing out of Liam's pores, Brig sent an inquiring thought into his mind to assess his condition.

Gathering his strength, Brig placed his hands on his son's fevered brow. A golden glow shone underneath his hands as he commanded the poison to turn inert. He felt Liam's temperature cool and finally return to normal. The wound on his leg quickly healed from the inside out. His eyes slowly opened and fixed on his father in surprise.

"Athair, how did you get here?" he asked weakly.

Brig lovingly brushed the hair back from Liam's brow. "There will be plenty of time to talk later, son. Right now just rest." With a gentle smile he sent Liam into a deep healing sleep. Brig's troops then carefully put him on a stretcher and sent him toward Nantuor with a large armed escort.

Brig ran into the forest and caught up with his Fianna. They relentlessly pursued Braen, who found himself cut off from the path leading down to the sea. Reversing course and making his way to the top of the cliffs, he plunged into the sea, barely avoiding being cut in two by a Fianna blade.

The angry Fianna showered the water with a hailstorm of arrows and glittering spears. Thinking quickly, Braen remained deep underwater and called to the great white shark that he had stationed at the base of the cliffs. He had it attack a nearby sea lion and waited as the blood spread through the water. Then he ordered the shark to show himself at the surface to dupe the Fianna into thinking he was dead.

Brig was not fooled. He whistled for Fiacra and waited patiently, his dark silken hair blowing in the morning breeze, the sunrise reflecting off his armor.

Having flown over Brig's troops and seen Liam being returned to Nantuor, Fiacra could hardly contain his joyful surprise at seeing Brig. The great eagle dropped level with the top of the cliffs. "Yes my lord?" he asked Brig respectfully. "What does the High King command?"

Brig smiled grimly at his old friend. "Take your children and seek out Braen. He must not escape."

"With the One's help my Lord, he will never see another sunrise," answered Fiacra fiercely. This evil creature had killed half his children and nearly killed his dear friend. His golden eyes were aflame as he soared high on the wind, calling his children to join in the hunt for the Lord of the Dark Elves.

Meanwhile, Braen held the tail of the great white as it slid through the water toward the tiny island where Braen's yacht was anchored. Above them the Eagle Clan swooped back and forth over the restless waves, striking the surface with their talons at the slightest hint of any movement underneath.

Braen was finally forced to emerge for a breath of air. Fiacra spotted him and dropped down from the sky like a giant thunderbolt. He slammed his talons deep into the surface of the water, the memory of his dead children burning in his heart.

Braen felt the searing pain of Fiacra's talons raking his back. He frantically dove down beneath the shark as several more eagles violently pierced the water and beat the sea into a foamy froth. Growing crazed by the smell of Braen's blood, the great white turned and attacked him, forcing Braen to put his knife through its brain. An eagle snatched up the shark's body and carried it high into the air, where another eagle joined in tearing the body to pieces.

Just when Braen thought his lungs would burst, he found a large piece of driftwood draped in seaweed. He cowered under it until dark, watching as the eagles circled the area, their bronze wings gleaming in the moon's silver glow. Finally the great birds' strength began to wane and they reluctantly headed back to Brisal.

Carefully and quietly, his eyes scanning the heavens for eagles, Braen started to make his way toward the yacht.

Chapter 21

A New Beginning

Fiacra and his sons flew back to Nantuor to report Braen's escape. Brig didn't blame Fiacra – the crafty Dark Elves excelled at evading capture. He thanked Fiacra for his efforts and left to see his son.

Recovering rapidly under his father's care, Liam could walk the terrace with his father by mid-afternoon. News of Brig's arrival had spread quickly over the island, sparking plans for a great celebration that night. Many of Brig's soldiers had already reunited with loved ones they thought they'd never see again. Many more elven families were expecting friends and loved ones to come through the Rift that night for the festivities.

As Liam looked out over the Royal Gardens, he felt the entire island reverberate with elven power radiating from the Rift and from Brig and his troops. His heart quickened as the power flowed through his body, uplifting his spirit and filling his mind with clarity. He had not felt this power for almost two thousand years, not since he and his people had surrendered it to protect mankind by placing the barrier around the Dark Elves.

Liam turned and walked to Ginger's room. Finding her sleeping peacefully, he looked down at her for a moment, his heart too full for him to speak.

His sons had been waiting for him in Ginger's room, having been instructed by Liam to stay there with her. They crowded around him, each trying to embrace him. "Are you alright Athair?" asked Rigalis. "We were worried when we heard the golden trumpets and you did not return with the others."

"I am unhurt my sons." smiled Liam. "Although a rest is in order before I go off on any more adventures."

His sons smiled and breathed a sigh of relief.

"I am glad to hear that," said Barram, "and I am sure Rigalis is too. An arrow in the chest should be sufficient adventure for at least a month."

"More like a lifetime," replied Liam with a royal frown. He turned and looked at Ginger. "If you will kindly remove the barrier, I would like to speak to my bride-to-be."

The four young elves dismissed the barrier with a wave of their hands. A few faint sparks crackled in the air above the bed and the air began smelling of jasmine. Liam looked at his sons with a raised eyebrow.

"We decided we needed a little more flair, so we have been practicing," explained Teagan. "It was my idea to add the sparks," he added proudly.

"And *our* idea to add the jasmine," said Owain, indicating himself and Rigalis. "Barram wanted to add fire and brimstone, but we thought it a bit much, and we were worried that the smell might disturb Lady Ginger."

"I imagine waking up to the smell of fire and brimstone would be enough to disturb any mortal," remarked Liam, slightly amused. "And now . . ." he said, turning back to Ginger.

His sons watched as Liam gently called Ginger from sleep. He kissed her forehead softly and looked lovingly into her eyes. She smiled sleepily at him.

"Hi," she whispered.

"Hello, my little dove," he responded, his voice lilting with elvish ardor.

"What happened?" she asked.

"The Dark Elves were wiped out and Braen will soon be hunted down." Liam leaned down and kissed Ginger gently on the lips. She shivered from a thrill of fear. *Braen is still alive.*

"Are you cold, precious one?" Liam asked, concerned.

"No," Ginger murmured sleepily. The thought of Braen faded from her mind as she grew sleepy again. "Not at all. I just feel so sleepy."

Liam tucked her blanket around her. He was about to send her to sleep when she drifted off herself with a happy smile. He looked around at his sons.

Teagan cleared his throat quietly. "We've been practicing that too," he explained.

"On what?" Liam inquired.

"Well," said Owain, "we thought it best to start on something small, so . . ."

"We have been practicing on chickens," Rigalis interjected proudly. "I can put a rooster to sleep in mid-crow."

"You didn't have to learn manipulation for *that*," smirked Barram impishly. When Rigalis failed to retaliate, Barram looked at him with a puzzled frown.

"We are too old to act so childish," said Rigalis stiffly. "We are warriors now."

"Ah, then you are too old to retaliate when I do this," laughed Barram. With a blur of motion he removed Rigalis' gilded belt, fled to the terrace, and climbed atop a large tree. An incensed Rigalis pursued closely, while Teagan and Owain watched the pair from the garden, at turns jeering and cheering at the spectacle.

Liam smiled at his sons. "It is indeed good to be home," he laughed softly to himself.

After Ginger's nap Liam took her for a walk. Finding the fresh air exhilarating, Ginger drank tea and chatted away with the royal couple Brig and Gwaynek.

Liam glanced at the terrace, where Oriana stood alone looking out over Nantuor. He briefly stood in shocked silence at what his healer's eye saw. Then he excused himself and joined her on the terrace.

"What troubles you Oriana?" he asked quietly.

Oriana raised tearful eyes to her king. Then her gaze went to Ginger who had joined them on the terrace.

"I have treated you with disrespect and hatred," she whispered. "I have no excuses for what I have done. The One has found it in His heart to forgive me my deeds. Can you find it in yours?"

Ginger's eyes brimmed with tears. "I already have, Oriana," she said softly. "I already have." She gave Oriana's hand a soft squeeze.

Oriana looked over at her king. "I have sinned against you even more, my lord. I acted as a traitor to my own people and against my own king. How can you forgive me that?"

"Freely, little one," Liam replied. "Just as the One freely forgives me my trespasses against Him." His voice was kind and gentle as he took Oriana's hand and kissed it in a gesture of royal forgiveness.

Oriana smiled gratefully and whispered, "Thank you, my liege."

With a calculated smile, Liam hid the shock he felt upon touching Oriana's hand. Her body had confirmed his previous suspicion. She was with child – Braen's child. He could not tell her the news now, but later he would have to take her to his study and break it to her gently. His heart ached with pity. *To be carrying the child of a Dark Elf*!

But still, he reasoned, the child was half Light Elf too. The good could always outweigh the bad. The child would have a will of his own – and Liam vowed in his heart to ensure the child chose good over evil.

Later that evening Liam led Oriana toward his examination room to check on her health and that of her unborn child. He broke the news of her pregnancy gently. Oriana stood in shocked silence for a moment. Then she suddenly announced she wanted to kill the child before he was born.

"I will not kill an innocent child, Oriana," he told her firmly.

"But it is Braen's child," protested Oriana tearfully. "It can only be evil."

"It is not just Braen's child, it is yours as well," counseled Liam. "And no child is born evil, Oriana. Doing evil is a choice made by individuals."

"Would it not be better to kill him in the womb before he can choose evil?"

"Killing a helpless, unborn child is a great evil in itself," replied Liam. "I will not allow it. If you do not want him, I will raise him myself, but he is not to be harmed, is that clear?"

She nodded and accompanied Liam into his study. As she sobbed quietly, Liam stepped outside to talk to his counselors, leaving Aili to watch over Oriana. Touched by the sound of Oriana's grief, the four elven warriors stood in silence for a moment before one of them addressed their king.

"I have described to Oriana Braen's depredations on the Light Elves and his role in the massacre of her entire family," shared Ranal. "She found the truth hard to accept, but she finally understands Braen's viciousness."

"She must be devastated," said Tiernan sympathetically.

"Yes," said Liam. "I have tried to explain to her that Braen had her mind ensnared, but she is filled with sorrow and shame nonetheless.

"She will need much kindness and understanding until her heart and spirit mend," said Ranal.

"Yes," agreed Egan. "And she should be watched until she has made her peace with the One. It would be tragic if she were to free herself from Braen's savage grip only to end her own life out of sorrow."

"She will be closely watched," Liam assured him. "There will be at least one comforter with her at all times."

"I would like to volunteer for that position, Liam," said Ranal. "After watching her so closely I feel I know her better than any of you. Perhaps the One will help me use that knowledge to comfort her."

"As you wish, Ranal," answered Liam. "Keep a watchful eye on her, old friend. Grief can easily overwhelm a wounded heart."

That night Ginger went to sleep early and seemed to be sleeping soundly. She suddenly awoke screaming. The "suggestion" Braen had planted in her mind had finally driven her to the brink of madness.

Brig and Gwaynek heard her scream and ran into the room. They found Ginger cringing on the far side of her bed staring at the vase in the corner.

Brig tried to assure Ginger there was nothing to fear. But she quickly grew agitated, insisting that he find a weapon she could use to kill the Dark Elf. Brig asked where the Dark Elf was.

"Are you blind?" Ginger asked indignantly. "He's right there in the corner, hiding behind that vase!"

"That poor little lamb," Gwaynek said in Celtic. "What she must have gone through to be left like this."

"No," Brig replied, "this isn't from torture. This is the work of a Dark Elf suggestion put into her subconscious. It will swiftly eat away at her sanity until she snaps." He looked at Ginger, whose eyes were still fixed on her unseen enemy.

"Oh Brig," said Gwaynek softly, "can this be undone?"

"Not easily. It takes much prayer and faith. In her case, it will take a miracle."

Brig slowly moved toward Ginger and gently lifted her to her feet. The wild look in her eyes worried him. He didn't want to put her under restraints.

Reading her husband's face, Gwaynek stepped quickly to Ginger and sent a calming warmth through her body that instantly soothed her into a drowsy, almost limp state.

Brig picked her off the floor into his arms and she immediately tensed.

"Do not be afraid, little one. I am only going to put you back in bed."

"Please put me down," she whispered, trembling.

"But," Brig started.

"Put me down!" she demanded, her voice rising.

"Put her down, beloved," Gwaynek told Brig.

He sat Ginger back down on the floor and stepped away. Gwaynek smiled kindly at Ginger, who looked uncertainly at her for a moment and then slowly smiled back.

"There there, little lamb, let me tuck you into bed," Gwaynek crooned softly as she gently stroked Ginger's cheek.

Gwaynek helped Ginger into bed and tucked her in. Meanwhile Brig looked into Ginger's troubled mind. He saw an image of the table and vase in the corner of the room, with a deadly looking Dark Elf hiding behind them. He saw other things as well, impressions that bothered him deeply.

Gwaynek stroked the hair from Ginger's face and pressed a tender mother's kiss on her forehead. She sent Ginger into a sweet, healing, dreamless sleep.

"Come, my love," Brig said softly to Gwaynek.

They both stepped out into the hall. Brig closed the door and turned to see Liam coming down the hall. Brig and Gwaynek moved to intercept him before he reached Ginger's door.

"Good morning, Mather," Liam said with a smile as he kissed her cheek. "Good morning Athair. I just thought I would see how my love is feeling this morning."

He stopped short at the look on his parents' faces. A spark of fear gnawed at him.

"Son, come with me." Brig took Liam's arm and started to lead him back down the hall.

Liam stopped. "Athair, what is wrong? Is Ginger . . .?"

The look in his father's eyes chilled him to the bone. The spark of fear exploded into an inferno. He turned to run for Ginger's door but Brig's firm grasp on his arm stopped him.

"Son, please do not disturb her. She is sleeping peacefully."

"Alright Athair," Liam said reluctantly. He turned and followed his parents down the hall and out onto the terrace. Liam's sons were seated at a large table there with breakfast laid out before them.

Liam sat down across from his sons with his parents on either side of him. The blessing was offered over the meal and several attendants moved in to serve the family.

Liam fidgeted with his food and then looked at his father.

"Athair, what is wrong with Ginger?"

Brig set his cup down and considered what to say.

"Son, your Mather and I looked in on Ginger this morning and found her cringing behind her bed, hiding from an imaginary Dark Elf."

The color draining from his face, Liam said nothing as he waited for his father to finish.

"I looked into her mind and found a Dark Elf suggestion." Brig watched as his son struggled to remain calm. His grandsons sat motionless, their faces pale with shock. The silence on the terrace was deafening; even the birds had stopped singing.

"She has had several horrendous dreams, son – dreams that no human could deal with."

Brig saw the grief in his son's eyes. He paused a moment, then continued.

"Her mind is so rattled by what it has had to endure . . ." he trailed off. "Perhaps with much prayer and treatment she could recover, but for the moment . . . she is quite insane."

Two days later Ginger awoke with a violent start, her body drenched in sweat. She lay trembling, too terrified to move. The nightmares were getting worse. In this last one, she was being roasted alive by a searing hot blast of green fire from a dragon's snout. She could smell the stench of her own flesh sizzling on the bone.

She knew Liam would arrive in a moment, his keen elven senses picking up on her latest bad dream.

She hated this. She hated feeling helpless and useless – helpless because she couldn't stop the nightmares, useless because she was so incapacitated by the dreams that at times she couldn't even dress herself. Instead, she would sit in a corner trembling and crying until Liam came. He would speak softly to her and hold her face close to his. Then she would feel a surge of tremendous power flow through her mind and chase the terror away – at least for a while.

She hated Liam seeing her in such a state. And much to her horror, she was beginning to hate Liam too.

She knew she still loved him, but she resented him as well. Liam was always in control, always remained calm. And more than anything, he pretended never to see the Dark Elves that were stalking her, even when they were standing in plain sight. He would just say something soothing and then go concoct some awful sleeping drought.

She sighed as she rubbed her eyes. Why put her to sleep? The Dark Elf would still be there when she woke up.

Liam sat back and looked at his father. "We will have to try to heal the damage done by the suggestion," he told him.

"I agree," said Brig.

Gwaynek nodded her agreement. The three elves rose and headed for Ginger's room.

When they arrived Ginger was sleeping fitfully. Brig stepped forward and touched her forehead, a slight glow illuminating her face and then fading away. She sighed quietly and fell into a relaxed, peaceful sleep.

"Thank you, Athair," said Liam. "She was suffering."

"You are welcome, son. Now, let us get down to business. We are here to heal her and we must not lose a moment."

As he spoke Ginger stirred a little and moaned uncertainly. The Dark Elf suggestion was re-entering her mind.

The three elves held hands around the bed and began to gather their healing power. Ginger moaned again as the suggestion grew stronger, stirring terrible dreams into faint remembrance.

Their power elevated, the elves began singing a song to the One, praising His power, love, kindness, and generosity, and asking for Ginger to be healed. Suddenly a brilliant light filled the room. An immense surge of healing power was felt by the elves. At first Ginger was overwhelmed, but then she breathed a quiet sigh and the feeling was gone. The song faded quietly and was done. Brig looked into Ginger's mind. It was clear of any Dark Elf influence.

The elves breathed a tired sigh of their own. The suggestion had been tenacious and they were spent.

Liam looked at his father. "Will she require a few days rest to recover?"

"I shouldn't think so," Brig said. "She should be just fine"

That evening the elves of Nantuor dressed in their finest clothes to celebrate their king's engagement to the Lady Ginger.

Everyone gathered on the main terrace. Brig's eyes lit on an elf he had not seen in five hundred years – and that was not long enough. He turned an irritable scowl on Liam.

"What is *he* doing here?"

"Who?" asked Liam, puzzled at his father's sudden change of mood.

"Him!" snapped Brig, pointing to a tall handsome elf in the crowd. The elf caught Liam's eye and began making his way toward the happy couple.

"Uncle Lucan?" asked Liam. "He's supposed to be here. We are celebrating our engagement."

"You sent him an invitation?"

"Of course I did. He's family." Liam stared at his father. "He's my uncle."

"I'm surprised he's not dancing on a table," snorted Brig.

The exchange surprised Ginger. "What's wrong with Uncle Lucan?"

"What isn't wrong?" Brig scowled. Seeing Ginger's puzzlement, he explained. "My parents in a brief moment of elven insight named him Lucan, Bringer of Light. But I have never met *anyone* who was harder to wring the truth from than him."

He took a swallow of wine and continued. "Elves usually try to live up to their given name, but my brother was a bigger miss than anyone I have ever seen."

He tensed up as Lucan joined the party.

"Did I hear someone mention my name?" he asked in a melodic voice, smiling at his brother.

"No," snapped Brig.

"Oh, but I'm sure I heard my name float over from this blessed corner of the room." Favoring Ginger with a brilliant smile, he raised an eyebrow at Brig and waited for an introduction.

Liam's elbow in his father's ribs stirred Brig to politeness.

"Alright!" he muttered sullenly. "Ginger, I would like to introduce you to Lucan, Liam's uncle. Lucan, this is . . ."

"I know," Lucan interrupted. "I heard. Come here and give your uncle Lucan a big hug."

He scooped up Ginger in an embarrassing bear hug.

"I'm so glad you came to our celebration," emerged Ginger's voice from somewhere inside the bear hug.

"Thank you, my dear," exclaimed Lucan as he released her. "I almost did not make it here. My invitation must have gotten lost." He stared in Brig's direction and added, "I had to hear about it by word of mouth."

Liam wheeled around at his father. "Athair!" he scolded.

Brig grimaced sheepishly. "Wait until I find out which big-mouth invited him," he muttered. He looked across the room and caught Gwaynek's inquisitive glance. Raising an eyebrow, she looked at Lucan and then at Brig, who had promised her to be nice if his brother showed up. Brig smiled and then turned to hide his scowl from her.

Lucan stepped back and looked at Ginger, his hands on her shoulders.

"My goodness but she is a pretty little thing, is she not?"

He leaned over and whispered conspiratorially into her ear, "I will just have to spend a lot more time in Nantuor so I can get to know my new niece, will I not?"

Ginger smiled at his attention. "You'll absolutely adore me once you get to know me," he told her.

"Not quite," admonished Brig. "You are coming straight back to the Realm with me after this is over. You cannot stay in this world and you know why."

"Why?" asked Ginger.

"Just ask some peasant girls in Old England," remarked Brig, warming to his task. "Or perhaps some merchants in ancient Egypt. Or, what about the poor soul in that European museum who still thinks they own the largest emerald in the world."

He turned to Lucan. Remembering Lucan's shady dealing with the museum's curator Brig remarked, "Is it not amazing how a "suggestion" can make a piece of glass look like a priceless artifact?"

"Brig!" came Gwaynek's soft voice in his ear. It stopped him dead in his tracks. "You promised."

"Oh, alright my dear," he growled. "I just want her to be forewarned."

"I don't need to be forewarned," Ginger interjected. "I used to be a Texas Ranger and I have met plenty of Uncle Lucans in my line of work. I think he's quite charming. We are going to get along just fine."

The others stood openmouthed as she took Lucan's arm and escorted him to the refreshment tables. They watched as Liam's sons fell on their Uncle Lucan with joyful hugs. The brothers were not dressed in their usual princely robes, but in the garb of the warriors they had become. They wore the emerald green tunics of an elven soldier, with gold buttons and a golden sword at their side. Their hair was in warrior braids.

"My goodness Brig," a lilting female voice spoke up behind him. "The last time I saw you, you had a scowl on your face. And two thousand years later, it is still there."

Brig turned to greet his sister Arlyn. She was beautiful in a white silk dress, her golden hair hanging in heavy waves to her hip. Her emerald green eyes, which had stolen the heart of more than one elven courtier, sparked with laughter.

"It is not the same scowl. It's a different one," Brig said as he hugged his sister.

"And who is it for this time?" the she-elf inquired.

"It is for whatever loud-mouth invited Lucan to this celebration."

"I am so sorry, Brig. I guess I am the loud-mouth," she confessed with a charming smile. "But I just could not come without Lucan. You should have seen the look on his face when I told him I had not seen his invitation. I just could not say no when he begged me to bring him."

"Oh yes," said Brig. "I am well-acquainted with that look. He used it whenever he wanted something from Athair."

"Now With, do not be that way."

"Brig. My name is Brig. You know I hate being called With."

"But that is part of your name dear – Brig Withell Midir. There's no escaping it, I am afraid."

Brig cringed when he heard his middle name, the source of his hated childhood nickname. "So help me Arlyn, if I hear that name one more time . . ."

"What name?" broke in Ginger. She had returned from the refreshment tables with Liam's sons and their uncle Lucan in tow.

"Never mind," muttered Brig as he glanced at Lucan.

"I think he means With. Isn't that right Brig?" asked Lucan. "You see my dear Ginger, his middle name is Withall. As children we shortened it to With. He hates being called With," he said, pronouncing the name loud and slowly.

Brig took a step toward him but once again was stayed by a look from his wife. He took a deep, calming breath and turned to Ginger.

"If you will excuse me my dear, I think I will go get a glass of wine."

"I would be absolutely thrilled to go get you a glass of wine, Wi . . . I mean Brig," chimed in Lucan.

"No thank you, Lucan," replied Brig with excessive formality. "I can get it myself."

He turned on his heel and glided regally toward the serving tables.

"Oh shoot," exclaimed Ginger. "I forgot to get a fork. Brig, would you mind very much getting me one on your way back?"

Brig stopped dead in his tracks and stood motionless.

"Brig?" Ginger asked uncertainly. He ignored Ginger as a frown spread across his face.

"Uh, well if it's too much trouble," began Ginger, "I can get off my lazy carcass and . . ."

Brig came to himself with a start.

"I am very sorry, my dear. I did not mean to ignore you. What were you saying?"

Liam was concerned by his father's apparent confusion.

"Athair, are you alright?" he asked, stepping toward Brig.

"I am fine, son." Brig said frowning. He looked at Liam.

"I sense the presence of an unfamiliar Light Elf nearby."

"An unknown Light Elf?" Liam was puzzled. "I thought we knew every Light Elf in our kingdom."

"I would not exactly call myself unknown, Liam," said a familiar voice behind him. "More like abandoned."

Liam and the others turned toward the voice but saw no one. A chuckle came from the stone wall in front of them. Suddenly the figure of a male elf formed before them.

Liam and Brig recognized him immediately.

"Cian Nuada!"

Brig watched in surprise as the Light Elf answered with a bow showing a little more attitude than respect.

"We thought you died in the hunts," Liam uttered in amazement.

"Apparently not, old friend," replied the handsome elf, his dark brown eyes flashing angrily. He was lean and muscular with long dark hair, and he moved with the grace of a panther.

"What happened to you, Cian?" asked Liam.

"We were cut off," Cian responded. "Why did you not wait for us?" he demanded quietly, the tightness in his voice betraying his anger.

"We thought you were dead Cian, and we could not wait any longer," said Liam. "The humans were about to overrun us. We had to leave or die. Where are the rest of you?"

Cian paused a moment then replied, "I am all that is left of my house, Liam. There is no 'rest of us.'"

In the stunned silence that followed, Liam recalled his dear friend's family; the many brave warriors, the beautiful, gentle she-elves, the elven children and infants, all those precious little lives gone from this earth forever. Liam would not see them again until he was with the One in heaven. His heart was full of grief for his friend's loss.

Liam moved to Cian's side and reached out to put a comforting arm around his shoulders.

"I am so sorry, Cian," he said softly. "We would have come to your aid if we had known you were still alive."

Cian angrily pushed his arm away. "So you say, cousin," he said bitterly.

The two stared at each other, Cian seemingly struggling with his emotions. Finally he sighed deeply and his shoulders sagged. His face grew tired as he spoke, his voice quiet.

"I know you would have come if you had known. I do not mean to speak with such resentment. It is difficult to be so alone, with no family, for so long. Only a few of us survived the hunts. We have formed an alliance to fight the evil ones among us."

"What evil ones?" asked Brig.

"Surely you don't think Braen risked all his forces in battle? There are Dark Elves among the humans. We have been fighting them since the hunts."

Liam shut his eyes and sighed. "Braen hinted as much," he said. "We must prepare to meet this threat with whatever force is necessary to stop them."

Cian nodded. "I will get in touch with the rest of my group and let them know I have found you. Then I will brief you on what we have done in your absence. We have a very efficient organization."

Liam was intrigued. "Indeed?" Then another question occurred to him.

"Cian, how were you able to hide yourself from us? You appeared as if you had been invisible."

Cian smiled mischievously. "The One gave us gifts to help us survive. We can create the illusion that we blend in with our surroundings. We can also sense the presence of a Dark Elf miles away and track his movements."

"Amazing!" exclaimed Brig. "What a powerful tool to fight the enemy."

"You are indeed blessed," said Liam.

"Not to mention lethal," added Lucan.

Cian suddenly began chuckling.

"What are you laughing at?" asked Liam.

"Don't you feel it?" Cian asked them.

The puzzled elves looked at each other. "I don't understand," Liam said.

"Your power," explained Cian. "When you were praising the One I felt immense power flowing through all of you, the human woman included," he said, indicating Ginger.

"The 'human woman's' name is Ginger Carter," Ginger said pointedly.

"My apologies, little one," said Brig. "I was so shocked to see Cian that I forgot to introduce you. Cian, this is Lady Ginger Carter, Liam's fiancé."

Cian took Ginger's hand and caressed it with an elegant kiss. "Fiancé? Liam's gain is my loss, beautiful one." His dazzling smile nearly took Ginger's breath away.

"Pleased to meet you," she said, struggling to keep her composure. He was definitely a charmer.

"I can see you are still quite dashing with the ladies," commented Liam as he took Ginger's arm possessively.

"And I can see you need to catch up with the times, Liam. People never say 'dashing' anymore." Cian looked at Ginger with an intensity that made her shift uncomfortably.

"Do you notice anything different, Lady Ginger?" he asked. "Does standing among Light Elves bother you in any way?"

Ginger thought a moment. "Actually, no. I don't feel on edge at all," she said glancing at Liam.

"I am not shuttered," Cian told her. He looked at Liam. "Unshutter, cousin."

Liam glanced at Ginger. She returned his nervous look with a reassuring smile.

Liam slowly unshuttered fully. Ginger showed no reaction. One by one all the elves in the room unshuttered and looked at Ginger.

"What?" she asked.

Cian was amused by Liam's open-mouthed amazement.

"Apparently the One has allowed your fiancé to tolerate the power of an unshuttered Light Elf. And speaking of power," he said to Liam with a grin, "do you feel any different? The One has restored you to your old magnificence. I can feel it all the way through my soul. Can you feel it?"

Brig looked at his son as he reached out to his mind, assessing his condition.

"He is right," said Liam. "We are back to normal."

A murmur of delighted chatter rippled through the Light Elves. Liam reached out with his mind, searching the elves around him. Their power had indeed been restored. He swept Ginger up in his arms enthusiastically and held her close.

"I could get used to this," she said giggling.

"So could I, my beloved," said Liam as he cuddled her close.

"Well, this is indeed a day for celebration," declared Brig. His joyous power streamed out from him in waves.

"I agree," responded Cian. He paused for a moment. "But I do have some more serious business to talk over with you . . ." He was cut short by Gwaynek's soft voice.

"We were celebrating Liam and Ginger's engagement. Surely this can wait a little while, Cian. A lady is entitled to her engagement celebration. I certainly was."

"Now, Gwaynek . . ." began Brig sternly.

Gwaynek stood looking directly into her husband's eyes.

Brig backed down. He knew that look.

"I really should brief Brig and Liam on our operations against the Dark Elves," insisted Cian. Catching Ginger's and Gwaynek's feminine stares, he sighed in defeat. He remembered his aunt's determination to cling to decorum and tradition.

"Perhaps afterwards would be a better time." He turned and retreated to the refreshment table with Liam and Brig. They were joined by Liam's counselors. Cian tasted a piece of honey quail. It was exquisite.

"You know," he said with a glint in his eye, "this island would make a wonderful staging area for our war against the Dark Elves."

www.ingramcontent.com/pod-product-compliance
Ingram Content Group UK Ltd.
Pitfield, Milton Keynes, MK11 3LW, UK
UKHW021416020425
5280UKWH00042B/493